**Corporate Responsibilities
and Opportunities
to 1990**

Arthur D. Little Books

A series of books on management and other scientific and technical subjects by senior professional staff members of Arthur D. Little, Inc., the international consulting and research organization. The series also includes selected nonproprietary case studies.

Acquisition and Corporate Development
James W. Bradley and Donald H. Korn

Bankruptcy Risk in Financial Depository Intermediaries
Assessing Regulatory Effects
Michael F. Koehn

Board Compass
What It Means to Be a Director in a Changing World
Robert Kirk Mueller

Career Conflict
Management's Inelegant Dysfunction
Robert Kirk Mueller

Corporate Responsibilities and Opportunities to 1990
Ellen T. Curtiss and Philip A. Untersee

Corporate Responsibilities and Opportunities to 1990

Edited by
Ellen T. Curtiss
Philip A. Untersee
ADL Impact Services Company
Arthur D. Little, Inc.

An Arthur D. Little Book

Lexington Books
D.C. Heath and Company
Lexington, Massachusetts
Toronto

Library of Congress Cataloging in Publication Data

Main entry under title:
  Corporate responsibilities and opportunities to 1990.

  1. Economic forecasting—Addresses, essays, lectures. 2. Business fore-
casting—Addresses, essays, lectures. 3. Industry—Social aspects—United
States—Addresses, essays, lectures. 4. Corporations—United States—Ad-
dresses, essays, lectures. I. Curtiss, Ellen T. II. Untersee, Philip A.
HD30.27.C67   301.18'32'0973   78-20737
ISBN 0-669-02848-7

Copyright © 1979 by D.C. Heath and Company

Published simultaneously in Canada

Printed in the United States of America

International Standard Book Number: 0-669-02848-7

Library of Congress Catalog Card Number: 78-20737

Contents

List of Figures

List of Tables

Corporate Responsibilities and Opportunities to 1990

1 Introduction: The Key Issues Confronting Business

Ellen T. Curtiss

The socioeconomic environment is changing and in turn is changing the role of the corporation, placing new demands on corporate and other institutional managers. In this book we investigate the following key themes, to help readers assess the kind of future they face:

1. What will be the dominant characteristics of the economic, social, and regulatory environment of the 1980s?
2. What will be the impact of this environment on the role of business and on business managers?
3. How does and should industry respond to the changing socioeconomic and regulatory environment?
4. What are some of the implications for corporations of the major technological changes that will affect society by 1990?

Many of the themes and issues in this book grew out of a major three-day executive forum attended by some 200 Arthur D. Little clients in June 1978 in Boston. At the forum, key corporate planners and investment research managers focused on the problems and opportunities confronting corporations in the coming decade, with the goal of gaining new perspectives on their opportunities and responsibilities and on the role of their organizations. Brief biographies of all the writers of chapters in this book are found at the end of this book. Many of the chapters have been expanded and updated since that meeting. The issues addressed have remained constant; only the world continues to change, requiring frequent updating of analyses in some areas.

Individuals concerned with the future, whether they be in business, government, or other institutions, are worried about and interested in *issues* as well as *specifics*. They want and need to know what kind of a world they will live in by 1990, what their role will be, and what their companies or other institutions will be doing.

In the consumer arena, they want to know whether they will live in the country, the suburbs, or the city, and whether they will walk, drive a car, or take a train to work. They want to know whether they will eat their meals at fast-food restaurants or whether they will eat food cooked at home in microwave ovens.

In the work arena, they want to know whether pressing employment

1

problems will change the ways they make decisions about automation, plant locations, and so on. They want to know whether inflation will destroy the purchasing power of entire classes of people and continue to exacerbate social welfare payments problems. They want to know how important international trade and investment will be, and how the world's major trading partners will view each other. They want to know what the regulatory environment will be, and they want to know what social values will be, as expressed in legislation and regulatory actions. They also want to know what role technology will play in solving society's problems—or in exacerbating them.

In short, they really *want* to know what kind of future they face, somewhat beyond the time frame they may ordinarily have the opportunity to look at. For many of us, caught up in our daily activities, even if we are fortunate enough to work in a research or planning environment, the distant future often becomes no more than the next 10 minutes worth of difficult decisions; it takes an effort of will to free up time to plan the next 6 months or year or few years. One reason we believe many readers will find this book an exciting one is precisely because most of us rarely have the opportunity to look this far in the future. As humans concerned with human destiny, we welcome the chance to exercise our crystal-ball-gazing muscles just a bit more than usual, to try to take ourselves and our readers on a journey to 1990. At the end of the journey we hope that all of us will have learned something about the kind of future we envision. We also hope that we will have received some encouragement that the corporation and other social institutions can balance the sometimes conflicting demands of the profit motive, social responsibilities, individual rights, environmental requirements, government constraints, and national employment and income goals.

In exploring the longer-term future, we must all walk a delicate path between listening too hard to those who forecast gloom, doom, and destruction and those who forecast joy and rapture unforeseen, accompanied by increasingly exciting technology at work and at home, increasing leisure time, and expanding economic and cultural opportunities. The truth, as always, lies somewhere between the two extremes. We cannot ignore the all too frightening possibilities of overpopulation, socioeconomic collapse, and warfare, but neither can we be deluded by promises of a brighter tomorrow. We cannot be paralyzed into inactivity by gloom about the future, and we cannot be mesmerized into inactivity by a false sense of security about the future. All of us, but particularly managers and planners, have the responsibility to understand as best we can what the future will be like and to chart the course of our businesses and institutions accordingly. Knowing there will be both calm and turbulent seas on any voyage, we must plan and be ready for both. It is our purpose in this book to provide some charts to help readers in their navigation. Readers will find some areas on these maps that could reasonably be labeled "uncharted waters," for the most marvelous characteristic of the future is that it is not completely foreseeable. Still, some of it can be foreseen, and we believe the charts we endeavor to draw will have enough well-mapped areas to aid readers on part of their journey and to warn them to be wary on other parts—to be wily, like Odysseus, on his 10-year voyage home.

Three of the key issues that will dominate corporate opportunity and responsibility in the next decade are the economic outlook, the energy situation, and strategic planning in the international environment. These issues are addressed by Dr. A. George Gols and Richard F. Messing, vice presidents and senior members of Arthur D. Little's professional staff, and by Robert Kirk Mueller, chairman of the board of Arthur D. Little. General James M. Gavin, Arthur D. Little director and former board chairman, gives his views on the crucial role of the business manager in shaping international strategy, and Gerard Piel, publisher of *Scientific American*, discusses the implications of the transformation of the social order in the United States and the emergence of world interests "beyond the economic problem." Other Arthur D. Little staff members discuss the 1980s from the perspective of new socioeconomic influences, the changing consumer, the challenge of meeting energy needs, and the critical issues that corporations will face internationally. Also addressed are specific issues concerning the future growth, development, and funding of corporations and other social institutions; the productive—and nonproductive— uses of technologies; and the far-reaching changes to be expected in information handling and communications at work, at home, and in travel.

Important progress has been made in dealing with the critical issues of the seventies, but none of the issues has been (or perhaps ever can be) totally resolved. The reason is that the critical issues—of unemployment and inflation; the provision of food, clothing, shelter, and health care; the enjoyment of opportunities to grow intellectually and spiritually—are endemic to the human condition. As society changes, our responses to the handling of these challenges must also change. Too often, however, our social institutions lag behind our social problems. Careful reading of Gerard Piel's thoughts will reinforce and clarify this notion. Dr. Gols points out that he expects an "environmental crisis" to come to the forefront during much of the next decade. Yet, in the 6 years since the energy crisis date of October 1973, our society has barely begun to put in place an appropriate organizational apparatus and legislation to deal with energy problems—let alone an environmental crisis. Much of the population still remains unconvinced there is an energy problem, even though many researchers have been studying the boundaries of this issue since the 1960s.

In the year 1990 there will be 5 billion people on this planet; there are 4 billion now. If we take Gerard Piel's numbers as a base, we could conclude that over half, perhaps approaching two-thirds, of the U.S. portion of the whole would be living outside the "market economy"—working in government, supported by transfer payments, and the like. That is one indicator of the different kind of world we are up against. Feeding, housing, clothing, educating, caring for the health of, and helping to provide for the physical, mental, and spiritual development of the total world population is a challenge worthy of Hercules. The best answer in democratic society to date is the corporation, and we believe that the corporation will continue to be the best way to attack the challenge. This book is an effort to help readers understand some of the issues they must address and we planners must help them address in maximizing the effectiveness of their role and their institutions' role in meeting these needs.

It seems appropriate to seek encouragement about the role of our present institutions by assessing progress made in recent years on several issues which have gummed up the wheels of progress in our society and which needed some work. One of the problems was that fewer and fewer of us held jobs relative to the total society (see table 1-1). We had more and more older people on welfare or transfer payments, often mandatorily retired whether or not they wanted to be (see tables 1-2 and 1-3). And we had many young people who could not get jobs whether they were or were not college graduates and who were excruci-atingly—and rightly so—disillusioned about their prospects in our society. Among the well educated we also had the in-between group—the overworked job holders, often workaholics, stunting their potential contribution with ulcers, heart disease, alcoholism, and a host of other problems. These problems have by

Table 1-1
Analysis of U.S. Population Not Employed/Unemployed/Employed, 1950-1990

	1950	1960	1970	1980	1990
Under 16	43.1	58.8	61.9	53.9	58.4
16 to 64	96.7	105.2	122.9	143.4	155.2
In labor force	60.8	68.7	82.6	100.9	113.4
(Civilian employed)	(56.0)	(62.7)	(75.5)	(93.1)	(106.0)
(Civilian unemployed)	(3.1)	(3.6)	(3.9)	(5.5)	(4.6)
(Military)	(1.7)	(2.4)	(3.2)	(2.3)	(2.8)
Not in labor force	35.9	36.5	40.3	42.5	41.9
65 and Over[a]	12.4	16.7	20.1	24.9	29.8
In labor force	3.1	3.4	3.3	3.1	3.1
(Civilian employed)	(2.9)	(3.1)	(3.1)	(2.8)	(2.8)
(Civilian unemployed)	(0.2)	(0.3)	(0.2)	(0.2)	(0.3)
(Military)	(–)	(–)	(–)	(–)	(–)
Not in labor force	9.3	13.3	16.8	21.9	26.6
Total Population	152.2	180.9	204.9	222.2	243.5
Labor force	63.9	72.1	85.9	103.9	116.6
(Civilian employed)	(58.9)	(65.8)	(78.6)	(95.9)	(108.9)
(Civilian unemployed)	(3.3)	(3.9)	(4.1)	(5.7)	(4.9)
(Military)	(1.7)	(2.4)	(3.2)	(2.3)	(2.8)
Not in labor force	88.3	108.8	119.0	118.3	126.9
Working	60.6	68.2	81.8	98.2	111.7
Not working	91.6	112.7	123.1	124.0	131.8
Percent Working	40	38	40	44	46

Sources: U.S. Department of Labor and Arthur D. Little estimates.
[a]Not adjusted for possible change due to elimination of mandatory retirement age.

Table 1-2
Labor-Force Participation of U.S. Population, 1950-1990

	1950	*1960*	*1970*	*1980*	*1990*
65 and Over					
Not in labor force					
Millions	9.3	13.3	16.8	21.9	26.6
Percent of total population	6.1	7.4	8.2	9.8	10.9
In labor force					
Millions	3.1	3.4	3.3	3.0	3.1
Percent of total population	2.0	1.9	1.6	1.3	1.3
16 to 64					
Not in labor force					
Millions	35.9	36.5	40.3	42.5	41.9
Percent of total population	23.6	20.2	19.7	18.9	17.2
In labor force					
Millions	60.8	68.7	82.6	100.9	113.4
Percent of total population	39.9	38.0	40.3	45.4	46.5
Under 16[a]					
Millions	43.1	58.8	61.9	53.9	58.4
Percent of total population	28.3	32.5	30.2	24.2	24.0

Sources: U.S. Department of Labor and Arthur D. Little estimates.
[a]Assumed all to be not in labor force.

no means been resolved, but legislation has been passed which eliminates the mandatory retirement age of 65, and there is talk of changing minimum wage requirements so that young people might be able to get some jobs that pay less than the minimum—and curiously enough, for someone who has no income, $2 or $3 an hour looks a good deal better than no dollars per hour. This is progress, but not enough. Still far too many educated young people cannot find suitable—or any—jobs. Surely there is something amiss in both our educational system and our economic system when we devote valuable resources to educating our young and then tell them society has no need for what they have learned. This problem will cause much more trouble and require much more work in the next decade. Our educational and business institutions must be brought into congruence with our social needs and the aspirations of our young.

Another substantive problem that has seen some resolution concerns how the corporation views itself. The lack of congruence between the corporation's traditionally defined role and society's needs appears to have diminished. Corporations are more concerned not just with *earning money*, showing a profit, but also with *understanding* that the true role of the company is to fulfill a basic human *need*, to provide a desired human service or a product needed by society. The understanding that a company out of touch with its marketplace is destined for difficult times has become sufficiently clear that more emphasis is being placed on understanding what the customer wants and less on what the supplier wants to supply.

Table 1-3
Percent of Population in Labor Force, 1950-1990

	1950	1960	1970	1980	1990
Under 16 plus over 65 not in labor force as percent of total population	34.4	39.9	38.4	34.0	34.9
Plus 16 to 64 not in labor force as percent of total population	58.0	60.1	58.1	52.9	52.1
Percent of population in labor force	42.0	39.9	41.9	47.1	47.9

Sources: U.S. Department of Labor and Arthur D. Little Estimates.

A major stride has been made in redefining business activities in terms of broader human needs, such as *health care* (instead of the drug industry or the medical supply business), or *information handling* (instead of the computer industry or word processing). We benighted business people still go back and forth between these broader "human need" definitions of business and narrower industry-focused definitions. We probably always will. More and more, however, we have tried to move toward broader definitions of functions of society or needs of the human race. In this context we can much more readily understand what a corporation can bite off as a challenge and what it can legitimately expect to be in business to do successfully. Such a perspective permits us to *stop* focusing too heavily on short-term business cycles and to *start* concentrating attention on serving long-term human needs that will not evaporate in 1 year, or 5 years, or in any set of business cycles, although demand for the services or products may fluctuate and change in its characteristics.

Another issue that has seen significant progress toward resolution is the problem of regulation and the corporate response to it. Earlier, business had cast itself in the role of the recalcitrant child that had to be monitored and admonished by an overprotective but presumably well meaning "regulator" or parent. Business is not separate from society, however, and business people increasingly appear to believe they should voluntarily take into account the impact of their decisions on the social situation. That impact can range from unemployment impacts, to impacts on water pollution, to foreign trade impacts, and what have you. Business interests increasingly appear to understand that unless business cleans up its own act, it must expect the government to write more and more laws to set up more and more bureaucracies to send more and more "little people" around to drive "business people" farther and farther up the wall. Given that choice, business people are well versed in tradeoff decisions.

Laws have not stopped being put on the books, and bureaucracy has not diminished. There are encouraging signs, however, that business people do increasingly acknowledge that regulation is in fact necessary and that a complex and maturing society cannot live without it. There is increasing recognition on both sides that the problem is not to have *no* or *too much* regulation, but to have *reasonable* regulation. Signs from many quarters in business indicate that business people are no longer acting as if their only function were to make money in isolation from society, but instead are realizing that they have social responsibility as well and must reach some reasonable accommodation with society—with government, with the consumer, and with other interests. There is increasing realization that instead of making that accommodation at the point of a gun, it may be infinitely preferable to take the initiative and to be known as the safe company, the good guys, the guys with the white hats. In advertising, many companies are striving for this image, and clearly there is some reality behind the advertising. Business people are proud of their role in contributing to this substantive progress—although they may not always feel free to acknowledge, parade, or broadcast their feelings, fearing group pressure. In fact, the most intractable problem in business may be the fear of being different, which, particularly in large organizations, stifles ingenuity, creativity, productivity, and every other measure of an energetic, growing society.

Surprisingly enough, despite the sometimes seemingly monolithic nature of corporate enterprises, individual business people do occasionally find some small opportunities, and sometimes even rather large opportunities, to influence the directions their companies take on specific issues. They are fortunate to have this responsibility, and they have demonstrated a growing concern for how wisely they exercise it. Such wisdom is essential, for if people in business are not wise in exercising their responsibilities, their freedom to make their own decisions will increasingly be eroded as the populace catches on to their stupidity or lack of wisdom, whichever the case may be.

Another issue of concern is the economic cycles in which we seem to have been so inexorably entangled and which make conducting business life more like riding out a storm than like conducting a rational human endeavor. Business people can help ameliorate these cycles—by trying not to overreact in response to either slack or boom demand. The price might be to suffer some opportunity loss by not taking full advantage at the peak, but likewise one would not suffer the loss resulting from having excess capacity at the bottom of the cycle. We think we see some improvement here.

It is crucial that business people understand how their efforts contribute to this and the other improvements we have discussed, because to be good managers they need to feel they can take actions that bring their world into a somewhat more rational framework. "Watching the Fed," waiting for "government initiatives," and "tossing it to the lawyers" to solve social, economic, and business problems are the very courses that lead to the government intervention so deeply resented by business people—and by all people, for that matter. The issue is one of freedom—at all levels—in business, in other organizations, and in our personal lives.

A closing thought: we do not think that the little black boxes known as computers, or any other version thereof, are going to solve many of our problems. We know they will increase the complexity of our lives and can also lessen our freedom if the issues of privacy and security of personal information are not well managed. To quote a colleague at Arthur D. Little, an ounce of thought is worth a ton of computer. The thought that all of us will give to the issues addressed in this book is the most important hope any of us has for the future of the corporation and for the freedom of the individual and society.

A great contribution was made to this book by Philip A. Untersee, who handles the day-to-day management of the ADL Impact Services research activity. He took the key role in coordinating this project. On the day we finalized our work, we reviewed what we had achieved against what we had set out to do. He said, "I'm even getting to be rather excited about this. This is going to be pretty good." Phil is an immensely self-contained individual, and, from him, that was quite heavy praise. I hope you will agree with him.

Part I
Overview

2 The Consequences of Conflicting National Goals

A. George Gols

Approximately 2 years ago, a persistent and very pervasive climate of gloom seemed to be blanketing the "psyche" of the U.S. business community. The depressed state of mind of the business community was directed particularly at the prospects of the U.S. economy, and that was understandable, since no more than a year had passed since the economy had emerged from the deep recession of 1974-1975—a recession which undermined the confidence of those who believed that our country still had great potential for growth, and a recession which had robbed some people of their personal wealth, if not of their positions and jobs.

We concluded then, however, that many of the worst fears were unwarranted, that business conditions would continue to improve, that unemployment and inflation rates would subside. And indeed, looking back, these things did happen, and they continued to happen—at least until very recently, that is, until the first quarter of this year. Then, developments again seemed to take a turn for the worse. Every economic indicator except the unemployment rate seemed to be going the wrong way. The worst fears harbored earlier seemed to be coming true. Inflation resurged—by some measures to double-digit rates; growth came to a standstill; the dollar's international value nosedived; and our balance-of-trade deficit ballooned. Economic analysts began to remind everyone that very few past economic recoveries have lasted longer than 3 years. Since that milestone was passed in 1978 interest rates have risen sharply and consumer confidence has dropped noticeably. "Anxiety fever" has reached a new peak.

Given these circumstances, is it surprising that some economists unveiled during 1978 dour recession forecasts for the second half of 1978 and/or early 1979? Yet we need not be too ready to accept such dismal prognostications. The principal reason for taking a more optimistic view is that our very concerns are likely to be the best *deterrents* to forestall the excesses that are generally the precursors of a recession. Actually, looking at the facts more closely, some hopeful signs are apparent.

While government took many steps that have spurred inflationary pressures (for example, higher farm supports, higher import restrictions, higher social security taxes, higher minimum wages, and higher import prices), it has more recently also initiated action to mitigate these pressures—by trimming the planned budget deficit, freezing and/or limiting government employee pay increases, and increasing interest rates. While these appear to be small measures compared with the former, at least one senses some urgency in the administration and Congress about containing the inflationary scourge.

Second, while our energy situation continues to be a cause for concern, many programs initiated by the private sector and government have already brought about some appropriate supply-and-demand, as well as price, adjustments.

Third, while our international trade balance is outsized and the value of our currency has fallen to an all-time low, perhaps at no time in the last two decades have U.S. goods been more competitive with foreign goods, and at no time has there been more foreign investment flowing into the United States, which is offsetting some of the dollar outflows.

Fourth, while our standard of living has not grown during the last 5 years, it has not actually declined sharply, considering the enormous effort that is being expended to pay for past profligacies—both of the short-term variety (say, some of the rather lusty speculations of the early seventies) and many of the longer-term variety (attributable to overexploitation of many valuable renewable and nonrenewable resources, including our social and biophysical environment).

Fortunately, there are still two sides to measuring performance. The chances that we are likely to grow slower in the future than in the past (not only in the short term but also in the long term) are very high. But these are not reasons to adopt the Dantean motto to "leave all hope behind." Is it so bad to grow more slowly? In many other human experiences, we are more positive in this assessment; we do not necessarily equate "quickness" with "soundness." In fact, inflation, which is the price for excessiveness, is making us more acutely appreciative of the merits of slower, but more stable, growth.

Having said that, what about living with the inflation we have created and solving its dilemmas? These are not simple tasks that will be taken care of by "quick remedies," by "instant" policy reversals, or by "jawboning" contests. We know that even a mere "leveling-off" of the inflation rate at 6 percent is not an acceptable goal. By standards of any period prior to 1973-1975, 6 percent is an extremely high inflation rate for the United States; it means purchasing power is cut in half every 12 years. True, some countries have lived with inflation rates this high and higher for many years, but our country's economic institutions are not readily adaptable to accommodating this rate as a steady diet. No political group supports it, not even the normally heavy spenders. Internationally, our country's role in the free world economy is too crucial to allow such a rate to persist. No leading country in the world has ever sustained such a rate of inflation in the last 300 years and remained a leader.

We find the getting-rid-of-inflation task equally difficult to accomplish. One problem is that there is really no unanimity now on what the real root causes of inflation are—too much money chasing too few goods is too simple a statement when, at the same time, there *are* excessive supplies of certain products (for example, steel, automobiles, television sets, shoes) and, above all, labor of the young and the unskilled. True, *excessive money supply*, which results from *excess debt creation* by *both* the government and the private sector, is one cause—but not the ultimate cause. Higher government debt is mainly the result of defense spending and social program spending outrunning tax revenues, which lag behind in a slack economy.

Private-sector debt results from people's spending outrunning people's income, which also lags in a slack economy. In addition, the general proliferation of credit cards, installment accounts, and the easy transfer of monies from different accounts—all of which encourage debt creation—is also encouraging us to spend faster than we earn. Thus, at no time in history has our consumer per capita debt been higher than it is now. If government were to rein-in debt creation, would the private sector do so too? Many of our institutional arrangements, including the tax system, encourage everyone (both government and the private sector) to borrow up to the hilt, and inflation abets the process. In fact, the process is self-feeding—for borrowing costs are generally tax deductible.

On the other side of the ledger, the *inadequate supply* of resources has also played a role in inflation. The depletion of many types of resources—nonrenewable and renewable—has increased replacement costs. Renewable resources may be replenished, but usually only at greatly increased costs.

Institutional arrangements have produced monopolistic supply constraints in both domestic industry and labor. Internationally, new supply constraints are growing. OPEC is an example par excellence—some are less obvious. Some cynics even believe that internationally there is a silent conspiracy in which nation groups are trying to out-inflate each other in a game of "chicken." The game is designed to see who can be made to "hold the bag" with the currency that has lost the greatest value—a sort of "musical chairs" of devalued currency game. Of course, as the 1920s and 1930s taught us, competitive devaluation results in only one loser—everybody.

Simple cures of sharply lowering money growth rates by lowering deficits are not necessarily instantly effective either. Inflation can persist for long periods, even if we induce high unemployment and recession. And the obverse is also true: unemployment can persist even though there is plenty of stimulus and inflation.

Our economic theorists and policymakers know this. Where they disagree is on what the proper balance should be. Even on such a basic question as "How should Federal Reserve credit policy respond to an OPEC oil price increase?" you will get quite opposite answers from such a presumably monolithic economist group as the "monetarists"—some say expand the money supply, some say restrict it. In capsule form, we are caught between conflicting goals and conflicting means to reach them. How will this deadlock be solved? Before we address that, let us first be very concrete on what our short-term and then our longer-term prospects are.

Prospects (The Next Year)

During the next year we should expect real GNP growth to decelerate. This should have a dampening effect on inflation, but it is also again likely to raise unemployment rates somewhat. Much of the slowdown is likely to result from higher interest rates and be accompanied by some demand saturation in the replacement cycles of automobiles and housing. All this will be tempered by a very cautious attitude by business in areas of inventory building and capital spending. However, this contraction is unlikely to bring inflation down sufficiently so that government can re-deficit-finance itself out of increases in unemployment.

We believe the deadlock out of which we will have to extricate ourselves will become the seedbed of new policy measures. We believe this effort will lead to the formalization of a new "incomes policy." This incomes policy will use tax incentives to encourage deceleration in the rates of price and wage increases. In terms of timing, however, and because implementation of this policy has plenty of practical problems, the "seeds" of this idea may not sprout until after 1980—that is, after the presidential election year. We doubt that such a new incomes policy will fly full staff on any political platform. In the meanwhile, more of the traditional fiscal and monetary and "jawboning" policies will be invoked to cope with the "stagflation" problem.

But "trial balloons" for new policy avenues will be launched. Principal industries that are most likely to be affected by any near-term slackening in expansion are the housing and consumer durables sectors, particularly autos. Investment spending will continue to remain modestly strong—even after the consumer and housing sectors' growth begins to weaken. The key reason that the moderate plans to expand productive capacity are not likely to be fully scrapped is that the slowdown is expected to be mild.

Internationally, slackening of aggregate demand growth in the United States will help our balance of payments by slowing the growth of imports—though only mildly in the oil sector. This should further improve the dollar's value. It will also take the United States out of the so-called locomotive role and place West Germany and Japan more into the "pulling" position, thus helping U.S. exports somewhat.

What will be some of the *noncyclical* policy influences that will accompany these shorter-term developments? We suspect the following. First, energy problems will continue to dominate the scene, but to a somewhat lesser extent than they do at present. Second, environmental regulation problems will move up to front center. Third, health care cost control and national health insurance policies will also move up to front center. And last, taxation policy, not only at the federal level, but also at the state and local levels, will draw more acute attention. Proposals like California's Proposition 8 and Proposition 13 to limit state and local taxing power will become popular in other states.

Long-Term Growth (The Next 5 to 7 Years)

Real GNP growth should average out at about a 3.0 percent rate through 1985, with a probability that we might see a notable speedup before the presidential election and a sharp slowdown shortly thereafter. Inflation will continue to average 5.5 percent—but not without some very sharp quarterly fluctuations, ranging from perhaps 3.0 to 8.0 percent. But longer-term unemployment rate trends should show some easing as labor force growth slows when the demographic changes (such as an actual absolute drop in the number of people in the highly vulnerable age groups of 20 and below) work themselves through the population structure.

The economic fluctuations we will experience could again be as severe as they were in the 1974-1975 recession—but only if there are major outside disturbances (for example, other foreign military ventures and/or natural disasters). Otherwise, the longer-term cyclical "peaks and valleys," based purely on economic policy management programs, could be shallower, and we may actually see better growth in productivity in the next 5 years than we have in the last 10 years (which is not saying much)—say, 2.0 versus 1.6 percent. It should be noted in this connection that longer-term productivity performance is influenced as much by the steepness of cyclical fluctuations and labor force composition as it is by research and development investments.

Internationally, we expect that in the next 5 years the United States will outdistance Europe in growth. This is so because, relatively speaking, general resources availabilities, competitive costs, and energy will favor the United States as compared with Europe.

As far as longer-term noncyclical policy issues are concerned, we expect that the "energy crisis" will vie with *environmental* issues for the number one problem spot. By the early 1980s, we believe, many of our basic, as well as high-technology, process and other fabricating industries will be the great "problem industries"—we include here mining, chemicals, paper, and even some categories of the electronics industry. Recent and further revelations on the health effects of processing nonfuel minerals and in many cases using their end products will spawn a mind-boggling brood of production restrictions. In the chemical industry alone, if the estimate is correct that there are over 70,000 different chemical products, a large fraction of which are candidates for testing for health-risk potential, the task will be absolutely staggering. Moreover, every year we introduce hundreds of new chemical products. These figures portend the possibility of the onset of a transformation of the chemical industry in the next 5 years as great as we have seen during the last 20. The chances are high that by the mid-1980s we will legislate a government organization that will regulate the chemical industry in a way similar to the manner in which the Food and Drug Administration now regulates its industries. Moreover, the possibility that many chemicals and other substances now in use may have to be quickly phased out of production because of identified hazardous effects could, in itself, create some major industry adjustment problems not unlike those we experienced during the oil embargo.

In fact, the transformation of product designs and materials to meet the administrative rulings of the Consumer Product Safety Commission on products in use, to accommodate the rulings of OSHA or EPA on production processes and workplace and living environment, will become a major, even tougher problem for many industries than it is now. Linking these issues with the problem of spiraling health care services' needs and then costs, to correct some of the adverse health effects induced by the environmental problems, you can conjure up your own kaleidoscopic visions of the kinds of domestic issues we will have to sort out in the early 1980s.

Implications and Consequences for Corporate Strategy

What implications and consequences does all this have for corporate strategy and planning in relation to opportunities and challenges? The consequences of these pressures reinforce the need to do more intense corporate strategy analysis. This will mean not just more sophisticated planning for economic problems, but the creation of more integrated planning approaches to accommodate the triad of economic-environmental-safety planning requirements. It will also mean continually reassessing immensely enhanced resource needs. Superimposed upon all this will be the emergence of a keen awareness of new litigatory risks that will blanket many activities. For example, in the corporate economic sphere, high inflation rates and/or government's new incomes policies will require more intense assessments of the inflation implications of profit potentials for specific investments and ventures. Stockholders and lenders will demand these assessments from management and seek legal recourse to elicit them when they are not deemed sufficient.

In environmental planning, regulations will not only require planning for safe environment production, but also planning for safe product performance and, something newer (already not so new in some areas), planning for product *disposal*. Thus, new product development and old product phase-out planning will be subject to much greater scrutiny to compare cost versus benefit not only for product life, but also for product death. It sounds a little macabre, but you may want to think of it in somewhat more ironic terms—namely, that the interest in people's trashcans, which, according to some authors, became something of a vogue during the Watergate "snooping period," will get its revival, but in a somewhat different context. Here, too, litigatory action will be prolific.

In fact, many decision problems in these areas will be dealt with under a canopy of a vastly expanding litigatory environment. Moreover, the litigious forces are likely to reach far into the "vital organs" of the corporate structure to seek remedies from and pinpoint liability claims for product and service performance—often on individual managers. The corporate "shield" protecting individual managers is thus likely to further weaken. Also, while the sixties and seventies were known as the decades of the corporate/financial man, the eighties may well become known as the decade of the corporate/law man. Thus we see the onset of a somewhat new economic order, and we will learn to live with it very fast. Only what will it be like? Will it necessarily be better or worse than what we have experienced in the past? We do not know. It certainly will be part of the price we have to pay for further material progress.

Fifty years ago, to some of our grandparents, today's workaday world might have seemed like one holding little charm—overregulated and tumultuous; but to many others, it might have appeared like a vision of a vast cornucopia, brimming with material wealth. A recent cartoon showed a tombstone which read: "The U.S. economy: victim of the energy/environmental crisis and mismanagement: circa 2000 A.D." This epitaph, we believe, is too pessimistic. More intriguing is the perspective conveyed in the ancient Chinese curse: "May you live in interesting times." One thing of which we are certain: during the next decade, we will not want for interesting times.

3

What Ever Happened to the Energy Crisis?

Richard F. Messing

Most forecasters of the energy outlook seem to fall in one of two camps: (1) doomsayers who feel that an energy crunch is inevitable, that it is already too late to deal with it, and that congressional and governmental inaction (as well as public attitudes) are responsible, and (2) those "true believers" who feel that the nation is accommodating successfully to change, that there are plenty of replaceable energy resources available for development, and that more emphasis on conservation will solve the problem. Much of our inability to deal with the "energy crisis" derives from this basic conflict, and finding a reasonable compromise is a difficult task.

The term *energy crisis* has itself led to a number of misunderstandings. The public can easily understand this terminology when there are long lines of cars waiting to purchase gasoline at filling stations or worker layoffs caused by a curtailment of natural gas deliveries to manufacturing plants. It is less able to grapple with the idea of crisis when we are dealing with issues of possible future shortages, especially when their timing and the extent to which they will cause disruptions in our lifestyle is uncertain.

The record shows that there have in fact been no significant shortages of energy during the past year. The Carter administration now takes the position that energy shortages are unlikely until the early to mid-1980s. Even though we may have succeeded in balancing the energy equation for the short term, those who view with alarm still see important danger signals. One is the large continuing drain of the U.S. balance of payments arising from requirements for imported oil. While few analysts will argue for elimination of oil imports, many feel that finding ways to reduce our dependency on imported oil represents an urgent national goal. Another area of concern involves the long lead times required to realize the benefits from new energy-producing facilities and the likelihood that any supply crunch which manifests itself before 1990 is quickly slipping beyond our planning horizon. Underlining both these concerns is an uncertainty over the pricing of various energy forms and the likelihood that price escalations will significantly exceed the rate of general inflation. Moves by consumers and regulatory groups to place more of the energy cost burden on large users may represent a significant threat to the viability of energy-intensive enterprises. Any break in the continuity of supplies of energy, especially crude oil and petroleum products from foreign sources, would obviously cause serious disruptions.

Recent signals from the energy-production front have all been generally positive. Domestic crude oil production has been augmented by the flow from the North Slope in Alaska; one result is that the West Coast is experiencing a glut of oil. Natural gas production in 1977 showed the first upturn since 1973, and many of the large offshore producers had continuing increases in production in 1978. The self-help programs involving oil and gas exploration by industrial and utility companies have shown positive results. Production of coal in 1977 increased about 6 percent over the previous year, and although the strike posed some problems, most utilities managed to weather this problem better than had been expected. The number of operating nuclear plants has continued to increase, and even though new orders remain stagnant, the contribution of new facilities to energy supply should continue to increase for the next several years even if no new plants are authorized. On the international front, foreign crude oil supplies are more than ample, and a significant amount of prospective production is shut in. Large-scale deliveries of liquefied natural gas from Algeria started in early 1978, and both Canada and Mexico have surplus gas reserves available for export to the United States by pipeline once regulatory and political hurdles are cleared.

These developments on the producing front have been accompanied by similarly positive signals from consumers. Most forecasters had expected that 1977 would show a substantial upturn in energy usage because of cold weather and the strong economic climate, but energy usage, which was reported on a preliminary basis at just under 76 quads, was up only 2 quads from the previous year, and the annual rate of growth since 1973 has been only 0.4 percent (see table 3-1). The most dramatic impact of conservation was evidenced in the industrial sector, which has shown an actual decrease of 2.3 percent per year in the level of energy use since 1973 (see table 3-2). Virtually all the major industry sectors have committed themselves to programs of energy conservation which

Table 3-1
Energy Consumption by End Use, 1973-1977
(Quadrillion BTU)

	Residential/ Commercial	Industrial	Transportation	Electricity Generation	Total[a]
1973	14.30	20.63	18.75	19.84	74.74
1974	13.89	20.72	18.25	19.97	73.04
1975	13.58	17.92	18.53	20.24	70.58
1976	14.69	18.37	19.32	21.37	74.00
1977 (est.)	14.95	18.87	19.66	22.47	75.95
Average annual growth	1.1%	−2.3%	1.2%	3.0%	0.4%

Source: Department of Energy.

[a]Total includes miscellaneous and unaccounted for.

Table 3-2
Industrial Energy Consumption, 1973-1977
(Quadrillion BTU)

| | Primary Energy | | | | Electricity | |
	Gas	Oil	Coal	All Fossil	Distributed	Total[a]
1973	10.05	6.23	4.34	20.63	2.63	23.26
1974	10.31	6.06	4.35	20.72	2.66	23.43
1975	8.55	5.54	3.82	17.92	2.58	20.53
1976	8.38	6.17	3.82	18.37	2.81	21.21
1977 (est.)	8.12	6.92	3.83	18.87	2.91	21.78
Average annual growth	−5.2%	2.7%	−3.1%	−2.3%	2.5%	−1.6%

Source: Department of Energy.
[a]Includes hydro, geothermal, and other.

are expected to yield similarly dramatic savings in future years. The residential and commercial sector also showed an impressive change from the historic momentum of energy growth, with an average annual increase in primary fuel usage from 1973 of only 1.1 percent. To some extent, electrical usage has been substituted for other primary energy forms, but even after making allowance for this replacement, overall annual growth in energy usage in the residential/commercial sector was only 1.8 percent over the period since 1973 (see table 3-3). The all-out pace of sales by the insulation industry has reflected the public's concern over finding ways to economize on energy use, as have sales of a variety of other heat-saving devices. The transportation sector has also shown a significant departure from the historic consumption growth rates, with an average increase since 1973 of only 1.2 percent per year (see table 3-4). While automobile production and registrations have continued to increase, roll-over of

Table 3-3
Residential/Commercial Energy Consumption, 1973-1977
(Quadrillion BTU)

| | Primary Energy | | | Electricity | |
	Gas	Oil	All Fossil	Distributed	Total
1973	7.32	6.69	14.30	3.71	18.01
1974	7.52	6.06	13.89	3.72	17.62
1975	7.59	5.75	13.58	3.97	17.55
1976	8.12	6.33	14.69	4.14	18.83
1977 (est.)	7.51	7.18	14.95	4.39	19.34
Average annual growth	0.6%	1.8%	1.1%	4.3%	1.8%

Source: Department of Energy.

Table 3-4
Transportation Energy Consumption, 1973-1977
(Quadrillion BTU)

| | Primary Energy | | | |
	Oil	*All Fossil*	*Electricity Distributed*	*Total*
1973	18.00	18.75	0.02	18.76
1974	17.56	18.25	0.02	18.27
1975	17.93	18.53	0.02	18.55
1976	18.73	19.32	0.02	19.33
1977 (est.)	19.06	19.66	0.02	19.67
Average annual growth	1.4%	1.2%	3.2%	1.2%

Source: Department of Energy.

the fleet to include more high-efficiency vehicles has been reflected in lower gasoline usage than would otherwise have resulted. Assuming that the automobile industry can meet the mandated new passenger car standards of 20 miles per gallon in 1980 and 27.5 miles per gallon in 1985, this trend should continue, with a likelihood of a leveling and perhaps even a slight downtrend in transportation fuel usage.

The electric generation sector has shown the highest average annual growth in consumption of primary fuels (3.2 percent), but this rate is less than half that which had been experienced in the 1960s (see table 3-5). Each of the major consuming sectors contributed to this growth in electrical usage, with residential/commercial showing the highest gain (4.3 percent per year).

While the developments just cited provide some reassurance for the near-term outlook, there is balancing evidence that we continue to face a longer-term problem in energy supplies. Some of the key indicators are as follows:

Table 3-5
Electric Generation, Energy Consumption, 1973-1977
(Quadrillion BTU)

	Gas	*Oil*	*Coal*	*Hydro*	*Nuclear*	*Total*	*Electricity Distributed*
1973	3.68	3.66	8.62	3.00	0.89	19.84	6.36
1974	3.51	3.48	8.52	3.25	1.20	19.97	6.41
1975	3.21	3.24	8.76	3.19	1.83	20.24	6.57
1976	3.13	3.48	9.69	3.03	2.03	21.37	6.97
1977 (est.)	3.27	3.81	10.33	2.40	2.66	22.47	7.32
Average annual growth	−2.8%	1.0%	4.6%	−4.7%	31.5%	3.2%	3.5%

Source: Department of Energy.

1. Although reserve additions for natural gas increased in 1977 by about 30 percent, they still fell considerably short of withdrawals, even though drilling activity in the industry was at a high level. Natural gas usage has been declining despite the overall growth in energy consumption, and a continued long-term downtrend appears inevitable (see table 3-6). A shortfall in natural gas supplies will have a major leveraging effect in demand for other fuels and for electricity.
2. Problems of compliance with the Clean Air Act Amendments create many uncertainties for both the utility and industrial users. No new coal-fired facilities have been committed by utilities except for those grandfathered by the act. Some hiatus in new commitments is likely.
3. Opposition to new nuclear facilities continues, and problems in plant siting will probably limit expansions to existing sites. Even at these sites, regulatory delays and design changes make nuclear power a less attractive expansion alternative for utilities.
4. New liquefied natural gas (LNG) import projects have experienced major roadblocks in securing the necessary approvals.
5. The overall ability of oil-producing countries to maintain and increase exports to the United States comes into greater question after the mid-1980s, since reserve positions of some producing countries will require a tapering rate of production. Growth in usage in the developing countries will tend to absorb the world surpluses. A major price increase becomes more likely as various links in the supply chain become strained.

In summary, the energy crisis has not gone away, and users should not adopt a relaxed attitude regarding plans for future energy supplies. Early decisions on choice of energy alternatives will be needed to accommodate the long lead times necessary to put new facilities in place. Most important, users must accommodate to the likely shifts in pricing of various energy forms. Because various sectors of the energy industry are partially or completely regulated, pricing levels for various energy forms will be significantly different in

Table 3-6
Energy Consumption by Fuel Form, 1973-1977
(Quadrillion BTU)

	Gas	Oil	Coal	Hydro	Nuclear	Total
1973	22.71	34.85	13.29	3.00	0.89	74.74
1974	22.03	33.41	13.10	3.29	1.20	73.04
1975	19.95	32.74	12.83	3.23	1.83	70.58
1976	20.21	34.94	13.75	3.06	2.03	74.00
1977 (est.)	19.48	36.97	14.43	2.40	2.66	75.95
Average annual growth	−3.4%	1.5%	2.1%	−4.7%	31.5%	0.4%

Source: Department of Energy.

future years. The penalties which must be borne by users to convert from one fuel form to another will be an important consideration in planning conversions between fuel forms. The possibility of using renewable resources may involve some early commitments to avoid obsolete investments. Close monitoring of the shifting energy scene is a clear responsibility for management over the coming years.

4

Thinking Internationally: The Importance of Being Strategic

Robert K. Mueller

Importance of a Strategy

This chapter stresses the importance of being strategic in our thinking and planning. We can illustrate the issue by a quotation:

> Every 60 seconds, 200 human beings are going to be born on this earth. About 160 of them are going to be colored: black, brown, yellow, and red. Of these 200 human beings, that are being born as I stand here in this 60 second interval, half are going to be dead before they are a year old. Of those that survive, another half are going to be dead before they are 16. Of those 200 kids that are coming into the world at this moment, 50 of them are going to survive past their sixteenth birthday and when you look at them and multiply by hundreds and thousands and millions, you see the human beings of this earth.

> During the next 25 years and thereafter, this is the way they are going to look. They are going to have an age expectancy of about 30 years. They are going to be hungry, tired, illiterate, and sick most of their lives. Most of them will live in mud huts, or tents, tilling the soil, working for landlords. Most of them will lie naked and hungry under the open skies of Asia, Africa, and Latin America, waiting, watching, and hoping. These are the human beings with whom we have inherited this earth.

These are the solemn words of Sol M. Linowitz, Ambassador to the Organization of American States. They were offered to a college audience only a short time ago. This perspective starkly indicates why we can no longer continue to be insular in our strategic plans and actions. Global interaction and interdependency are forcing us to think and plan strategically. In addition, we must remain alert to opportunities where we may have distinctive competence and, of course, include them in our development program.

As we know, a thoughtful strategy can force us to form a dynamic perspective of a complex situation. It does this by dealing explicitly with (1) what our objectives are, (2) what others' perceived objectives are, (3) what others are doing, (4) what the environmental situation is and is likely to be, (5) the alternative options for achieving our objectives given these interactive circumstances, and (6) the consequences and tradeoffs involved.

One of the most neglected areas in strategy building is that of *internal* strategy. The purpose is to deal with organization styles and changes, conflicts and tensions that result with most corporate development thrusts. These forces are primarily concerned with the problems of changing ongoing organizations. Anyone familiar with physical chemistry will recall how Le Chatelier's principle of mobile equilibrium works—not to fight back, but by moving its point of equilibrium along a scale, to counterbalance the effect of an outside force. The system does not collapse or react violently, it simply adjusts its own internal relationships so that the effect of the change is offset.

The *key* is to take total strategy formulation responsibly, and this includes organizational strategy, business strategy, and international strategy. When we are not thinking internationally, our strategic performance in overseas situations will reflect an incomplete approach to a host of vexatious issues. We cannot afford to be like the two British housekeepers who were talking over their problems at work—one said, "The lady I work for says that I should warm the plates for our dinner guests. That's too much work. I just warm hers and she never knows the difference."

Worldviews

Some basic hypotheses have been made in recent studies at Arthur D. Little. These identify global trends affecting the future environment for institutions. The requirement, both for more corporate leadership and more strategic thinking about these probable endstates, is clear. Some of the movements which call for new thinking and new abilities are as follows:

1. The internationalization of political and economic institutions is increasing in other than the large industrialized nations. The less developed countries (LDCs) are rising!
2. There is a growing dependence of developed nations on the availability of key external resources obtainable mainly in less developed countries. The equation balance of physical survival and economic health versus political relationships is shifting.
3. As developing countries reach a more advanced state, different patterns of government and business relationships enter the international competitive arena. This causes increased uncertainty in the conduct of international business and a strong sense that there will be a transition to new patterns of institutions, business, government, and international relationships.
4. A political explosion in the formation and reformation of new nations increases the number of actors on the global stage. A rapid increase in sophistication of these participants is occurring, whether they are new governments, political aggregations, cartels, culture groups, new private enterprises, new suppliers, or consumers.

5. Basic value systems are changing. There is a strong drive toward egalitarianism resulting from the growth and affluence of developed nations. This causes a growth in interdependence among nations, which creates a search by individuals and institutions for a stronger sense of identity.
6. All this causes a requirement for more clarity (legal, strategic nature, social, political) in the interrelationships of institutions. It presages a change in the relative maturity of industries and societies.
7. Connections and conflicts between fundamental driving forces and systems will gradually develop to provide special incentives and some differentiation. These will be based on self-value, egalitarianism, and, of course, market values in free world areas.
8. The impacts of technology will affect industries, social-economic maturity, and the balances between nations and social force systems. This will be a continuing cause for future turbulence.

The attitude that if government, activists, communities, unions, and shareholders will only leave the corporation alone, everyone's welfare will be served just does not fit the prospective future complex society anymore than it works today.

The Mandala Scheme

One way to approach this worldview of increasing complexity is to perceive organizations as multivariate systems. At least four interacting variables loom especially large around a central core. These are the variables of (1) objectives and purpose, (2) resources, (3) structure, and (4) actors or people. The core is the governance concept for the system—a fifth major variable.

Perhaps not too strangely, these four variables and the fifth core variable can be represented in the geometric or radial form of a mandala, which is the Hindu or Buddhist graphic symbol for design of human and world affairs.

By way of background, the esoteric Buddhist sects concentrated on the production of painted mandalas as pictorial representations of complex situations. These involved map-like representations of the Buddhist cosmologies. The concept of mandala consisted of two elements: a core (*manda*) and a container or closing elements (*la*). Mandala designs consist of both simple and complex sets of satellites arranged around a center. These designs occur with such insistence at various levels of Hindu-Buddhist thought and practice that anthropologists were invited to probe their representational efficacy in the past. Drawing on their findings, these concepts may also aid us as we approach the complexities of the future.

The mandala scheme proves helpful in providing a structural approach and a protocol for dealing with inordinate complexity. So let us go from mythology to the notion of four interacting variables and their governance core in a twentieth-century context. This notion is well known to corporate planners and to many thoughtful leaders of institutions. There are, of course, more than five variables which can be placed in our mandala scheme, but let us keep it to the simple five-unit design for this illustration.

The first variable in strategic thinking and planning is that of *task* or *objective*. This concerns the objectives of our institution on a long time frame. This embraces not only domains of activity or sectors in which the corporation expects to function, but also the geographical areas, the identity, ideology, philosophy, and very nature of the business. More profoundly, it means the purpose and business concept of the activity itself. Often we find in consulting work that objectives of the owners of corporations are mixed, sometimes conflicting. Frequently, they are unclear. We need not take time here to stress the importance of clarifying where we want to go and where we want to be before attempting to devise a strategic plan to cope with any internal and external forces.

The second variable is that of *resources*. In twentieth-century context this includes technology, facilities, materials, money, time, and intangible assets such as intellectual property, goodwill, going-concern value, and skills, both on and off the balance sheet. Interdependency between objectives and resources is obvious. We must tailor our aspirations to the resources available. One does not go into the navy business or build a battleship because one owns a sailor suit.

Perhaps the least tractable resource is that of time itself. The temporal aspects of strategic thinking are critical to international activity. A little later we will indicate some of the turbulent governance issues on the international scene which make timing of our future moves a most formidable task.

The next variable in our mandala design is that of *structure*. This refers to the institution's legal structure, ownership patterns, organizational scheme, systems of communication, power, authority, and work flows. It is obvious that depending on the resources available and on the objectives sought, the structuring of the activity may differ. These three variables are interdependent, interactive, and must be juggled conjointly.

The fourth variable in our oversimplified mandala design is that of *actors*, usually people. Experienced managers know not to design an organization and then stick people in boxes on a chart. Organization structure must be designed around talents and capabilities of individuals who are available and committed. There is always a compromise here, so that structure and actors are two interactive interdependent nodes on our mandala. The relationship of actors to the available resources and to the objectives also forms interdependent couplings.

Thus we have an elementary geometric radial design. The four units are deployed around a central point where the interactive forces meet. It is at this point that the board of directors and key management sit. This core deals with the governance process variable.

If we are to think strategically both inside and outside of our organization, we must add another representation to this cognitive mapping of complexity. Take the mandala design and encircle it to represent the shifting environmental envelope in which we find ourselves when dealing with complex external problems. The environment is not only that of "space-ship earth," but also of the regulatory and legal climate, the social, cultural, and economic setting surrounding the corporation. This varies, of course, by geographical region and its time or place in various economic and other cycles of industry and business.

Now we have the ancient concept of mandala. The core of key management and governance with their satellite elements, a minimum of four in number. Satellite units can be more numerous, but these four are essential in dealing mentally with the dominant variables which usually exist in a complex enterprise situation. This radial construct is the concept around which some of the advance trends in organizational thinking provide fluidity and an open style for the future. More about this later.

New Trends in Corporate Governance: The Key Fifth Variable

A recent study in which Arthur D. Little participated was conducted by Business International for their clients and centered around looking at trends taking place in corporate boards of directors. In addition to our knowledge of these governance trends, a few highlights of this study can be revealed which are unusual in the context of our thinking strategically about international activities.

There is no question but that wide-ranging experimentation and innovation is most prevalent in the United States. The main changes deal with the composition of boards and their different roles and functions. The U.S. phenomena, however, will not be further discussed here.[1] Canada is following the United States slowly, and Australia is moving also in a parallel direction of boardroom experimentation.

More interesting, perhaps, the European Common Market leads the world in institutionalized participation by labor in company governance, in management, and toward employee shareholdership. The European Economic Community (EEC) is currently working on two measures: the Statute for the European Company, hammered out by the EEC Council of Ministers, and the Fifth Directive, devised by the EEC Commission. The Statute for the European Company is a regulation rather than a law and will introduce the "$2x + y$" formula. This means boards will be composed of one-third shareholder representatives, one-third labor, and one-third public interest representatives. The Fifth Directive, when adopted, will call for a two-tier board structure consisting of a supervisory board with worker representation probably constituting one-third of all board membership and a managing board.

In the Netherlands in the late sixties, the principle was established that employees' interest in the enterprise was equal to that of a shareholder. This serves as a basis for worker participation and corporate decision making through the works council mechanism. The Dutch Parliament has before it a proposal that would require disclosure of information on salary structures on all corporate levels including top management and honoraria paid to company directors.

Traditionally, French boards have been composed of "wise men, primarily influential bankers and businessmen or the representatives of major shareholders, often members of the founding father families." This is changing, however, with more of an emphasis on board members having competence.

Sweden's Democracy at Work Act of 1976 is perhaps the most drastic version of labor participation in governance. It gives labor an effective veto right over all corporate decisions from work schedules to plans for expansion, acquisitions, and mergers, and to investment abroad. The next target of Sweden's powerful unions is what is called "economic democracy," or collective ownership of companies.

One of the problems of the representation of interest groups on boards in Sweden is that it has changed the attitude of board members. They formerly concentrated for the good of the company; now they must think about the interests of those who have elected them. This has a built-in conflict, and further interest representation will mean that boards lose their ability to function. The problem in Sweden is that employers and unions have become management's partner in decision making but are not considered partners in overall responsibility or liability. Interestingly, the percentage of women on Swedish boards is the highest of any industrialized country, totaling 10 percent now and expected to rise.

Norway is the first country in Western Europe with plans to make mandatory the presence of local officials on boards in certain sectors under certain conditions.

As a general rule, Japanese directors are appointed by the chairman in consultation with the president. Representative directors who can sign promissory notes and other financial obligations usually represent the company in financial, governmental, and outside matters. The other kind are the inside directors whose functions are limited to intracompany activities. Typically, these are managing directors or division and staff heads. It is interesting that since directors, including the Japanese version of inside directors, are legally not employees of the company, they can be fired without violating the lifetime employment system. In addition, directors are elected every 2 years.

Strangely, these days in Japan, if the company wants to indicate to a senior manager that he will not make it to the top, it appoints him a director. This in effect gives him 2 years notice to find another job. This move, known as "a pat on the back," is comparable to our Western "percussive sublimation" technique.

Under this system, the question of a director's personal liability becomes moot. It is so moot that none of the Japanese companies consider it necessary to insure their directors.

India makes a convoluted contribution to new trends in corporate governance. A proviso is attached to all large loans to companies which (1) makes part of the loan convertible into equity at the option of the financial institution making the loan and (2) gives the financial institution a seat on the company's board. Since all financial institutions in India are nationalized, this means, in effect, that the government now sits on the board of most sizable companies. The Indian innovation is a back-door entry into the corporate boardroom that appeals to developing countries, haunted by myths of corporate decisionmaking to their detriment.

Indian boards have many problems with the considerable government intervention, often with a heavy hand. For example, the government sets directors' fees for both outside and inside directors. The ceiling now, for outside directors, is rupees 500. With the rupee eight to one exchange, the fee is ludicrously low per meeting. The result of this government clumsiness is that many senior executives refuse to serve on the boards of their companies since to do so will get them into a hassle over their compensation with the Indian bureaucracy. Regulations also require shareholder approval for the hiring of any family member as an executive of the company.

Iran's innovation is important in that it may set a precedent, not only for developing countries in general, but specifically for the oil and cash-rich countries of the Middle East. Iran has a mandatory equity spin-off system whereby companies over a certain size must offer 49 percent of their equity to employees. In Iran, employees can buy their shares from the company or from two national financial institutions that serve as underwriters/brokers.

An intriguing board compensation system exists in Iran. The law allows for a reasonable attendance fee for outside directors. While that fee used to be minimal or nonexistent, it is more in step in recent years. Now it averages between $100 and $300 per meeting for the larger companies. The new twist, however, is that a big chunk of director compensation derives from the law that permits board members to become compensated with up to 5 percent of distributed profit in a public joint stock company. This can come up to 10 percent in a private joint stock company. (Whether Iran will maintain its past approaches under its current governance is unclear.)

This concludes a sampling of current international experimentation affecting the governance core of our mandala concept for dealing with complexity. As can be seen, all the issues are not homebased. This recalls what Dean Rusk said when, as Secretary of State, he was addressing the House Foreign Affairs Committee: "The world is round. One-third of its people are asleep at any given moment; the other two-thirds are awake and probably stirring up mischief somewhere!"

Thoughts in Conclusion

So much for winds of change in the boardroom—that center core of our strategic governance system. Here are half a dozen suggestions on how we might think internationally and strategically about the future:

First, create a flexible attitude around your corporate strategy. The worldview is one of continual uncertainty, conflict, tension, and transition from one state of disequilibrium to another. Instability is a natural condition of most developing enterprises.

Second, be realistic about international social, economic, and political problems and opportunities. The value systems and environments are widely variable. Cultural context and legal systems are not comparable. For instance, one of my Arthur D. Little colleagues recently observed these differences in laws and regulations: in Britain, you can do it provided it's not forbidden; in Germany, you can do it if it is allowed; in France, you can do it even if it is forbidden; and in Russia, you cannot do it even if it is allowed.

Third, withhold our biases about how best to organize for managing and governing future enterprises. An open style setup may be very useful in dealing with normative strategic plans in a turbulent future. The mentality which accepts past organization structure as appropriate for the future may be passé. The basis for future organizational structure may rest more on social and political imperatives than on economic, technological, or historical factors. A fluid approach to governance will be useful. The board of directors will grow in importance in the corporate scheme of things.

Fourth, future leadership will demand that the leader influences the institution more than it influences him. No longer will the leader be the "wave pushed ahead by the ship," as Tolstoy wrote. A recognition of the companionship of art and science of management is called for in our strategic actions.

Fifth, unusual degrees of career and individual freedom will be required if we are to retain and motivate top talent for our future organizations. Continual sharpening of intellectual and business capabilities with less dependence on a central-life interest in one corporation will be more characteristic. Acceptance and understanding of such a culture is necessary.

Sixth, individual's issues of choice and the selection of tradeoffs will require more sophistication and more thoughtful perception of the very nature and purpose of our activities. Responsible thinking on an international canvas will tax our managers who, in the past, have often gotten by without full appreciation or acknowledgment of the social-political-cultural and ideological sanctions and demands of our societies around the world.

Note

1. For further discussion, see Robert K. Mueller, *New Directions for Directors* (Lexington, Mass.: Lexington Books, D.C. Heath, 1977).

5 Beyond the Economic Problem

Gerard Piel

Nearly 50 years ago, John Maynard Keynes held out a generous vision: "that the economic problem may be solved or at least be within sight of solution within 100 years. This means the economic problem is not, as we look into the future, *the permanent problem of the human race.*"

For readers who might not have encountered the economic problem, Keynes defined it: "that struggle for subsistence always hitherto the primary, most pressing problem not only of the human race but of the whole biological kingdom from the beginnings of life in its most primitive form."

Today we can say, for the one-third of all of us that live in the industrial—the "rich" or the "developed"—countries, the economic problem is behind us. For the rest of mankind, it can be said that the technological fix is in.

A century from now, we can see the world population stabilized at a total number of 8 to 12 billion. People then will look back upon the population explosion of our time as a benign event. For most of our history mankind experienced not population explosion but population growth, on the Malthusian plan of equilibrium with misery. People maintained their fertility resolutely at high rates to offset the high death rates that held human life expectancy down to 25 years for almost all of history. A century from now, almost everyone will live to see their grandchildren. The world population will then have returned to zero growth or near zero growth rate, but at low death rates and low birth rates. Mankind will have achieved stable population not by birth control but by making it possible for every individual to live out a full human biography—that is, by economic development.

We can make this prediction with confidence from the experience of that one-third of us who have made the demographic transition to near zero growth at low birth rates and low death rates. We inhabitants of the industrial countries are able to count ourselves members of the world middle class. We are the first beneficiaries of the technological fix.

The technology that has thus fixed our estate does not belong to us; we are its trustees for all our fellow men, for technology embodies the accumulative experience of our species from the beginning of our biological evolution. In the great task of economic development that now faces the rest of mankind, our role—our duty—is nothing more than to share our heritage with them. We need have no concern about the cost of this enterprise; technology is knowledge, the one resource that increases in the using and the sharing of it.

33

That this declaration may sound high flown—that the great task of promoting the economic development of the underdeveloped countries is scarcely represented on the agenda of contemporary U.S. politics—locates the principal obstacle to the attainment of the vision of mankind securely at home on the only planet we will ever inhabit. The obstacle is presented by our institutions and the values that sustain those institutions.

The Original Sin was slavery. Slavery made possible the building of high civilization. From the institution of slavery, however, there persist in all contemporary societies institutions that rest upon scarcity and inequity and blind us to the new dispensation of equity and abundance.

As an example of our institutional and moral incapacity, consider that we find ourselves paralyzed by an energy crisis at the very hour when science and technology have brought infinite sources of energy within our reach.

In addition to gigantic, central nuclear power stations, we can look forward to securely ballasted, decentralized electrical power generated by solar collectors on rooftops. Bruce Chalmers, at Harvard, is now satisfied that his technique for rolling out large single-crystal sheets of silicon will bring the capital cost for solar cell power systems within the competitive range of $500 per kilowatt. Melvin Calvin, the distinguished student of photosynthesis at Stanford, tells us that botany is going to deliver generous supplies of energy from the biomass.

Most of mankind faces a want more urgent than energy, that is, food. Roger Revelle, the oceanographer who came ashore to get the salt out of the Pakistani farmlands, estimates that the application of demonstrated agricultural technology to the established arable land of the world will feed a population of 45 billion. That is many times more people than we need plan for, providing we work the technological fix.

Beyond demonstrated agricultural technology, molecular biology is bringing into agriculture new command over the genetic capacity of plants. Industrial laboratories as well as university laboratories are already engaged in isolating the genetic apparatus that fixes nitrogen in the bacteria and fungi that do this work in association with the legumes, such as soybeans and alfalfa; they will then transplant those genes to the plants themselves, not only into the legumes but into wheat and corn and other crop plants as well.

To fix their own nitrogen the plants will have to divert some solar energy away from the production of edible tissue—you see, not even in molecular biology do you get a free lunch. Other genetic engineers propose, therefore, to transplant the carbon-fixing apparatus of the so-called C-4 plants, which conduct photosynthesis more efficiently, into our standard field-crop plants.

The new generation of agricultural scientists envisions the design of crop plants that will fix their own nitrogen, yield 10 tons of edible tissue per acre, do so on half an acre foot of water, and thrive in all latitudes from the far northern prairies deep into the tropics.

Here we collide again with our value problem. America is ill-prepared for the next revolution in the plant sciences. The financing of university biology by the national health agency—preoccupied with the afflictions of the middle aged and the middle class—has diverted the energy of American life scientists into zoology and human biology. The result is that we have all too few scientists trained for effective contribution to the task of feeding the world.

If we are to find our way around the confusion of our values brought on by the impact of technology upon our institutions, we must face those impacts honestly. The values by which we live derive from the simplifying compulsion faced every day by old Adam, "When do we eat?" As Samuel Johnson said, "If a man knows he is to be hanged in a fortnight, it wonderfully concentrates his mind." It is no wonder that the relief of that compulsion, that our transit through the economic problem, should afflict our society with the symptoms of the bends. Keynes himself foresaw our plight when he wrote that essay nearly 50 years ago.

"I think with dread," Keynes said, "of the readjustment of the habits and the instincts of the ordinary man bred into him for countless generations which he may be asked to discard in a few decades. Must we not expect a general nervous breakdown?"

The model of our society that we carry in our heads and to which we refer grave public decisions comes from the golden age of America as an agrarian republic. It is an agreeable model. Describing the yeoman England from which the colonists came, the British economic historian R.H. Tawney wrote: "Whatever the future may contain, the past has shown no more excellent social order than that in which the mass of the people were the masters of the holdings which they plowed and of the tools with which they worked and could boast, with the English freeholder, 'It is a quietness in a man's mind to live upon his own and know his heir certain.' "

Our agrarian republic was a myth even in the eighteenth century, for 25 percent of the labor force of the colonies was in slavery. We have come a long way now to the industrial state. While we know our heirs certain, just about every one of us present here is an employee. Technology has undermined and overthrown the central pillars of our social order: property and work.

Consider, first, property. Property ownership no longer confers power in our society. Power resides in that most revolutionary of all institutions, the U.S. industrial corporation. Through that agency, power has been disjoined from ownership and has been taken in the hands of self-selecting, self-perpetuating managements. Those managers know most vividly that the security and vitality of their corporations resides not in their real property nor their fixed assets, but in the capacity of their people to innovate. Power issues from the brains of those organizations, not from the assets on the balance sheet. The deployment of resources in research has become the fulcrum of decision making; it determines what business the corporation will be in a decade from now.

This kind of power is essentially political. Indoors, it is the bureaucratic-political sorting out of human capacity that brings managers to the top of these huge enterprises. At the top, these managers find their days preoccupied with the external politics of public regulation, which constrains their relations with investors, employees, customers, and competitors, and now such third parties as the pressure groups that speak for the environment and have compelled us to recognize that we cannot buy progress and amenity at the price of destruction of the values of the natural world around us.

Nor is this system of corporate political power peculiar to the American economy. That heroic Russian physicist, Andrei Sakharov, in an essay that the censors keep his fellow citizens from reading, tells us, "The development of modern society in both the Soviet Union and the United States is now following the same course of increasing complexity of structure and of industrial management, giving rise in both countries to managerial groups that are similar in social character. We must therefore acknowledge that there is no qualitative difference in the structure of the two societies. . . ."

The disappearance of work raises even more sensitive and troubling ethical and moral issues. There is no way to avoid the conclusion that we have become a workless economy. Mechanical horsepower long since displaced human muscle from the production process. Now the fleapower that activates the circuits of the computers and the robots is displacing human nervous systems, not only from the production process but from a rapidly lengthening list of white-collar functions as well.

The profusion of economics has devoted considerable talent to reassuring us that we face no technological unemployment. The most recent grand-scale effort was that of the National Commission on Technology, Automation and Economic Progress appointed by President Johnson and chaired by Tom Watson. On the efforts of this commission to assure us that all was right with the world, Wassily Leontief, a Nobel prize winner in economics, observed, "The debate about technological unemployment is always charged with emotions that are raised by the human or the inhuman implications . . . " of the very term. To help his readers take those emotional hurdles, Leontief rewrote the report as a parable of the horse. A National Horse Commission convoked early in the century would have remarked "the past steady growth of the total employment and per capita output of horses" and, from those cheerful figures, would calculate "how much aggregate demand would have to be increased to secure satisfactory employment opportunities for the steadily increasing equine labor force."

In truth, the average productivity per horse on the American farm would go on soaring until tractors had displaced the horse population entirely. What happened to horses, Leontief concluded, "must under no circumstances be allowed to happen to human beings in a world in which more and more productive tasks can be performed better and more cheaply by machines."

Our country has done remarkably well in absorbing the shock of technological unemployment. Today we are concerned about employment not in order to increase the national product but to secure its distribution—to qualify consumers with the effective demand of a paycheck, each to purchase his share of the growing abundance of our workless economy. Our success is reflected in the restructuring of our labor force over the last 25 years.

During that period, the output of U.S. manufacturing industries, measured in constant dollars, more than doubled. The number of blue-collar workers increased, however, by less than 20 percent. The white-collar payroll of industry, by contrast, doubled; it is in these ranks that we find the swelling number of high-paid managers and technologists who move knowledge from the laboratory to the production line. In consequence of this primary impact of technology, our labor force went through a revolutionary transformation.

In 1950, more than half the labor force, 55 percent, was engaged in producing goods. By 1975, the producers of goods had shrunk to less than 30 percent of the labor force. With more than 70 percent engaged in the services, we had made the transit to the world's first service economy. What most economists fail to acknowledge, however, is that we have maintained employment by creating half and more of the new jobs for a 50 percent larger labor force outside of the economy as we customarily define it. The government, by political and not by market decision, made those jobs. Public employment in America swelled from 7.5 million in 1950 to 17.5 million. This was not by any reckless inflation of the federal payroll, which increased by less than 1 million to just under 3 million in that period. The great expansion came in state and local payrolls which are concerned with meeting such essential human needs as medical care, education, and public safety.

To those employed on the government payroll, we must now add another 11 million employed by the political decision that makes purchases from the private sector. That 11 million does not include those employed by the Keynesian repercussion of those purchases, but only those directly employed by government purchases. The total of the paychecks generated outside the market economy now, therefore, employs more than 30 percent of the American labor force, compared with 18 percent in 1950.

To that 30 percent we should now add the employees of a most significant and characteristically American sector, that is, the not-for-profit private sector. This is the locus of our hospitals and our universities principally, but also of other volunteer citizen enterprises too numerous to mention. The employees of this sector equal 7 percent of the total labor force. This brings the citizens employed outside of the market economy up to nearly 40 percent of the labor force.

When we reckon up the numbers from the consumption side, we find still more of our fellow citizens living outside the economy. To the 30 million employed in the public sector by paychecks, we must now add those increasing numbers who are receiving transfer payments, that is, payments for no work. They now outnumber those who receive paychecks.

We must reckon first with the million or so who are at all times chronically incarcerated in jails and mental hospitals. They must be regarded as recipients of pure transfer payments because, surely, those institutions see neither to their rehabilitation nor their therapy.

There comes next the 2 million who at all times are running through their unemployment insurance benefits. To them must be added the growing numbers on welfare. There are 7.5 million of them, and that does not count their dependent children.

Then there is the largest group of all: the 21 million who live on social security. We have abandoned the fiction that their incomes flow from an insurance trust fund. The premiums are called "payroll taxes" and the benefits are counted in the executive budget. Perhaps not all the beneficiaries can be counted as public-sector people, for some live also on incomes from other sources. More than half, however, have no such other sources; they have only their social security check or the pittance they are allowed to earn without jeopardy to their social security income.

If we add all these public sector denizens together—the receivers of paychecks and the receivers of transfer payments—we find 50 to 60 million of our fellow citizens living outside the economy. If we add their dependents, starting with the 10 million dependent children on welfare, we get a total of more than 100 million. This is more than half the American population.

Plainly America has crossed a major watershed in the transformation of its social order. That the 100 million and more who live outside the economy are supported by less than 40 percent of the gross national product shows us that the public sector remains America's poorhouse. Poverty in America is a social institution maintained by incomes or transfer payments that are set by political decision.

Along with poverty, most of the denizens of the public sector must accept shame with their incomes. Public employment in America remains suspect except, perhaps, for the status we accord to judges and generals. Yet the public sector is also the habitation of people engaged in those occupations which Sigmund Freud called the most demanding of all: "to govern, to teach and to heal." To these occupations and people society has been looking, over the past 25 years, with increasing recognition of its dependence upon them for realization of the values and amenities of the material abundance generated by our workless economy. The chances are that we will look to them in even greater dependency in years to come.

The picture we have sketched here does not show that "excellent social order" recalled by R.H. Tawney. We cannot regard the passing of that social order without regret. We have tried to exhibit the major structural features of the society we are actually living in.

There is always the danger that history and evolution can carry the real world out of congruence with the model of the world we carry in our heads.

Most of us form that model in our adolescence or, at the latest, in the latter years of our formal education. Albert Einstein, in one of his great generalizations, said: "Common sense is a deposit of prejudice that is laid down in the mind before the age of 18." Such loss of touch with reality is dangerous enough for the individual; it becomes a downright peril for society as a whole if the world model of its decisionmakers goes very far out of phase with reality.

With the economic problem behind us, we are faced at last with our real, our permanent, problem. The lifting of the compulsions that simplified life for old Adam sets us free to discover how to be human beings—in the words of J.M. Keynes, "how to occupy the leisure which science and compound interest have won for us to live wisely, agreeably and well." If that seems too difficult, there remains, for at least the rest of the century, the task of helping the other two-thirds of our fellowmen to get beyond the economic problem.

World Roundup: What Corporate Enterprises Will Face in the 1980s

James M. Gavin,
Nicholas Steinthal, Oscar A.
Echevarria, Polyvios C.
Vintiadis, and Yoshimichi
Yamashita

America's Future: Its Hopes and Problems
James M. Gavin

National power can no longer be expressed in terms of weapons systems alone. It is now a function of domestic and economic conditions as well. This means that businessmen—not military men—are in the front tier of national defense in today's increasingly competitive world. Their leadership is crucial because national strategy must be based on economic, technological, and societal considerations.

In view of this shift, we must take a new look at our defense needs and the balance of power in the world today. Many people are concerned over the concept of power in its own right, and the manner in which it is wielded by the United States, the USSR, international coalitions, and more recently by the OPEC nations of the Middle East.

Although the United States has technological power, this has proved to be a mixed blessing. Those responsible for meeting the hardware needs of our armed forces have an admittedly difficult job, which they have pursued by exploring every bit of new technology for its possible contribution to our weapons systems. Since newly developed technical information has been coming at us almost too fast for comprehension, our weapons become obsolete the moment they are in inventory.

This has been the picture over the past 20 years and more, a time during which this country could have, for example, bypassed silo-built static missiles for the more secure and less-detectable mobile system that is now being proposed for deployment by 1980 at a cost of $35 billion to $45 billion. In the meantime, the current obsolescent systems must be maintained.

We can no longer afford the huge expenditures for fielding redundant systems. When these have been questioned, we are usually told that the newest one is a blue chip on the bargaining table in the SALT talks, or references are made to commitments in Southeast Asia. These and other old dogmas and clichés must give way to a more sensible and responsive national defense posture.

41

The reasons are the changes in the very basis and nature of power that have emerged within the last decade. The most dramatic is oil power, which is slowly gaining political leverage. There has been with us for some time the problem of commodity power, defined in such terms as Jamaican bauxite and Moroccan phosphates. The United States is particularly vulnerable to this form of power. Seven major minerals come from Third World sources. In addition, we import one-third of our requirements for thirteen out of fifteen raw materials.

New technologies in the world also represent new bases of power. For example, Brazil is learning how to replace imported oil with ethyl alcohol from sugar cane and other crops. Other inroads include the use of enzymes in industrial processing, obtaining rubber from a desert bush, and of course, solar energy. Accordingly, it is technology plus the knowledge of how to apply it that constitute a nation's true strategic resources. In this sense, technology has replaced weapons systems as the major consideration.

Add to this the fact that the power of the states per se has also grown. The bipolar world of 20 years ago, in which the United States and Russia confronted one another, was replaced by a five-power world in which the European Economic Community, Japan, and China joined the original contenders. Now countries in South America and Africa are vying for a share of the power. These shifts can be traced, in part, to the control of new technologies, commodities, and resources.

The problem is how to accommodate ourselves to this new political world while providing an adequate defense establishment. Our true strategic interests now lie in the economic and social realms, while the military sphere has actually become a tactical area.

This shift has developed since the post-World War II era when our air power was considered as strategic, since it was not opposed by any comparable force and was free to attack nonmilitary targets, such as cities, factories, and power plants. Simultaneously, our tactical forces were kept in a high state of readiness. Twenty years ago, however, the strategic role of both our long-range aircraft and our missiles ceased to exist as such. The primary mission given these forces was to engage and destroy their counterparts that had grown up in enemy territory, and thus they became long-range tactical forces in nature.

Parallel with these developments, the world itself has become a small tactical theater, owing to improved communications and transportation. Today we are witnessing the development of fiber optics, which can bring about a sixtyfold expansion of communications channels at one-tenth the cost of copper. Similarly, a team of atomic physicists predicts that the first human message could be sent through the earth—rather than around it—as early as 1979.

With these profound changes in communications, we are forced to examine the domestic condition in countries where the overriding concern is growing populations and diminishing resources. For the Third World countries, and others as well, adequate food and fresh water, housing, health care, education, and the economics of obtaining them are problems of the first magnitude.

This means that in order to focus on the strategic questions of economic and domestic conditions, expenditures for tactical forces must be based on the hardest of decisions in order to avoid duplication, redundancy, and waste. With these kinds of problems before us, it is auspicious that the Joint Chiefs of Staff are at long last being examined with a view to possible reorganization. There has been too much of a tendency in the past for each of the armed services to support the programs of the others, receiving support in turn. This has led us to acquire weapon systems that are not only redundant and extremely costly, but sometimes designed more to meet the needs of the individual service than national requirements.

In the October 1978 issue of *Scientific American*, two members of a Boston study group, Professor Philip Morrison and Paul F. Walker, have proposed a drastic change in the composition of our military forces. Their article is based on their recent book, *The Price of Defense: A New Strategy for Military Spending*. After a careful and thorough examination of the changing pattern of weapons systems, they come to the conclusion that an adequate defense budget could be provided by the 1980s at a total of $73.2 billion. This compares to the present budget of $120.4 billion. If realized, this change would significantly enhance the position of the dollar and, if handled properly, go a long way toward helping to balance the budget. These two events alone would significantly help our national defense posture. Their proposal, if nothing more, emphasizes the need for a reexamination of our strategic position in world affairs.

The View in Europe
Nicholas Steinthal

Europe is a very heterogenous region. How can one generalize about an area which includes Basque nationalists, British aristocracy, a large Italian communist party, and social welfare systems ranging from the world's most luxurious (Sweden) to the most rudimentary (Switzerland)?

Therefore, let us first briefly touch on the key issues facing the major European countries—and only then attempt to generalize about the main factors of change which, in our view, will impact to a greater or lesser extent on Europe as a whole.

Issues Confronting Major Countries

Germany, after a postwar period of rapid growth and labor shortages, will need to learn how to live with low growth and an increasingly high cost of social services

France faces the still unresolved and profound conflict between labor and management. This is a potentially explosive situation, barely contained during the recent elections.

The United Kingdom faces the challenge of using its (time limited) oil wealth in order to create a viable society and economy.

Italy will need to find ways to make the country governable, given its left-right political polarization.

Spain will struggle to establish viable democratic institutions as a precondition to joining the European Economic Community (EEC).

The challenge to the EEC as a group is, of course, how to accommodate these diverse pressures (and presumably a number of potential disasters) and still forge a political framework to support its existing and increasing economic interdependence.

Key Areas of Change

If we now try to find a common denominator for our European pressure cooker, what areas can we identify where business planners should be alert to change and where change will have a profound impact on the business climate?

The keynote for the eighties will be set by two factors:

1. Economic growth will be very slow, due to stagnating populations (the German population is actually declining), the continuing worldwide economic difficulties, and high energy costs.
2. Pressures for the redistribution of wealth, deeply rooted in the postwar socialist tradition of Europe, will increase.

The consequences of these two tendencies will, of course, be manifold. For the businessman, some of the more relevant developments can be summarized under the headings of social change, investment trends, and market factors.

In the *social arena*, we need realistically to anticipate changes which will complicate the management task. The rigidity of industrial structures will increase; it will become even harder to close factories or to lay off labor. Due to government pressure, management will be at least as much concerned with preserving and creating jobs as with profitability. Worker participation in company decision making will increase—the currently high levels of codetermination in Scandinavia and Holland will be reached first in Germany, and later in the southern tier of Europe. And finally, the cost of social services will increase and will be borne by fewer people, due to aging and stagnating populations.

The *investment picture* is also changing dramatically. Outside investment will be increasingly welcome (even in France) because of persistent unemployment problems. But there will also be fewer investment opportunities. The investor, therefore, will need to be highly selective, relying on technological strengths and on building synergism in his U.S. and European business portfolio. And there will be increasing European investment overseas, particularly in North America. This desire by Europeans for both direct and portfolio investments could spell opportunities for the North American business community.

Within the European *marketplace*, changes will occur. Companies and competition will increasingly become Europe-wide, rather than remain contained within individual countries. Economies of scale will improve, but managing European enterprises will be more complex in such areas as distribution, labor relations, antitrust matters, and key executive personnel. And because of the increasingly high quality of life, demand will shift to high-value goods and services.

In summarizing these thoughts, one cannot avoid the conclusion that the European scene in the eighties will be far less attractive than in the postwar years. Clearly, U.S. business cannot ignore the large and wealthy European markets, but it will take high levels of management skill—especially sophisticated and perceptive strategizing—to identify and to capitalize on opportunities.

Latin America's Business and Social Environment
Oscar A. Echevarría

Businessmen interested in Latin America are primarily concerned with performance, which is dependent both on the economic characteristics of the region and on the social characteristics of its population. This essay provides a frame of reference to facilitate the task of understanding by (1) providing a socioeconomic profile of Latin America, (2) assessing the impact on business of the most important economic characteristics and social attitudes, (3) identifying probable areas of opportunity and responsibility, and (4) suggesting key strategy considerations. Although official data from Latin American countries, as in any developing countries, are subject to much uncertainty, the statistics used for this document permit drawing general relative qualitative and quantitative conclusions about the different Latin American countries.

The Economy

Major Countries. Making generalized statements about a heterogeneous region composed of twenty-seven different countries deriving their origin principally from five different nationalities but with recent immigrants from all over the world appears difficult. However, the great majority of these countries are Iberian in origin. Furthermore, seven Latin American countries—Brazil, Argentina, Mexico, Venezuela, Chile, Colombia, and Peru—account for 80 percent of the total Latin American population of 330 million, 88 percent of the total GNP of $450 billion (U.S. dollars), 74 percent of the total exports of goods of $55 billion (U.S. dollars), 73 percent of the total imports of goods of $50 billion (U.S. dollars), 85 percent of the total net foreign debt of $55 billion (U.S. dollars), and 82 percent of the total foreign reserves of $27 billion (U.S. dollars).

In both GNP and population, these seven countries combined represent a market larger than any country except for the United States, the Soviet Union, Japan, and West Germany. These seven countries are generally divided by international lending institutions into two groups: the larger, more populated, and/or industrialized countries, including Brazil (seventh in world population and tenth in GNP), Argentina, and Mexico (twelfth in world population and sixteenth in GNP), and the smaller, less populated, and/or industrialized countries, including Venezuela, Chile, Colombia, and Peru. Each of the other Latin countries has no more than 30 to 40 percent of Chile's, Colombia's, or Peru's level of economic activity.

By most demographic and economic indicators, Brazil accounts for approximately 30 percent of Latin America in size. Argentina and Mexico combined account for an additional 36 percent. Of these three countries, Brazil ranks first by almost every statistic; Argentina and Mexico differ in levels of development and economic size measured by different economic or social indicators.

The second group of countries—Venezuela, Chile, Colombia, and Peru—combined accounts for about 20 percent of Latin America's main demographic and economic statistics. These countries have been traditionally of comparable economic dimension and development. But recently Venezuela has begun to grow at a faster pace, and today it is of an intermediate size between the first group of countries and those still remaining in the second group.

Any effort to assess business opportunities in Latin America can be greatly simplified by concentrating the analysis on those seven countries. However, excellent opportunities also exist in other countries as a result of the value of specific natural resources, strategic locations in relation to other markets, or acceptable import substitution opportunities despite small market size.

Economic Performance

Rate of Growth of Gross Domestic Product (GDP). The growth of gross domestic product (GDP) for the region as a whole has been relatively stable over the past decade and a half. The annual percentage change in GDP was on the order of 5½ percent per year in constant dollars from 1961 to 1970, a rate of growth which increased to about 6.9 percent per year through 1974. In 1975, GDP grew at only slightly over 3 percent, mainly reflecting the world recession, but in 1976 it grew 5 percent.

The primary sector—agriculture and mining—contributes about 18 percent of economic activity and has been growing at a rate lower than the average for the economy. The secondary sector—which includes manufacturing, construction, utilities, transportation, and communications—constitutes 37 percent of GDP and has been growing slightly faster than the whole economy. The manufacturing sector has been growing at a fast yearly pace—between 6 and 10 percent in recent years. In Ecuador and the Dominican Republic, the industrial sector has posted yearly increases of over 11 percent in several recent years. Value added by transportation and communications economic activities is strongest in Brazil and Argentina. Finally, the tertiary or services sector—which includes commerce, finance, government, and other services—maintains a 45 percent share, at the average growth pace for the economy.

Investment. Gross domestic investment in constant dollars increased at about 4 to 5 percent per year between 1961 and 1967 and about 12 percent per year from 1968 to 1975. The highest increases in the last 6 years have been in Brazil, Ecuador, and the Dominican Republic, where gross domestic investment has reached between 18 and 20 percent per year. Domestic investment in Latin America accounts for approximately 20 percent of GDP and was valued at close to $60 billion in 1976 (in 1973 U.S. dollars). During 1970-1973, the seven largest countries in Latin America financed between 80 and 100 percent of all investment domestically, as measured by the ratio of net savings to gross domestic investment.

The flow of external financing has increased rapidly over recent years, from $5.1 billion for 1972 to $6.6 billion for 1973 and $7.6 billion for 1974. In 1975, financing from International Development Bank, the World Bank, and the Eurocurrency markets amounted to $8.3 billion. External financing has become a greater proportion of total investment, increasing from 7 percent in 1961-1966 to 9.2 percent in the 1967-1970 period, to 12.2 percent in 1971-1974, and to over 10 percent in 1971-1975.

The seven largest countries which received most of the external financing also account for the largest portion of external debt (about 85 percent). The total debt for Latin America was around $80 billion in 1976 and has been growing at 17 to 20 percent per year recently. The average composition of the debt is 28 percent due after 10 years, 26 percent between 5 and 10 years, and 46 percent in the next 5 years. About 52 percent of the debt is from public creditors and 48 percent from private sources, including banks (20 percent) and suppliers (16 percent). The ratio of external debt service to exports of goods and services averaged around 14 percent in 1976 and appears to be increasing.

Inflation. The factors influencing inflation vary by country, and further distortions are introduced by relatively frequent changes in monetary policy. However, the most important reasons for inflation in Latin American countries generally include expansion of monetary supply to finance government deficits for social programs and for increased capital and consumption expenditures by the central governments and government-controlled companies, devaluation of currency, and recently, the impact of external or world inflation. Of these three major factors, world inflation has had a significant impact in Latin America, where average prices for import commodities grew 5 percent per year in 1971-1972, 13 percent in 1973, and 45 percent in 1974.

Latin America as a whole has shown a tendency toward inflation rates higher than worldwide inflation. Until the late 1960s, most countries had stable conditions, with inflation at rates below 5 percent per year. But very few remained in that category in the early 1970s, although five had returned to it by 1976. Until the late 1960s very few countries had consistently high inflation rates of over 15 percent per year, but in 1976 eight countries were in this situation. The trend since 1970 has been one of increasing numbers of countries posting these high inflation rates. Most recently, economists have coined the term *hyperinflation* to describe extremely abnormal situations such as those occurring in recent years in Argentina, Chile, and Uruguay. The 1975 inflation rates for these countries were 180, 360, and 80 percent, respectively, and in 1976 they were 347, 174, and 51 percent, respectively.

Economic Integration. An important consideration in any analysis of business opportunities in Latin America is the impact of the constraints and regulations imposed by the regional economic associations. At present, five main groups with different memberships are active on different fronts of economic activity. The Latin America Free Trade Association (LAFTA) includes all the Latin American countries. The Andean Subregional group, or ANCOM market, includes three Pacific countries (Peru, Ecuador, and Colombia), Bolivia and Venezuela. The latter group probably has created the greater amount of constraints, such as Decision 24, for its member countries. Two common markets operate in Central America and the Caribbean Economic Community that replaced CARIFTA, the previous economic association in that area. A smaller association in the center of South America, called URUPABOL, regulates special trade and industry agreements between Uruguay, Paraguay, and Bolivia.

In addition, in 1974 the Latin American countries met and established SELA, a Latin American economic system aimed at helping coordinate the efforts of all the other major integration groups. Several industry associations also exist for specific areas of common concern, such as steel and oil.

Population

In the 1980s Venezuela and Peru are expected to show a marked reduction in population growth rate. Mexico and Brazil are not expected to decrease their relatively high population growth rates by significant amounts even through the year 2000. Chile and Argentina have traditionally lower growth rates, and these are expected to decline slightly.

The area is characterized by high population concentration in urban centers. However, the migration trend from the farms into the cities of the last few decades is being reversed, and new population growth is expected to be higher outside the cities. Argentina, Venezuela, and Chile, with urban concentrations of around 80 percent in 1974, are expected to show diminishing urban population concentrations of 60 to 70 percent by 1980. Mexico, Peru, Colombia, and Brazil had urban concentrations of around 60 percent in 1974. By 1980 there will be more than 350 cities with populations exceeding 50,000 people. Almost 40 percent of the urban population is expected to be concentrated in seven large cities, averaging 8.2 million people each: Mexico City, São Paulo, Buenos Aires, Rio de Janeiro, Limae-Callao, Santiago, and Caracas.

Implications

Some of the socioeconomic characteristics just described imply excellent business opportunities without a countervailing negative trend. Some of the main examples are the size of the market, stable economic growth, increased value of exports of basic commodities, and greater institutionalization of government, regardless of the method of access to power. Other characteristics, however, can be considered a mixed blessing. For example, the positive aspects of population growth and increased urbanization, which facilitate production and marketing, are increased market size, greater availability of labor, and a larger geographical concentration of population. Among the negative aspects, which contribute to social pressures and instability, are real estate inflation; overtaxed cities, unable to provide adequate services; a larger proportion of younger, nonproductive population; and larger unemployment.

Another mixed blessing from a business point of view is the improved education and skill of the labor force. The positive side is that education increases productivity, but on the other side, a more educated labor force has rising expectations about standards of living, social mobility, and participation. These expectations lead to greater governmental intervention in business and labor relations, costly social reforms, and welfare programs that contribute to inflationary pressures.

Third, a more technocratic government contributes to greater efficiency and stability. However, since technocrats have a professional bias to increase their participation in the economic affairs of the country, their role leads to the expansion of the government role. Increased government participation in basic industries is also a cause of production inefficiencies resulting from the lack of autonomy of public firms' managers in making sound economic decisions, social pressures to increase employment or subsidize consumption, or the inability or unwillingness to exert adequate discipline over the production factors. And national businessmen displaced from their logical areas of expansion are prone to turn to foreign firms as their alternative to new business opportunities.

Fourth, on the positive side, concern for the quality of life increases production opportunities by expanding the consumption mix to the model of a developed country. On the negative side, however, it creates social tensions when the economy cannot grow and develop at a pace sufficient to provide the quality and diversity of goods and services that the population demands.

Fifth, concern for the environment contributes to new business opportunities in the production and installation of environmental control devices, but it increases the cost of doing business.

And last, a more sophisticated entrepreneurial and middle class provides better potential business associates or partners and greater social stability. However, this class will be more demanding in its relationship with foreign businessmen as well as have rising expectations, which, as in the case of labor, will also be a cause of social instability but will have stronger implications because increasing expectations are being felt by the leaders of the country.

Finally, some Latin American trends negatively impact business opportunities without beneficial side effects. The most important of these is the continuous inflation in some countries such as Argentina and Chile.

As mentioned before, inflation has been generated by government actions in reply to the pressures of a pluralistic society with rising expectations. This has moved the government toward larger deficits and distributions of benefits to competing groups over and above the capacity of the economy. Deficits are also created by the inefficiencies of some government enterprises. And finally, a large component of imported inflation is tied to currency-exchange problems, particularly the devaluating dollar.

Social Attitudes

Opportunities are also a function of the attitude toward foreign investment and business. Some social attitudes have contributed to a reduction of uncertainties. For example, the nationalization of major industries has clarified the area available to private enterprises, both foreign and domestic. Regulations of foreign business and trade have been completed in all major countries and, in general, are similar in nature to those of ANCOM Decision 24. The attitude toward foreign investment is becoming more liberal. One example is the recent Decision 24 amendment increasing the remittance of profit from 14 to 20 percent of registered capital and also allowing the reinvestment of excess profit in designated areas and permitting the yield of such reinvestments to be exported. Nonetheless, there still is a need for divestment by many foreign investors or change in the nature of their presence in the country. Therefore, a suitable divestment strategy must be selected among several options. All these options entail opportunities for continuous business, such as management contracts, technological assistance, or the provision of key raw materials and equipment. There are also good opportunities for large projects in partnership with the government and private local entrepreneurs.

In addition, in many cases new investment permits will be tied to commitments to generate export opportunities. And in general, establishing a Latin American business will require a suitable domestic partner, since the time of the wholly owned subsidiary is coming to an end. Other opportunities will open through association with Latin American entrepreneurs to penetrate other areas of the developing world, since the Latin Americans can be considered by underdeveloped countries as acceptable technological and cultural intermediaries.

As for investment abroad by Latin Americans, the official attitude is divided. It is generally accepted if government-owned or promoted, but it is not well thought of if it is private or direct investment (considered a flight of capital).

Major Opportunities

The size and nature of the major Latin American markets and the attitudes of their government and economic leadership suggest that the major areas of opportunity are as follows:

Agribusiness. Given the need for food, both worldwide and in the region, and the availability of land and manpower, this is a prime area for foreign firms with adequate know-how.

Housing. This is needed because of the deficit created by the rate of population growth, which is more rapid than the worldwide rate, and because of the rising standards of living and demand for improved housing.

Production of intermediate and capital goods. This is an opportunity area since the governments would like to encourage more integrated industrial development.

Environmental control products and technology.

Alternative energy sources.

Joint ventures with Latin Americans in other developing countries.

Responsibilities

Any relationship implies a responsibility. What is the expected conduct of foreign businessmen as far as Latin Americans are concerned? Any sophisticated Latin American clearly understands that business is not for charity, but also expects it not to be predatory or irresponsible. Thus some key questions must be answered with regard to any new business venture. For example:

> Are the plant scale and technology adequate for the market or are they ill-designed and likely to cause an increase in the price of the domestic product over competitive imports, which must then be taxed to protect national production?

> Is the diversity of equipment technology or goods proposed compatible with the country's needs?

What are the answers? Possibilities include (1) cooperation among competing foreign companies who try to see the needs of the country as well as their own needs, or (2) division of territories. There is a need for innovative solutions, for example, the possibility of "enclaves in reverse," in which a Latin American country might purchase a manufacturing facility in a foreign country in association with the developed-country partner.

Conclusion

The opportunities of Latin America are many, and in contrast with what is known about other areas of the world, this continent might be one toward which businessmen should be looking in the 1980s.

A final warning is needed, however. There is no such thing as a general investment in or business relationship with Latin America. Investment and business are done with a particular country in a specific sector, in a determined market, with a defined product, and with concrete persons. Therefore, each opportunity has to be assessed by itself, not solely with macroeconomic concepts. The worthiness of a business opportunity can be estimated like a mathematical expectation of an event based on a combination of the attractiveness of an economy and the probability of success of the specific venture. The first, the attractiveness of the economy, is exogenous, since no one can really influence the size, the structure, or social characteristics of any particular country. But the second, the probability of success, can be improved by working carefully with individuals knowledgeable about the specific countries and business areas involved. The interpreter or intermediary provides both language and cultural capabilities; that is, he must be able to understand Latin American ethics and expectations as well as the foreign partner's own motivations and limitations.

The View in the Middle East
Polyvios C. Vintiadis

It is normally difficult to talk in generalities about the Middle East, simply because what is conveniently called the Middle East is in fact an amalgamation of fifteen or so countries, each of which has a different political structure, social and economic plan, long-term objective, amount of funds available, and the like. Furthermore, given the profound transformation the area has been going through since 1972-1973, it is difficult to describe what the Middle East is today, let alone to project to 1990.

At present the region represents a market with great potential. Newspapers and trade journals report that public and private expenditures for new infrastructure and industry are immense. Even allowing for the fact that actual spending normally lags behind planned outlays, and also that certain governments are planning to curtail expenditures in order to combat inflation, actual outlays will still amount to tens of billions of dollars, probably in excess of $60 billion annually, for this year and the coming few years. Obviously, the Middle East represents a very large potential market for Western companies.

When we talk about present and future Middle East markets, we have to bear in mind that some countries are undergoing much more rapid economic development and have more funds to pay for it than others. For example, on a relative scale, the present big spenders are Saudi Arabia, Iran (although in that country there is political upheaval and continued indications of financial strains and reassessment of plans), Iraq, Kuwait, and Abu Dhabi. In the future, however, Kuwait and Abu Dhabi will not represent as large a potential once their requirements for infrastructure and industry are satisfied. Egypt should become a more important market, assuming that its open door policy is strengthened and its financial benefactors continue their support.

An important question one should ask is whether the market, while attractive in terms of size, is also attractive in terms of profitability. Those who have not been in the area and who read about the billions of dollars spent annually on development projects could assume that all companies operating in the region are "making a killing" or at least making profits in excess of those they are accustomed to back home. Unfortunately, the facts tell a different story. Although some companies are enjoying high financial returns, many others have met with disaster, and many have made normal or below normal profits, which, given the higher-than-normal risks the companies are operating under, should be considered as marginal at best. On the surface some of the contracts appear to be quite profitable, and in certain instances they may seem to be exorbitantly so. However, one should take into consideration the extremely expensive business development process that one must go through to obtain the contracts, the difficulties in carrying out the work, the scarcity of skilled labor and professional management, the high levels of inflation (frequently with no compensating escalation clauses), and the unanticipated difficulties of working in another culture which the contractor may encounter after signing the contract and starting work. Given these factors, one begins to understand why many companies have achieved less than they hoped for in their activities in the Middle East.

This situation is changing rapidly, and an increasing number of companies are better prepared and are therefore doing much better now. Furthermore, the Middle East governments and other Middle East principals are themselves better prepared and more experienced, thus creating a more stable business environment.

On the basis of work carried out by Arthur D. Little in recent months, it is apparent that notwithstanding the difficulties encountered in the Middle East, Western businesses are definitely planning to expand their operations in that region. Almost all companies with whom we are dealing believe that the Middle East will continue to be a promising market in the next decade, particularly for industrial plant and equipment and construction services and products. (Incidentally, many companies also say that Middle East business has helped them survive slumps in domestic markets.)

Unfortunately for the countries of the Middle East, much of the current building is of low quality in terms of infrastructure, private housing, and industry. Furthermore, standards of maintenance have been deficient, and there has been inadequate provision for the costs and other requirements of maintenance. Although this is changing, the quality of maintenance today is poor, and this problem is aggravated by the shortage of skilled or semiskilled manpower. If today we can predict anything with accuracy to 1990, it is that after the current period of hectic development, the Middle East is bound to go through a second cycle of development to replace and/or upgrade infrastructure and modernize and enlarge industry.

If present plans are implemented, and it appears that they definitely will be, the Middle East by 1990 will become one of the world's biggest oil refining and petrochemicals centers. This activity will be jointly owned and run by local and foreign, mostly Western, interests. But generally speaking we do not foresee that the region will become by any means a large world industrial center.

Meanwhile, we should expect that the Gulf area will become an inceasingly important trading and banking center. By 1990 a significant amount of international financing will be arranged by Saudi, Kuwaiti, and Bahraini banks, and most of this financing will be denominated in Saudi riyals and Kuwaiti dinars.

At present, most of the governments in the region are spending heavily on education and are sending a large number of students overseas to Western universities. At the same time, governments are making an effort to distribute the oil wealth more equitably to their populations. Both these factors will produce a larger, more educated middle class, which will take an increased interest in the affairs of the country and the running of the government, a development which will create some strains in the political structures of some of these countries. In spite of this, the area in general will remain conservative and Islamic in character, with strong central governments (whether controlled by royal families or a sole political party) and with relatively limited political freedom for individuals.

In several countries in the region there are controls on foreign investment and imports, while in others the environment is more liberal toward outside participation. Although there will be an increased tendency to encourage private enterprise, even in the countries where production is now government owned, the trend is toward more control of foreign investment and imports. The process of Arabization which has started in most of these countries will continue to be the rule in the key economic activities such as banking and some strategic industries. In fact, the key piece of advice for companies interested in the Middle East may be that the time is getting late for concerns not already involved. The doors will soon be closing, and entry will become more difficult, both because of competition from companies which are now getting entrenched and because of new restrictive regulations.

With regard to overseas investments by governments and wealthy families in the area, these we would expect will be characterized by conservatism. Government investments will by and large continue to be made in government bonds, and private investments will go to secure or low-risk investments, such as real estate, stocks of blue chip companies, or bonds. We do not expect that there will be significant action in terms of takeovers, since the Arabs and Iranians, while having financial resources, do not have significant managerial or technological resources to offer to potential acquisitions.

In general we believe that the current intensive development activity will continue to 1990, that the Middle East will gradually become an easier area for Western companies to do business in, and that conservatism will characterize the region in the social, political, and economic areas. As these countries develop their own domestic capabilities, become more organized, and introduce more up to date legal and business systems, they will apply more controls and, in some instances, new or increased restrictions on foreign participation in various industrial and commercial activities. Therefore, the time is now if someone is interested in entering this geographic area for the long pull and wants to exploit the opportunities that are being offered and will continue to be offered not only through 1990, but even beyond.

Japan in the 1980s
Yoshimichi Yamashita

Key Problems

The economic problems that Japan faces in the 1980s are the following:

1. To secure energy sources. Japan has an 88 percent dependency on imported energy and a 75 percent dependence on imported oil. This critical factor says much about Japan's future problems.
2. To balance its international trade—and to handle the increasing trade conflicts with Europe and the United States that are already emerging.
3. To change its industrial structure to meet changing world markets.

In the *political* arena, Japan is quite stable internally. However, it is subject to problems caused by its international role. It will have to work carefully to maintain its strength as a trading nation. Positive participation in international politics will be requisite.

In the *social* arena, the immediate future will see some turmoil as a result of the impact of international events on the Japanese situation. The Japanese economy is so closely interconnected with the international economy and with international political events, which are difficult to predict, that the future of the country will continue to be subject to upheavals resulting from changes in other areas. Most of these will not be under the control of Japan.

In the *social* and *economic* arenas, an increasingly difficult problem for the country will be to cope with its aging workforce.

Basic economic indicators characterizing the Japanese economy in the period through 1980 will be as follows: GNP growth, 5 to 6 percent net; inflation, 5 to 6 percent; wage increases, 5 to 7 percent; and unemployment, 2 to 3 percent. The economy probably will not grow as rapidly as in the past. The country was growing over 10 percent annually before the oil crisis erupted, but GNP growth will probably be 5 to 6 percent per year at most in the early 1980s.

In addition, some structural changes are likely in the national economic system. The so-called Japan Inc. was an export-oriented economic system, based largely on the use of imported oil. Japan has become a kind of technical process center. To alleviate trade conflicts, this economic system must change rapidly to one that is well balanced and coordinated with world economic systems and more receptive to imports from overseas.

In the industrial area there must be a change toward more high-value-added industries and services and away from low-value-added industries, where Japan is being displaced by developing countries. There must be further evolution beyond mass-production areas to the service areas.

Further, increasing requirements for multinationalization of Japanese corporate enterprises are probable. Although these requirements will be extremely difficult to meet, in part because of strong differences in language and culture, they appear to be imperative if Japan is to maintain its role in the world economy. This is one of the limited options open to Japan to maintain its role.

Concentrated research and development efforts will most likely be focused on new energy sources, because of the great Japanese dependence on imported energy. Concentrated efforts focused on high-quality mass-production technologies in strategic industries formed the basis for the successful national production center that came to be called Japan Inc. This historical success gives rise to hope that future success may stem from concentrated energy research.

In the political arena one can expect a move toward the "medium right" for the majority of the population. Stable labor-management relationships are likely, but not participation by labor yet in the management of private enterprise. The increase in the older portion of the population will increase requirements for social security and place increasing strain on the socioeconomic system.

Government Attitude toward Investment
by Foreign Firms and Imports

Since balancing the Japanese economy and maintaining its role in the international economy will be a primary political issue facing Japan in the 1980s, the Japanese government will continue to encourage imports of foreign products and also investments by foreign firms. Success or failure by foreign firms will be largely a matter of the extent of efforts by foreign firms to understand Japanese requirements, to choose product and service areas carefully to minimize competition and maximize success, and to develop strategies to break through language barriers and minimize other cultural problems. Foreign firms have to take a long-term strategic approach toward the Japanese market to gain a foothold and then a greater share as time goes on. Unfortunately, many foreign firms still hold the same image about the Japanese market as they held 10 years ago, when the Japanese market was small and much more strictly regulated.

Government and Corporate Attitudes toward
Domestic versus Foreign Investment and Exports

Since Japan must earn U.S. dollar credits to buy imported energy, the Japanese Government will continue to encourage exports. Its posture will become more moderate, however, so that it can attempt to alleviate international conflicts and encourage a more comfortable international position. Private Japanese companies will be increasingly interested in investing overseas to solve problems stemming from the international trade imbalance, to circumvent international trade barriers, and to avoid problems arising from the fluctuating exchange value of currencies. We would expect that at least 30 percent or so of the Japanese Gross National Product will continue to be directed toward foreign markets.

It is important to note that Japanese companies find it very difficult to train management staff to manage investments in overseas countries having different cultural and language environments. This problem will impede, but probably not prevent, Japanese companies from taking a larger role in foreign investment.

Investment Opportunities for Domestic and Foreign Firms

There are a number of investment areas in Japan which hold good opportunities for both domestic and foreign firms. Chief among these are those related to energy, including nuclear and coal power plants, utilization of coal in industry, and mechanisms for energy conservation, including new engines, new transportation systems, more and better insulation, and more effective engineering of new buildings to conserve energy.

Engineering applications will provide a number of opportunities for investment in Japan. The automation of industry to offset increasing wages will also be important. Here, increasing use of electronics, particularly microprocessors and computers, will be important.

The health care industry will be a key investment area, in particular because it is one of high political exposure. Investments toward improving the quality of life and services to consumers will also be important. The housing industry, which is in some respects Japan's poorest consumer area, will provide fertile opportunities. High-quality food products will provide growth opportunities, as will leisure industry and services and educational services.

For foreign firms in particular, non-mass-production items, items which require reduced maintenance, items which provide a high-quality image, and items which are being encouraged by the government will provide the most promising opportunities. These might include industrial electronics; space- and aircraft-related developments; power-plant-related developments; health care equipment and supplies; specialty building materials and products, including interior finishing products and furniture; specialty food products; and specialty chemicals.

**Part II
Socioeconomic Issues**

7

Inflation: A Global Perspective

A. George Gols

World Inflation Trends

Chapter 2 alluded to the impact of U.S. inflation trends on the world economy. This chapter focuses on world inflation trends in general. First, world inflation has slowed somewhat recently but is still exceedingly high compared with earlier periods. Inflation in the world today is running at about 8 percent (see table 7-1). This is down from approximately 10 percent in 1975-1976 and 12.5 percent in 1974. But this average masks a performance ranging from 1.5 percent for Switzerland to over 100 percent for Argentina. In the major industrialized countries, the rates range approximately from 4.5 percent for West Germany to 11 percent for Sweden.

In May of 1977, my colleague, Kirk Bozdogan, in an ADL Impact Services report entitled *World Inflation Outlook*, indicated that "we do not expect a return to the pre-1973 rates of generally under 5-6 percent per year in the late 1970s and early 1980s in the world economy." He also identified a "lack of effective control over the growth of international liquidity" as a serious impediment to the control of world inflation. There is no question that Dr. Bozdogan's forecasts are being validated. Nevertheless, for some countries the inflation rate is subsiding at this time, but there is serious question as to whether, and how long, this trend can be expected to be sustained. Those who see money supply as the key cause envision further inflationary spurts as some of these countries try to restimulate their economies. Those who believe that "cost-push" will be the major function in driving inflationary forces see OPEC actions and other institutional factors as being a prime cause for future inflation pressures. Whatever the underlying reasons and whatever the future may be, there is no question that inflation has already profoundly affected world economic relations, world trade patterns, and many other institutional arrangements.

Key Inflation Impacts

First among the major inflation impacts is the fact that the international monetary system has undergone a profound metamorphosis. The U.S. dollar,

Table 7-1
International Price Trends, Consumer Prices: Percent Change

	1973	1976	1977	Estimated 1978
OECD Countries				
Canada	10.6	8.0	9.1	8.0
United States	10.5	5.5	6.5	7.5
Japan	24.5	9.5	6.1	5.0
France	13.7	10.5	9.9	8.5
Germany	7.3	5.0	3.6	3.6
Italy	19.1	20.0	18.6	12.0
United Kingdom	15.6	16.0	13.1	7.0
Total OECD	13.2	8.0	8.0	7.5

Sources: Organization for Economic Cooperation and Development and Arthur D. Little estimates.

once considered the world "yardstick" reserve currency, can no longer be expected to function adequately in that role.

Second, the abolishment of gold-backing of the international dollar, the freeing of exchange rates, and the instability in the international value of the dollar as a reserve currency—which are all, in major part, inflation-induced consequences—also mean that there is no effective control over the growth of international liquidity, save that exercised by central banks, which is inadequate for transnational jurisdictions.

Third, sharp world currency fluctuations are making it increasingly difficult and expensive for corporations to anticipate or plan for the impact that such fluctuations create on foreign-derived corporate profits.

And last, the destabilizing forces of inflation on world currency fluctuations, when superimposed upon the accumulating trade deficits in industrialized and less-developed countries caused by the huge cost of oil imports from OPEC, will continue to distort world trade and investment patterns and force countries to seek refuge behind trade barriers.

The Chances of a New Worldwide Recession

There is a question as to whether these factors will precipitate a worldwide superrecession. The rest of this chapter centers on this problem and explores potential alternative scenarios of developments and consequences for corporate planning.

First, insofar as possible world recession is concerned, we do not think that will be an immediate problem. Some countries, as already noted, have been able to decelerate their inflation to the point where they are able to take more stimulative, or "locomotive," action to buttress world growth. We refer here primarily, of course, to West Germany and Japan, where inflation rates are close to 4 to 5 percent and where fiscal and monetary policies have become more expansive.

For many other major Western countries, the near-term inflation trends are also favorable; for example, inflation is subsiding in Great Britain, France, and even Italy. In Latin America, inflationary forces have retreated somewhat in Brazil and Argentina, but they have come to a peak in countries such as Peru. In other parts of the world, such as the Middle East and Asia, inflationary forces are still high, with Israel and Saudi Arabia leading the parade at about 20 percent per year. Indonesia and India are examples of less-developed countries that are also fighting to be able to unwind a double-digit inflation rate.

The Eastern European countries and the Soviet Union are also facing inflationary pressures—which even the price-control mechanisms of the Central Planning Agency find difficult to mask. In addition, Canada and Mexico, our most immediate neighbors, have inflation rates that even exceed those of the United States.

Longer-Term Implications

There is no question that the potential exists for world inflation to persist at close to an 8 percent rate. There is a question, however, as to the corrective actions that can be instituted to unwind some of the inflation pressure. Inflation rates at 8 percent per year for the world are sufficiently destabilizing to endanger the world economy and world trade. We must find ways to defuse this inflationary time bomb. What are likely to be some of the means by which this might be done?

We have already outlined what we believe will be a major possible policy course to be adopted in the United States. Frankly, this is likely to be a "middle-ground" alternative to mandatory price controls, on the one hand, and letting extreme inflationary pressures be controlled mainly by traditional monetary/fiscal policies, on the other.

Second, in other countries, such as Canada and Great Britain, which also have had relatively disappointing results with price controls, possibly similar types of policy approaches may be instituted unless economic conditions show a considerable improvement.

Third, in countries such as West Germany, the continuation of a social contract between labor and management which is the result of codetermination practices (or the participation of labor on the management boards of companies) is very likely to be an ongoing instrument for balancing conflicting employment and inflation goals.

For Japan, modest stimulation and relatively tight central bank monetary policies may be the answer. In many of the less-developed countries, price and wage controls may be the main instrument for controlling inflation.

In the longer term, many of these measures may turn out to be simply "bandaid" policies offering no final cure. Therefore, over the longer run, some monetary compact between nations will probably be formed with an attempt to orchestrate a closer coordination of the control of international liquidity. This may be done under the aegis of the IMF, OECD, or some other supranational organization. Until this is accomplished, however, we will continue to be under the threat of tremendous world economic price inflation instabilities and therefore possible worldwide stagnation. Certainly, it will be a period of greater disorientation, with the proliferation of sundry experiments aimed at efforts to find a better stabilizing mechanism.

8 Issues in the Availability of Nonfuel Resources

Kirkor Bozdogan

Introduction: Are We Entering a New Era Dominated by the Economics of Scarcity?

A basic question facing us during the remainder of this century is whether we are entering a new era dominated by the economics of scarcity. During the past several years, this question has been gaining increasing momentum, for two major reasons.

The first is the emergence of a "limits to growth" mentality, created by the doomsday outlook painted by the *Limits to Growth Study* sponsored by the Club of Rome. The message here was simple: sooner or later (and sooner than we surely wanted to hear) the exponentially growing demand for basic materials, including energy and nonfuel resources, will outstrip their supply. This has raised the specter of a world economic collapse—the vision of a future society depleted of essential resources, running out of energy and choking in its own exhaust fumes. Of course, the severe commodity "shortages" and sharp price increases of 1973-1974 only inflamed these apprehensions.

The second reason can be traced to the success of OPEC, the oil cartel, and the resulting "energy crisis." The energy crisis then became linked to a potential "nonfuel resources crisis," by extension. The success of OPEC spurred fears of new OPEC-like cartels controlling the flow of critically needed resources to industrialized countries. Along with the threat of new cartels came the increasing demand from the Third World countries for international commodity agreements.

Bauxite, copper, chromium, lead, zinc, cobalt, and a broad range of other nonrenewable (or exhaustible) mineral resources have been available to the industrial countries in the past, generally without much of any problem. Today, the disruption of these mineral supplies would cripple the economies of these countries. What is the myth and the reality of the growing concern over the availability of these nonfuel mineral resources? We can first examine this question from a global viewpoint and then look at the situation from the perspective of the United States.

**Sources of Concern Over the Future Availability
of Nonfuel Resources: A Global View**

Taking a global view, a number of key issues need to be addressed. These concern the prospects for the depletion of essential nonfuel resources, the threat of new OPEC-like cartels and the outlook for international commodity agreements, and finally, whether we are entering a period characterized by insufficient investment in nonfuel resource industries in terms of exploration and development.

We will skip over essentially short-term issues, which have to do with possible short-run supply-demand adjustment problems. These are caused largely by conditions of cyclical volatility, which is common to many basic resource industries.

*What Are the Prospects for the Depletion
of Nonfuel Resources?*

There are two opposite and conflicting views concerning the depletion of essential mineral resources: the physical view and the economic view. The logic of the physical view is quite simple. The total available supply of any mineral is a fixed stock by definition, since the earth is finite and contains only so much of any substance. Meanwhile, demand, which is a flow variable, continues year in and year out. Sooner or later demand has to consume or exhaust the available supply. The end is likely to come sooner rather than later, because demand is growing exponentially. This, of course, is the argument inherent in the *Limits to Growth Study*.

While the resource base for any particular mineral commodity is a fixed stock, its reserves are not. Reserves represent not a static but a dynamic concept; reserves change as prices and technology change. At current rates, the resource base for all the mineral commodities identified would sustain production for millions, in some cases billions, of years. Thus, if the resource base rather than reserve estimates is used as a measure of mineral availability, at current rates of production the physical depletion of minerals becomes an extremely remote problem.

Economists, however, see a more serious problem in the physical view of depletion. They maintain that long before the resource base for a mineral is exhausted, extraction and processing costs and prices will rise, so that demand will be stifled, or alternatively, demand will shift to available substitutes. This has been true, of course, since prehistoric times.

What Is the Threat of New OPEC-Like Cartels
and What Is the Outlook for Third World Demands
for International Commodity Agreements?

The United States, Western Europe, and Japan are the major consumers, outside the Communist Bloc, of all mineral resources. They are, therefore, in principle vulnerable to the emergence of new cartels and to Third World demands for international commodity agreements. Over the last few years, a number of associations of major exporting countries have been formed, covering copper, bauxite, iron ore, mercury, and tungsten. As far as the future is concerned, and in the normal course of events, we do not think the outlook for them is very bright. We must qualify this, however. For example, they should not be altogether ruled out, especially in cases where world exports, output, and reserves are concentrated in a few countries that can band together, where demand is inelastic, and where supply outside the cartel is very limited.

As far as international commodity agreements are concerned, they too seem to have met with limited success so far. During the last few years, the Third World countries have been demanding the establishment of an integrated set of price-stabilization agreements through the creation of buffer stocks. They seem to have given up hope, finally, in recent months.

The outlook for the threat of new cartels, as well as for international commodity agreements, may be sharply reversed during the next few years if economic recovery and growth in the industrial countries accelerates and takes a more steady course and if the United States faces a general capacity constraint or bottleneck in the basic resource industries in the 1980s.

Is There Sufficient Global Investment in
Basic Nonfuel Resource Industries?

The exploration and development of mineral resources require the commitment of large amounts of capital. Further, new mines and processing plants are not built overnight. It takes 2 to 3 years, for example, to expand a copper mine and about 7 years to construct a copper smelter, from engineering design to shakedown.

The basic point is that during the postwar period there has occurred a fundamental change in the structure of key mineral resource industries world-wide (such as copper) through the wholesale nationalization of mining and processing operations by a number of host countries. There is now growing evidence that the move toward nationalization or more active participation by governments has stifled mineral investment. A World Bank survey recently showed that between 1970 and 1973 more than 80 percent of total expenditures on mineral exploration in the nonsocialist world was concentrated in only four countries: Australia, Canada, South Africa, and the United States.

In other words, in recent years it appears as though new private investment in the development of the mineral resources of the developing countries has all but ceased. Such a development, combined with a possible and general capacity constraint or bottleneck problem in the United States, could have ominous implications for the early 1980s.

The Mineral Resource Position of the United States in World Perspective

Let us now briefly turn to potential problems facing the United States in the 1980s. It is, of course, impossible to give a complete assessment of the nonfuel resource position of the United States in a brief summation. We can say that generally, however, except for chromium and perhaps a few other minerals, the United States has an abundant endowment of nonfuel resources. All that is needed is the technology that can competitively exploit these resources. As I see it, over the next decade or so, the basic issue for the United States will be a growing and sharp conflict between the desire for clean environment and increasing dependence on foreign supplies of key nonfuel resources. The point is illustrated by a concrete example: the case of the U.S. copper industry. Arthur D. Little has recently completed a study for the Environmental Protection Agency (EPA) on the copper industry which concluded that the impact of environmental regulations on this industry over the period 1978-1987 will be extremely serious. It concluded that the environmental regulations would not only lead to increased production costs (because of compliance costs), but would also, and perhaps more seriously, constrain domestic smelter capacity growth over the next decade.

The study provided detailed impact conclusions in terms of effects on production, consumption, prices, imports, etc. The capacity impact problem only is extremely serious. In summary, the currently promulgated air pollution control regulations will effectively constrain (and could even reduce) domestic smelter capacity between now and 1985 and would require major expenditures for capacity maintenance between 1983 and 1988.

If the Arthur D. Little findings on the copper industry do not represent an isolated case but rather a more general phenomenon, we will, in all probability, face a serious capacity bottleneck problem in the 1980s in a number of key nonfuel resource industries. As a consequence, our import dependence is quite likely to rise.

Although the prospects for resource depletion worldwide most certainly appear remote, the United States may be entering a period over the next decade or so where it faces a basic policy tradeoff between clean environment and increasing dependence on foreign supplies of key nonfuel resources. Such increasing dependence on foreign supplies of key nonfuel resources may, in some cases, prove costly and even dangerous, especially if domestic capacity constraints in basic nonfuel resource industries (with or without more "robust" economic growth in the United States and in other industrial countries) invite the emergence of new cartels and/or ignite renewed Third World demands for international commodity agreements on terms not entirely favorable to the United States or to the other industrial countries.

Patterns of Growth in U.S. Industry

Vince P. Ficcaglia

Over the past several years we have witnessed a sharp increase on the part of many corporations in efforts to better understand the relationship between their business, markets, or industry and the general economy. Such efforts have been in large part a response to a growing realization that business planning at an industry, product, or market level cannot proceed independent of events of a more macroeconomic nature. The experiences of the 1970s, with its wage-price controls, oil embargo, energy woes, double-digit inflation, and growing involvement by the federal government in the private sector, served to convince even the greatest skeptic that microplanning must be carried out with an awareness and understanding of macroeconomic events.

The response on the part of many corporations has in part been to beef up their staffs, especially in the areas of market planning, even creating new positions with such novel titles as Manager of Econometric Analysis, Director of Environmental Assessment, and even Corporate Economist. Along with this came an explosion in model building. Either with their inhouse staffs or with the help of consultants, many corporations have gone the route of constructing models embodying mathematical relationships which are purported to identify and quantify the interaction between a particular industry, market, or product and the overall economy or major segment thereof. Efforts to date have been quite numerous, and success, no matter how limited, has proven to be very educational. For the producer of wooden panels, the link to the macroeconomy is fairly direct. By tracking movements in residential home building and, perhaps, nonresidential construction, sales prospects can be fairly accurately determined. The implications of higher or lower levels of new building activities can also be directly translated into faster or slower gains in output.

However, for many corporations, the task has proven more difficult. For example, a manufacturer of styrene has no direct connection with major end-use markets of the overall economy. His product, which can be converted into a variety of intermediate and processed chemicals and then used in numerous applications, is well back in the economic chain of product flow through the economy. As a result, demand for his product is derived from his customers, who in turn may be dependent upon numerous other intermediate manufacturers or fabricators ultimately tied to an end-use market such as autos, appliances, apparel, or construction. Despite this separation of product and final market, it behooves the styrene producer to identify and understand the flow of

71

his product through the economy. Only in this way can meaningful and more reliable assessments of the influence of macroeconomic events be translated into changes in product demand. Needless to say, the further back in the product flow chain a producer is, the more difficult the task. However, the more imperative such a task undertaking becomes. The identification of a product's flow from producing stage through the economy ultimately to an end-use application, no matter how complex or less than comprehensively achieved, does allow the user to better understand his position vis-à-vis the economy and better monitor changes that can feed back—directly or indirectly—on his business.

For many corporations, their modeling efforts have been focused on quantitatively tying their business to movements in appropriate macroeconomic variables—GNP, consumer spending, capital outlays, etc. Changes in these components provide the principal force for growth in many industries. Note the previous reference to the wood panel manufacturer and his direct relationship with new building activity. Other industries that also have a large fraction of their performance determined directly by macroeconomic variables include aircraft producers, machine tool manufacturers, auto producers, and beverage producers. However, superimposed upon these and other less macro-oriented industries is another important determinant of growth which has not truly received due attention—in part because many analysts are not aware of it, believe that it is relatively less important for some industries, or believe that it cannot be quantified. This force is technical/structural change. It is this determinant of growth that explains why gains in the electronics industry have greatly exceeded those in all other industries, why chemical industry production continues to advance at about twice the rate of GNP, and why growth in plastics exceeds and growth in steel is less than that of their respective principal end-use markets.

Technical and structural changes can take various forms. However, the contributing factors generally comprise four broad categories.

Substitution of one material for another in the production process. The substitution of lightweight materials for steel in making an automobile is an example. Consequently, sales of plastics to the automotive sector will grow faster than automobile production, reflecting the use of greater amounts of plastic per auto. This in turn will have a positive effect on suppliers to the plastics industry, for example, petrochemical feedstocks. In like fashion, sales of steel to the automotive sector will advance at a rate slower than total auto production. The slower rate will blunt the demand for coking coal, limestone, industrial gases—all inputs in the steel-making process.

Technical change in the production process of an industry. For example, the increased use of oxygen converters instead of the open hearth has led to a greater penetration of oxygen (that is, industrial gases) in the iron and steel industry. Similarly, the expanding use of electronic components in various applications is generating a rate of growth in the production of integrated circuits well above that in its major end-use markets.

Introduction of *new products* within an industry. Microwave ovens, medical scanning equipment, and solar-energy-related materials are just a few of the myriad of new products introduced within the past few years. Their introduction has meant new opportunities for growth in such diverse industries as plastics, electronics, aluminum, and various chemicals.

Design changes in existing products. Growing concern for energy conservation has led to important changes in the design features of new (and to a lesser extent, existing) structures. For example, new homes are being constructed with greater amounts of insulation materials in walls and attics, while existing homes are being retrofitted with additional insulation. As a result, the pace of production in the fiberglass industry is well above that of new homebuilding or expenditures on home improvements. Similarly, design changes in products such as new cars, household appliances, and television sets are leading to new demands for plastics, electronics, rubber, and various chemicals. These increased demands then cascade into new opportunities for various supplier-related industries.

As previously discussed, structural and technical change can have both a positive as well as a negative effect on industry performance. While plastics and aluminum are making new inroads into the automotive market, steel is losing market share. Discrete semiconductor devices and electronic tubes are being displaced by integrated circuits and microprocessors as the technological boom in the electronics industry continues. Conservation efforts are resulting in structural/technical changes in the economy that are having an adverse impact on demand for gasoline and gasoline stations. Thus the historical relationship between the total number of autos registered, miles driven, and demand for gasoline is undergoing change.

A recent Arthur D. Little study forecasts about a 15 percent per year real rate of increase in the production of integrated circuits over the next 10 years. About 70 percent of this growth will be due to changes of a technical/structural nature. The changes take the form of new applications and increased market penetration by integrated circuits and are expected in markets such as motor vehicles, medical equipment, computers, communications equipment, and process instrumentation. Growth in plastic resins production is expected to be about 3 to 4 times as great as that for the overall economy as measured by real GNP. About 60 percent of this growth in plastic resins production will be due to technical/structural changes, with a concentration in autos, packaging, and building applications. Among other industries in which technical/structural factors will play a very significant growth determining role are organic chemicals, alkalies and chlorine, aluminum, computers, communication services, business services, and automatic temperature controls.

At the opposite end of the spectrum are many industries in which technical and structural factors are having an adverse impact on demand. Such industries are losing market share because of materials substitution, design changes, etc.

For these industries, the growth inherent in their final demand markets (the macroeconomic factors) is being eroded by these adverse technical/structural changes. For example, growth in such industries as electronic tubes, zinc, iron and steel, copper, and veneer and plywood products will be less than that of their major end-use markets.

Arthur D. Little recently examined the problem of cyclicality in the chemical industry and the relationship between growth in the chemical industry and growth in the U.S. economy. Analysts have often hypothesized a multiplier relationship between growth in these two sectors; that is, on average, chemical industry production has been thought to advance 2 to 3 times as fast as GNP. The recent performance of the chemical industry has led many industry analysts to question the continued existence of such a relationship and to ponder the value of this multiplier today. The brief analysis which Arthur D. Little undertook showed the following:

On average, growth in chemical industry production has exceeded and continues to exceed that of GNP by about a 2 to 1 ratio.

While the overall chemical industry multiplier has remained unchanged, there have been significant changes ongoing within various segments of the chemical industry.

Whereas growth in synthetic fibers contributed strongly to this multiplier relationship, especially during the 1960s, this sector has reached a mature stage in which fiber penetration into new markets has slowed substantially.

In like manner, synthetic rubber has undergone a similar maturing, especially in its principal market—tire production.

Maintaining the overall multiplier relationship today for the aggregate chemical industry is growth in plastics, which continue to benefit from new applications and increased market penetration.

As a result, while the overall macroeconomic relationship between the economy and the chemical industry has shown little change, technical/structural factors are generating significant changes within the industry, affecting growth prospects in various chemical segments.

The implications of change due to technical and structural factors are significant for U.S. industry and its corporate participants. They speak directly to the marketing, sales, and planning functions within a corporation. Hence there is a need to be able to identify, understand, and assess the impact of technical and structural change upon individual markets, industries, and entire corporations.

Where technical and structural relationships are working against an industry, any sales or market forecast that does not explicitly reflect such factors would err on the high side. The implications for stockpiling, market pricing, and overall corporate performance may very well be severe. Similar problems would result for corporate decisionmakers in industries which are being favorably impacted by technical change.

For corporate decisionmakers concerned with acquisition and diversification opportunities and strategic planning, the need to understand the forces at work upon a prospect is paramount. Market penetration levels, requirements for research and development, industry position, and product lifecycle stage can be influenced sharply by technical and structural factors. An attractive corporate marriage may turn unexpectedly sour if the suitor is unaware of change ongoing in its new marketplace and is unable to position itself to accommodate such change. On the other hand, a timely acquisition of a firm in an industry experiencing rapid technical/structural shifts on the plus side could help to offset some of the downside risk generated by the cyclical swings in the macroeconomic environment.

On balance, it behooves corporate decisionmakers to demand of their sales, marketing, and planning staffs assessments of corporate performance that adequately and accurately incorporate change due to technical and structural factors. It is necessary, therefore, that the means and methods employed in preparing such assessments be structured so as to account for the influence of such factors.

10 Planning to Meet Social Impacts of Large-Scale Projects

Michael C. Huston

Environmental impact assessment is increasingly used as a tool for integrated planning in the industrialized world. The first national legislation giving rise to environmental impact assessments was started in the United States in 1969. Between 1971 and 1977, some 9,000 formal impact statements were registered.

Canada, Germany, France, and Japan have similar legislation. Other countries, including Norway, Sweden, and the United Kingdom, preferred to incorporate environmental impact assessments in existing governmental procedures for physical planning and pollution control. Proposed environmental impact assessment legislation is now being discussed in Austria, Switzerland, the Netherlands, and within the European Economic Community (EEC) in Brussels.

In Eastern Europe, the Council for Mutual Economic Assistance is developing a methodology at a project programming level for economic and noneconomic evaluation of man's impact on the environment based on the practical experiences of Czechoslovakia and Hungary.

Several international institutions that finance development projects [such as the World Bank and the International Development Association (IDA)] now give top priority to helping developing countries avoid some of the potentially dangerous economic infrastructure and environmental consequences that often result.

In order to incorporate environmental considerations into a decision or a decisionmaking process, it is necessary to develop an adequate understanding of the possible and probable consequences of a proposed action on the environment. However, prior to this understanding, a clear definition of the environment must be constructed.

The word *environment* means many different things to different people. To some the word conjures up thoughts of woodland scenes with fresh, clean air and pristine waters. To others it means their man-modified neighborhoods or immediate surroundings. Still others relate *environment* to *ecology* and think of plant-animal interrelationships, food chains, threatened species, and so forth.

Actually, the environment is a combination of all these concepts, plus many, many more. It includes not only the areas of air, water, vegetation, and animals, but also other natural and man-modified features which constitute the totality of our surroundings. Thus transportation system characteristics, community structure, and economic stability all have one thing in common with carbon monoxide levels, dissolved solids in water, and natural land vegetation—

they are all characteristics of the environment. Thus the environment is made up of both biophysical and socioeconomic elements which should be considered in environmental impact analysis.

But what is meant by *impact analysis*? Simply stated *impact* means change—any change, positive or negative—from a desirability standpoint. Therefore an environmental impact analysis is a study of the probable changes in the various socioeconomic and biophysical characteristics of the environment which may result from a proposed or impending action.

In order to accomplish the analysis, it is first necessary to develop an adequate understanding of the proposed action. What is to be done? What kinds of materials, manpower, and/or resources are involved in building and operating the proposed facility? Second, it is necessary to gain an adequate understanding of the affected environment. What is the nature of the biophysical and/or socioeconomic characteristics that may be changed by the action? Third, it is necessary to project the proposed action into the future and to determine the possible impacts on the environmental characteristics, quantifying the changes whenever possible. Finally, it is necessary to report the results of the analysis in a manner such that the analysis of probable environmental consequences of the proposed action may be used in the decision-making process.

The exact procedures to be followed in the accomplishment of each environmental impact analysis are by no means simple or straightforward. This is due primarily to the fact that many and varied projects are proposed for equally numerous and varied environmental settings. Each combination results in a unique cause-condition-effect relationship, and each combination must be studied individually in order to accomplish a comprehensive analysis.

However, most industrial companies attempting to analyze environmental impact on a solely individual basis soon find themselves at a loss. No individual industrial company possesses the skills and the range and depth of knowledge necessary to address adequately all aspects of the environment in an environmental impact analysis. In view of this fact, environmental studies are usually conducted in a systematic and interdisciplinary manner by teams of specialists.

The original United States National Environmental Policy Act (NEPA) was passed in response to concern about degradation of the physical environment caused by industrial facilities, mines, highways, ports, power plants, and similar developments. However, in the nearly 10 years since passage of the NEPA, standards have been or are being established to regulate the amounts of pollutants which can be discharged by a new facility and to establish areawide pollution standards (for example, limiting the overall concentration of a given pollutant in an entire air basin or body of water). As these standards have been established, the range of potential impacts on the physical environment which may be generated by a proposed project has been narrowed. As a result, greater attention is now being paid to the socioeconomic impacts of development and its short- and long-term effects on a community's population and infrastructure requirements.

The NEPA and the subsequent guidelines for the preparation of environmental impact assessments provide little specific guidance on the scope and level
of detail of the socioeconomic impact analysis. The principal requirement is that
when an environmental impact assessment is required (that is, when there is
likely to be a significant impact on the physical environment), consideration
must also be given to possible population, economic, and social impacts. Because
of the trend toward greater community involvement in the environmental
impact assessment process, there have also been nonregulatory (that is, not
dictated by law or by practices of the lead agency) pressures to increase the
scope and detail of the socioeconomic impacts even when a project is not
expected to have significant impacts on the physical environment but may have
large population impacts.

In recent years there has been increasing disenchantment with the idea of
uncontrolled industrial growth. At one time, industrial plants were sought and
welcomed by almost every community, no questions asked. Today, most
communities are selective in the types of industry they seek, and an increasing
number of them have adopted a controlled-growth or even a no-growth policy.
While special inducements to incoming industry, such as favored tax treatment
or the provision of water or sewage service at a discount, are still common in
some communities, a number of other communities have adopted or are
considering the imposition of impact fees. Where the emphasis was once on the
economic benefits to be derived from company payrolls, more and more
attention is now being given to the impact the facility will have on the
environment and the services of the community.

Often communities do not have full-time public officials and administrators
or the capital budgeting, planning, and land-use control programs that their
situations call for. With a rapid population influx, their housing, commercial
facilities, and public services soon fall far short of growing community needs.
The consequences may include unsafe or insufficient water supplies, increased
taxes, scarce and high-priced housing, inadequate transportation, crowded
schools and medical facilities, and inadequate law enforcement and fire protection services. Public concerns center on a deteriorating quality of life; uncertainty as to what, when, and where development will take place; and questions
of who assumes the responsibility for public infrastructure investment. Communities which are unable to deal with the impacts may pay a heavy price in
social disruption, employee discontent, declines in productivity, increased costs
of production and services, and wasteful use of resources. Residents of impact
areas are likely to look at potential developments in a "cost-benefit" framework,
weighing expected gains in income and service against the potential costs in
higher taxes, increased congestion, or declining environmental quality. Citizens
of communities expected to be impacted by new developments have become as
concerned about degradation of the quality of life as about degradation of the
physical environment.

In these areas of socioeconomic and environmental impact assessments,

Arthur D. Little has undertaken a number of evaluations for proposed large-scale projects. Examples of recent projects are the new Trident submarine base in Washington state, very large crude carrier (VLCC) oil terminals located 30 miles offshore of Texas and Louisiana, liquid natural gas (LNG) terminals in California, the new Saudi Arabian city of Yanbu, and most recently United States Steel's proposed new 7 million ton steel-making facility.

Arthur D. Little has developed a number of models to evaluate the air- and water-quality impacts of large-scale projects. In addition, Arthur D. Little has developed a computerized system that simulates the impact on the socioeconomic environment. This system is referred to as SIMPACT. It was applied by Arthur D. Little to assist in the preparation of the environmental impact assessment for United States Steel's proposed $4 billion steel-making facility on the border of Ohio and Pennsylvania. Its primary purpose was the estimation of socioeconomic impacts directly and indirectly related to the plant, as required under the terms of the NEPA. However, it was also designed for maximum detail and flexibility to be responsive to the needs and concerns of federal, state, and local governments, planning agencies, and area residents.

The computer-system approach was taken because of the sheer magnitude of the proposed project—the proposed facility would require as many as 10,500 construction workers during the peak year and employ about 8,500 permanent operations workers. It would be located on the border of two states, effectively doubling the number of jurisdictions which would be directly impacted (state, county, and local governments and school districts). Impacts would need to be analyzed in terms of different political structures, tax policies, local regulations, etc.

Perhaps of greatest importance was the level of public interest in the proposed project. No new steel mill has been built in the United States for more than 15 years. The proposed plant site—on Lake Erie between Erie and Cleveland—is in a relatively rural area which has a fairly large amount of agricultural land. A significant concern for local residents was thus the tradeoffs to be expected between increased employment and income and the preservation of a rural environment and lifestyle.

Preparation of the United States Steel environmental impact assessment required inputs from 200 Arthur D. Little, Inc. professional staff members. Professional disciplines ranged from engineering to economics, and the staff included experts in environmental engineering, steel industry technology, regional planning, health care, biology, computer science, and many others.

Two principal considerations dictated the general approach to the socioeconomic impact assessment and the environmental impact assessment preparation. The first was the desire to prepare the assessment in a cooperative environment. Federal, state, and local agencies were involved from the outset of the project, providing input to the profile of the existing environment and reviewing each section as it was completed. The second consideration was the need to expedite the process as much as possible so that project construction could begin on schedule about 2 years after the environmental impact assessment was begun.

Arthur D. Little's approach to the preparation of the environmental impact assessment was to work with the various agencies responsible for review of the document. Meetings were held with concerned federal, state, and local agency representatives in order to present the proposed scope of work and methodology and to discuss principal assumptions. Agencies reviewed and commented on the major sections of the work before publication of the draft environmental impact assessment. In this way, United States Steel hoped to be able to address all major areas of potential concern or conflict in the draft document and eliminate the need for time-consuming and costly revisions or additional documentation in response to comments received during the review period prescribed by the NEPA. United States Steel also hoped that by involving various local agencies and groups from the beginning of the environmental impact assessment preparation, the potential for opposition to the project would be reduced.

SIMPACT was used to handle the huge amount of socioeconomic data required for this analysis in a consistent and cost-efficient manner. In the initial stages of the environmental impact assessment preparation, the SIMPACT design served to illustrate to agency representatives the approach which would be provided in the analysis. It was also possible, through use of the SIMPACT design, to illustrate the methodology which would be used to estimate impacts for each of the individual socioeconomic impact topics.

The forty-seven individual impact topic sections of SIMPACT (economics, housing, education, water treatment, taxes, etc.) were designed based on the recommendations of specialists familiar with methods for estimating impacts in each area and responsible for the analysis of results. These specialists determined the most appropriate methodologies for their subject areas based on the level of detail required, data available for the area under consideration, and the requirements of other topic specialists. For example, it was determined that housing requirements could best be estimated on the basis of household size and income. Therefore, it was necessary for the preceding population and economic analysis to provide a detailed breakdown of the new resident population for these two variables. Similarly, because of the emphasis on the fiscal impacts on local governments and school districts, each topic specialist dealing with an area which required publicly funded infrastructure had to develop a method to estimate public costs for both facility construction and facility operation. These public costs, separately derived for each subject area, were aggregated to determine the revenue requirements of each local jurisdiction and the associated impacts on taxes.

One of the principal objectives of the SIMPACT design is to provide a consistent framework for socioeconomic impact analysis. In essence, because of the size of the data base and number of computations required for this project and the desire to provide a method for assessing alternative assumptions, the system was constructed to take into account all the implications of assumptions made at any point in the analysis. In the simplest sense, the initial assumptions about facility employment and the number of in-migrant workers required to fill available jobs lead to impacts on population, housing, and so on. Changing the number of in-migrant workers required or the timing of hiring these workers would affect all other estimates of socioeconomic impacts. However, there are many relationships among other topic areas (for example, the residential allocation of in-migrant workers by community determines the extent to which each school district is affected). Moreover, there is input from almost every subject area into the overall fiscal analysis. The SIMPACT structure ensures that any change made at any point in the system data base will be carried through to all related areas and none of its implications will be overlooked. For example, a change in the type of housing expected to be built in a community will be reflected in impacts on land use, street requirements, assessed valuations and tax base, construction employment, etc. Similarly, it becomes very simple to examine the sensitivity of various topics to assumptions made at earlier points in the system's structure. For example, to what extent will school district tax rates be affected by a small increase or decrease in classroom size? How will secondary (that is, indirect and induced) employment be affected by different assumptions about the percent of construction workers who will be daily commuters? Would a possible construction delay of 1 year and the need to increase employment significantly in the following year to keep the project on schedule cause unacceptable strains on local services?

Any of the many techniques for projecting socioeconomic impacts must involve some basic assumptions and simplification of causal relationships. In practice, the purpose of an environmental impact assessment is to identify the impacts expected to occur under a "most likely" set of circumstances. Obviously, it is not possible for such an impact projection to incorporate possible future economic, legal, or technological changes which could dramatically alter this set of circumstances. In most cases the implicit assumption is that, with the exception of the specific assumptions set forth, all else remains on course. Events of recent years (recession, the "energy crisis," inflation) reinforce the need for sensitivity test capability in order to estimate a range of potential impacts both before and after any development.

Typically an environmental impact assessment for a large-scale project requires 2 to 4 years to prepare, review, and finalize. However, experience indicates that some of the initial assumptions under which estimates were prepared are no longer valid by the time the report is ready to be published. The SIMPACT structure permits response to these changing conditions and inclusion of new estimates either as revised report sections or in the responses during the public comment period (depending on the magnitude of the change). Examples of these structural changes occurred during the preparation of the United States Steel environmental impact assessment. Springfield Township, one of the jurisdictions expected to be significantly impacted, enacted a zoning ordinance with the potential to restrict severely the types of housing which could be built. In effect, this ordinance meant that many of the in-migrant workers who had been allocated to Springfield would have to be reallocated to other communities.

SIMPACT is designed to permit the distribution of employment into four categories—original residents, movers, commuters, and weeklies. Each category has its own unique set of socioeconomic characteristics, and the proposed project's ultimate impacts will be quite sensitive to the allocations of workers among the categories. *Original residents* are those workers hired locally. *Movers* are those employees who move into the area with their families as a result of being employed at the project. *Commuters* drive to work daily from outside the region, while *weeklies* are workers who reside in the area temporarily from Monday through Friday, returning to their permanent homes on weekends. (Weeklies are particularly common in the skilled construction trades.)

Original residents who are employed at the project will spend their income (creating increased business volume and related secondary employment) and generate additional income and sales taxes in the area. However, because they are living in the area even without the proposed plant, their infrastructure (for example, housing, school, sewage treatment) requirements will have already been accounted for under projections of conditions without the project. Commuters spend almost no money locally and, obviously, have no local infrastructure requirements; they affect the area only by generating increased traffic and by increasing revenues in communities which tax all payrolls earned within their boundaries. Weeklies have a somewhat greater impact than commuters in that they spend money locally for lodging and food. However, the majority of their earnings is spent outside the area. They make relatively minor demands on local infrastructure. It is the movers which are of principal concern in any analysis of socioeconomic impacts. These workers bring their families to the area and require new housing, education services, police and fire protection, utilities, etc. All measures of socioeconomic impact are highly sensitive to the share of the project workforce expected to be movers.

The structure of SIMPACT provides estimates for each year of plant construction and the first 10 years of plant operation. The annual structure of the model allows the identification of short-term impacts and their duration to permit planning for mitigating measures. (An example is school enrollments, which may exceed capacity in some districts for a few years and then decline. An appropriate action in this case might be the leasing of portable classrooms or the renting of space in another building rather than the construction of new school facilities.) Other time-phasing problems occur for public expenditure requirements. Some jurisdictions begin to experience expenditure requirements before they begin to realize increased revenues. The expected duration of this lag will help to determine the appropriate alternative action.

Almost all infrastructure components of the SIMPACT model incorporate provisions for excess capacity. This step allows use of existing excess infrastructure capacity for absorption of new population before determining new infrastructure requirements.

The focus of the analysis of impacts on the physical environment is the facility itself. However, to the extent that a project induces population growth, it will also generate secondary population-related impacts on the physical environment. These direct and secondary physical impacts must be evaluated to determine overall effects on land use, air quality, water quality, etc.

The SIMPACT system was also designed to estimate these secondary environmental impacts resulting from population growth and related development. The vehicle miles traveled (VMT) analysis (that is, traffic), which is based on the distribution of employees by place of work and place of residence, is used to determine auto and truck air pollutant emissions. Emissions are also determined for residential and commercial/industrial energy use. These population-related air emissions are in turn used as inputs to the regional air quality modeling analysis.

Other population-related impacts on the physical environment include additional residential, business, and infrastructure land use, with particular emphasis on the amount of open space converted to various developed uses. As part of this consideration of land use, the amount of new paved areas is estimated to determine increases in surface runoff. Sanitary wastewater, solid waste, and water supply impacts are determined as part of the infrastructure requirements analysis, but these also have direct bearing on the physical environment.

In essence, the SIMPACT system, as applied to the environmental impact assessment process, goes beyond the identification of socioeconomic impacts. SIMPACT uses the population, economic, and infrastructure requirement estimates to determine secondary environmental impacts, ensuring that the overall environmental assessment will be as complete as possible in terms of addressing all project-related effects.

A further application of the SIMPACT system is its use as a project-monitoring and ongoing planning tool. As mentioned, the eventual impacts of a given development are likely to differ to some extent from the most likely set of circumstances described in the environmental impact assessment. As these impacts are determined, they can be used as inputs to the system to estimate the longer-term implications of deviations from the environmental impact assessment scenario. In essence, planning officals can use the SIMPACT structure to perform additional sensitivity tests based on actual project-related data (for example, the number of in-migrants who actually move to each community of the study area during the first year of project implementation) rather than the best estimates developed for the socioeconomic assessment.

A small but growing number of companies are beginning to find ways of expediting the environmental impact assessment procedures. From the very outset of the proposed project they are in contact with environmental planners, engineers, and economists. Their intent is to assess the environmental impacts of the proposed facility prior to actual design. This affords the opportunity to "design away" many of the negative impacts and to allow for mitigative measures such as vegetative buffer zones, inplant controls, and process changes. It also permits the public and the regulatory agencies to be kept informed about the project as it develops.

The environmental assessment for a project is, of course, not an end in itself. Rather, it is a vehicle by which a vital, worthwhile project is carried from conception to the commencement of construction. In between these two points, the assessment process provides information to concerned citizens and agencies; it gathers and assembles pertinent data; it assists the design engineers in minimizing the negative aspects of the proposed project; and it produces a technical document for review by the government agencies which ultimately decide whether a project should be built. Done properly, these events can take 1 to 2 years. But the end product is of significant value; it is an environmentally compatible facility which pleases the company, the concerned citizens, environmental groups, and the regulating government agency.

11 Attitudes of Washington Thoughtleaders toward the Role and Competitive Position of the United States in World Trade

Kenneth Schwartz

Introduction

As the mid-July 1978 Bonn economic summit approached, Opinion Research Corporation's (ORC) Public Opinion Index examined how the international trade problems of the United States were perceived by members of Congress, the executive/regulatory branch, the Washington media corps, union leaders, and leaders of public interest groups interviewed during the Index's Washington Thoughtleader Survey. Their attitudes were compared with those of top- and middle-management executives.

This chapter presents the findings based on intensive personal interviews with 104 Washington thoughtleaders, conducted during the period February 28, 1978 through March 28, 1978. Of those interviewed, 47 were in the legislative group, 21 were executive/regulatory officials, 12 were union leaders, 13 were public interest group leaders, and 11 were members of the media. The individuals interviewed in this study are not representative of any particular group but should be considered "purposive" samples of people prominent and highly influential with regard to government affairs. Attitudes of executives are based on intensive personal interviews with a sample of 507 top- and middle-management executives representing the 500 largest manufacturing companies and 50 each of the largest commercial banking, utility, transportation, and life insurance companies. Interviewing was conducted by ORC Caravan Surveys in the offices of respondents from January 16 through February 13, 1978.

The Survey

Washington thoughtleaders, like the nation's executives, believe overwhelmingly in the importance of international trade to the total U.S. economy. At the same time, the degree of importance thoughtleaders attach to international trade is even greater than that expressed by executives (using the same rating scale)—

nearly half of the thoughtleaders (47 percent) versus less than a third of executives (29 percent) say that international trade is of *vital* importance to the U.S. economy (a score of 10 in figure 11-1).

Thoughtleaders as a whole, unlike executives, are more optimistic than pessimistic about the outlook for an improved competitive position for U.S. products in world markets 5 years from now. Legislators, in particular, are more inclined to be optimistic, whereas other thoughtleader subgroups disagree among themselves over whether the competitive position of U.S. products will improve or deteriorate. At least two members in ten of most thoughtleader subgroups expect the general competitive position of U.S. products to stay about the same over the next 5 years. *None* of the union leaders hold this view, however.

Although they recognize the need to alleviate America's energy problems and reduce oil imports, thoughtleaders who are optimistic about the competitive outlook for U.S. products in world markets over the next 5 years believe this

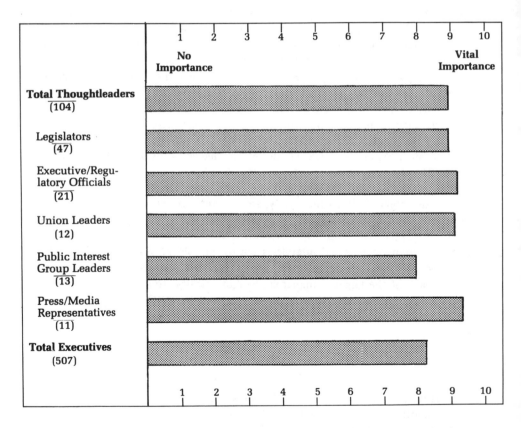

Figure 11-1. Importance of International Trade to the Total U.S. Economy.[1]

nation has many opportunities for significantly increasing its exports, especially with strengthening foreign economies allowing other countries to buy more U.S. products. Working to benefit the United States, they believe, will be a growing world market for agricultural exports, the superiority of American technology, more aggressive foreign marketing strategies by U.S. companies, and a growing awareness among Americans of the importance of exports. They made responses such as these:

> Our technology is so advanced, especially in computers, that other countries will be getting it from us. A lot of services will be obtained from the U.S. Hopefully, our domestic energy sources will be improved so we won't be importing so much oil [congressional aide].

> The development of alternative energy sources and the planned reduction of the importation of petroleum, coupled with a dramatic increase in the sale of agricultural products in overseas markets. We can, over time, substantially improve our balance of payments position [Senate aide].

> The economies of our trading partners—West Germany, Japan, etc.—are growing at a faster rate than ours. It will increase their imports of our products. The dollar is becoming a natural adjuster of the trade balance [union leader].

> Hopefully, we will be successful in greatly expanding our programs for agricultural exports, which are the most important component of our exports, overall [Senate aide].

Several thoughtleaders believe that the decline of the dollar has benefited our trade position, while others think that our competitive position will improve once the dollar strengthens or stabilizes. They expressed these opinions:

> We will muddle through. Things are so bad right now, but, generally, the trend is for some improvement. The dollar is cheap, which should boost our exports over time [press/media representative].

> The American dollar has shrunk. The devaluation of the American dollar means more imports of American goods [union leader].

Some thoughtleaders have faith that the administration's actions on the trade front or more cautious economic policies at home will improve our competitive position worldwide, while a few foresee increasing foreign labor costs or the prospect of some modernization of U.S. plants working toward our competitive advantage. A sampling of their comments follows:

> I think we are on the right track: (1) people in the administration are working on this; (2) during the time frame, the relative strength of the American economy, with trading partners, will slow up in our favor [congressman].

I believe some other major trade countries will cause a closing of a gap—such requirements as pollution control, human rights, minimum working conditions, where, currently, U.S. standards present significant competitive handicaps [public interest group leader].

The government, private business, and leaders of major unions are beginning to understand that plants need to be modernized and wages and prices need to be competitive with the plants, wages, and prices of foreign companies [press/media representative].

Not overlooked among thoughtleaders' comments is also the idea of the growing interdependence of world economies. As one Congressional Aide noted, "The U.S. realizes that a trade policy is a two-way street and that we must be sensitive to the needs of other countries as well as our own economic needs."

Thoughtleaders who expect the U.S. competitive position to *worsen* during the next 5 years focus on higher U.S. production or labor costs, specifically those caused by government regulatory requirements. They also cite the lack of capital investment by U.S. companies in new plants or equipment. Specifically, they observed the following:

Other nations are becoming more competitive in their industrial capacity and are producing at a cheaper rate because they have greater commodity access and lower wage rates [press/media representative].

Because of the debasement of U.S. currency and the continuing problems with the U.S. labor market. Mainly at fault are federal laws which protect unions and union political activity. The U.S. market can't be competitive [public interest group leader].

It relates to U.S. labor. Many of our products are labor intensive and we are not able to compete with almost any other country in the world. Another problem is that we will not significantly be able to reduce our oil imports during the next five years [Senate aide].

Low productivity trends in industry. Cost of production is rising, so our goods are less competitive. Low rate of capital formation in the United States, so our plants are not as efficient as our European and Japanese competitors' and they are more costly [press/media representative].

Some thoughtleaders are concerned about increased competition from developing nations, the technological capabilities of other countries, or the superior quality of some foreign goods, as well as the possibility that our energy problems may not be solved. One respondent put it this way:

In underdeveloped countries, the goods they can produce and their technology are increasing very rapidly, particularly in Taiwan and Korea. The U.S. is continually transmitting technology to other countries—like our steel mills in Europe. The other countries are then becoming much more competitive.

Several thoughtleaders are concerned about the protectionist actions of other countries versus the failure of the United States to protect domestic industry. These reasons were cited:

> Because foreign governments subsidize their products, particularly Japan. Also, the President has indicated he won't act on tariffs on steel and ball bearings. For some U.S. companies, it is cheaper to make the products abroad [congressional aide].

On balance, thoughtleaders appear more inclined to want U.S. trade policies to *stay the same* rather than become either more or less protectionist. However, like executives, they offer little support for more protectionist policies on the part of the United States (see figure 11-2).

Among the subgroups, at least half of legislators, executive/regulatory officials, and public interest group leaders would prefer to see U.S. trade policies remain the same. But three-fourths of the union leaders support *more protectionism* (see figure 11-3).

On the other hand, thoughtleaders as a whole are divided over the outlook for a swing to more protectionism in the United States, while the majority of executives believe that such will be the trend (see figure 11-4). Like the majority of executives, most union leaders and a majority of press/media representatives expect increased protectionism in the 1980s (see figure 11-5).

Thoughtleaders who say that U.S. trade policies will become *more protec-*

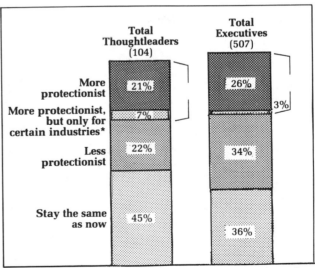

"In general, do you think our trade policies should become more protectionist, less protectionist, or stay about the same as now?"

"Don't know" omitted   *Respondents volunteered this reply

Figure 11-2. Should U.S. Trade Policies Become More Protectionist?

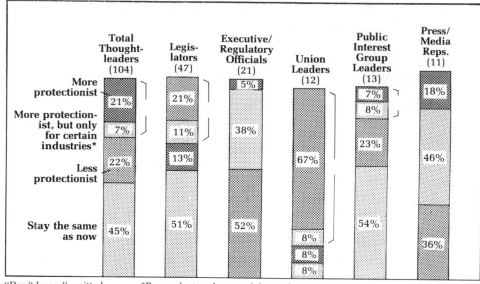

"Don't know" omitted   *Respondents volunteered this reply
¹See question wording above

Figure 11-3. Should U.S. Trade Policies Become More Protectionist (Subgroups)?

"Looking ahead to the 1980's, and forgetting your own feelings for the moment, in general do you expect the United States to become more protectionist than it is now, less protectionist, or do you think there will be little change from our current international trade policies?"

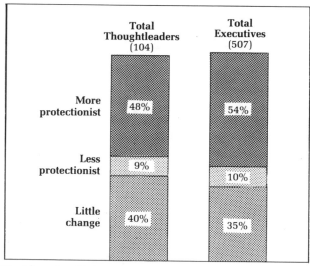

"Don't know" omitted

Figure 11-4. Will U.S. International Trade Policies Become More Protectionist in the 1980s than Now?

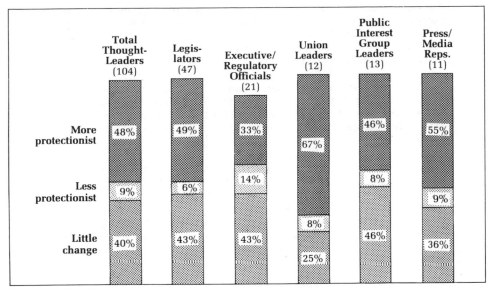

Figure 11-5. Will U.S. International Trade Policies Become More Protectionist in the 1980s than Now (Subgroups)?

"Don't know" omitted
[1]See question wording above

tionist in the 1980s anticipate increased pressure for protectionism from all sides. They point to the U.S. trade deficit and the need to protect U.S. jobs:

> There seems to be a growing concern in the business sector about imported products. This will translate into political pressure to create higher tariffs, or whatever has to be done to impede importation of foreign goods [congressman].

> Politically, as our trade balance continues to deteriorate, there will be increasing pressure by trade unions, major corporations, and other public interest groups to impose additional tariffs to protect American business and incomes [executive department official].

> We are losing too many jobs in this country and too many American-based multinational companies are locating plants overseas [congressional aide].

Some thoughtleaders who think a more protectionist approach to world trade will be taken say that the United States' competitive position is deteriorating, that our open trade policy is not working, or that our trading partners are protectionist. Among their comments:

American industry has lost its competitive drive and incentives to excellence in production. It can't compete in terms of labor costs with other countries which can turn out better, lower cost products than we do. Given that base, the only solution I see industry leaders grasping for is protectionism [press/media representative].

We find ourselves in an unfair competitive position with foreign countries and with protectionist policies themselves. Our free trade policy has worked to our disadvantage. We must give protection to our basic industries essential to our economic welfare, such as steel [union leader].

I feel there is a growing realization that the United States has positioned itself over the years to such a disadvantage with our trading partners that we have exported jobs and total industries. Our unemployment, balance-of-payments, and energy problems, among others, are a direct result of a free-trade attitude while our trading partners have been highly protectionist. The specter of retaliation is illusory because we have been retaliated against ever since the end of World war II [Senate aide].

Others feel that increased protectionism seems to be the trend. This Senate aide's comment was typical: "It is the trend I see in the Congress to try to protect industries like steel, agriculture, and electronics that are hurt by trade imbalance. The general feeling in the country is that our own industries have to be looked after. They expect the government to protect domestic industries."

The four in ten thoughtleaders who say the U.S. trade policies will *not change* much recognize the importance of international trade to the U.S. economy and believe that, for a number of reasons, the pressures for protectionism versus free trade will cancel each other out and a balance between the two approaches will be maintained. They made these observations:

I feel that the forces pulling in either direction may become primary for short terms, but in the end, we will wind up the same as we are now—the forces of protection on one hand, and free trade on the other [regulatory agency official].

The opinion of the country is so closely divided we can't move in either direction. The country is such that there will be no fundamental shift in the balance [public interest group leader].

The Carter administration is finding an acceptable middle ground between protectionism and absolute trade. This ground developed by the Carter administration, will set a pattern for the next decade [congressional aide].

Others who anticipate little change feel that increased protectionism will not solve the United States' trading problems. Some say that other countries will retaliate if the United States becomes more protectionist. According to an official from the executive department, "There will be a realization that if we become protectionist it will diminish our ability to sell abroad. Other countries will retalitate with their own protections, and, in a situation like that, we have more to lose than gain. I don't think most Americans are aware of the importance of our exports. They will become more aware and realize that protection isn't good."

Thoughtleaders are virtually unanimous, as are executives, in their feeling that the U.S. trade deficit is a serious problem. In fact, majorities of both groups think the problem is *very* serious. Only among public interest group leaders do a notable minority fail to regard the trade deficit as a serious problem (see figure 11-6).

Both thoughtleaders and executives focus on the amount and cost of oil

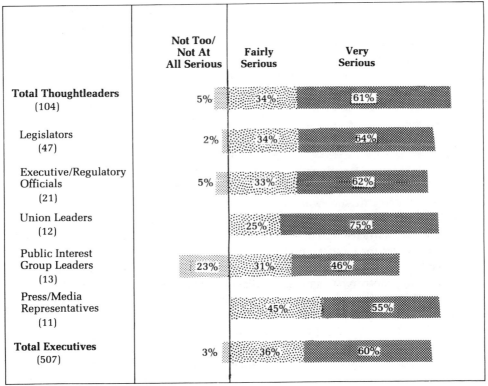

	Not Too/ Not At All Serious	Fairly Serious	Very Serious
Total Thoughtleaders (104)	5%	34%	61%
Legislators (47)	2%	34%	64%
Executive/Regulatory Officials (21)	5%	33%	62%
Union Leaders (12)		25%	75%
Public Interest Group Leaders (13)	23%	31%	46%
Press/Media Representatives (11)		45%	55%
Total Executives (507)	3%	36%	60%

"Don't know" omitted
[1]"As you know, the U.S. is faced with a very large and mounting trade deficit. Do you think the trade deficit is a very serious problem for the United States, fairly serious, not too serious, or not at all serious?"

Figure 11-6. How Serious a Problem U.S. Trade Deficit Is Thought to Be.[1]

imports as the most important reasons for the country's current international trade deficit and trading problems. In fact, thoughtleaders' appraisal of the various listed factors generally parallels executives' evaluation, with two exceptions: executives are more likely than are thoughtleaders as a whole to blame this country's trade deficit on high U.S. labor costs (also a factor of third-most importance to press/media representatives) or on a lack of productivity of U.S. workers (see figure 11-7).

Not surprisingly, union leaders are much less likely than other thoughtleaders to focus on high U.S. labor costs or on lack of productivity of U.S. workers (they regard the latter as *least* important). While *all* thoughtleader subgroups rank oil imports (amount and cost) at the top of the list of important causes for the trade deficit, union leaders are just as concerned about U.S. companies transferring manufacturing operations abroad and about foreign "dumping" of products into the United States.

Measures to reduce oil imports receive the strongest support from thoughtleaders and executives alike when they are presented with a list of twenty proposed solutions to our international trade problems. (To determine their reactions to a number of specific proposals that have been advocated for decreasing our trade deficit and accompanying problems, thoughtleaders and executives were asked, "For each proposal on the list, please circle the appropriate numerical score to indicate how strongly you favor or oppose the statement. If you don't have a feeling one way or the other about a proposal, please give it a score of zero." Respondents could select a positive score—ranging from "Slight Favor" (+10 in figure 11-8) to "Strong Favor" (+100 in figure 11-8)—or a negative score—ranging from "Slight Opposition" (−10 in figure 11-9) to "Strong Opposition" (−100 in figure 11-9).)

Although both groups favor the concept of energy sufficiency, thoughtleaders, overall, are somewhat less likely than executives to favor incentives for U.S. companies to develop domestic energy resources as a means of achieving such energy sufficiency. They also are far less likely than executives to support tax incentives for business investment. The comparably lower level of approval toward these two proposals on the part of thoughtleaders as a whole reflects the underlying controversy among Washington subgroups. In fact, not a single proposal, including even the reduction of oil imports, is ranked among the top four by *all* thoughtleader subgroups.

Thoughtleaders and executives both react most negatively to the idea of restricting the export of U.S. technology as a way to solve our international trade problems. Among Washington thoughtleaders, only those who represent unions *favor* limiting the export of technology. They alone also are strongly in favor of restricting the transfer of U.S. manufacturing operations abroad. Indeed, union leaders are the most protectionist of all thoughtleader subgroups when it comes to specific proposals for alleviating U.S. trade problems.

Thoughtleaders as a whole register neither approval nor opposition for six of the twenty proposals rated:

Establish worker-management councils like in West Germany—giving workers more say in management decisions in the hope of increasing productivity.

Have the government provide severance pay for U.S. workers displaced by foreign imports—70 percent of their pay for up to a year, or whatever shorter time it takes to find a new job.

Work toward the establishment of a "Greater Common Market" consisting of the United States, Canada, the Western European countries, and Japan, in which each country would give up some autonomy in the hope of greater economic and political cooperation.

Impose economic retaliation on OPEC if it further increases the price of oil.

Establish a series of "reference" or "target" prices—minimum amounts that foreigners could charge for their products in the American market.

Continue or expand the tax benefits on the export earnings of domestic international sales corporations.

Both thoughtleaders and executives take a neutral position on such controversial proposals as economic retaliation against OPEC and the establishment of a "Greater Common Market." But significantly, though tax policy changes to encourage individuals to invest in U.S. companies attract some degree of support from both thoughtleaders and executives, the proposal to continue or expand the tax benefits on the export earnings of domestic international sales corporations (DISCs) receives measurable support from executives only.

Thoughtleader and executive attitudes toward the treatment of U.S. workers hurt by imports also differ. Executives are largely negative toward the concept of severance pay for these workers, while thoughtleaders are withholding a decision at present. And, as noted previously, executives are less enthusiastic than thoughtleaders about the suggestion to have the government help find jobs for U.S. workers displaced by foreign imports.

When asked to suggest their own solutions for decreasing our trade deficit, thoughtleaders, like executives, focus overwhelmingly on the need to solve our energy problems. They offered these ideas:

The major one is to make efforts to reduce our dependence on foreign petroleum. Also, development of present domestic reserves and new energy sources. More attention to conservation policies [Senate aide].

A strong market-oriented energy policy encouraging domestic production and conservation. I'm an advocate of a dollar or more a gallon on gasoline [public interest group leader].

Solving the energy situation. Less dependency on foreign sources. Getting back to self-sufficiency, with more production of domestic oil

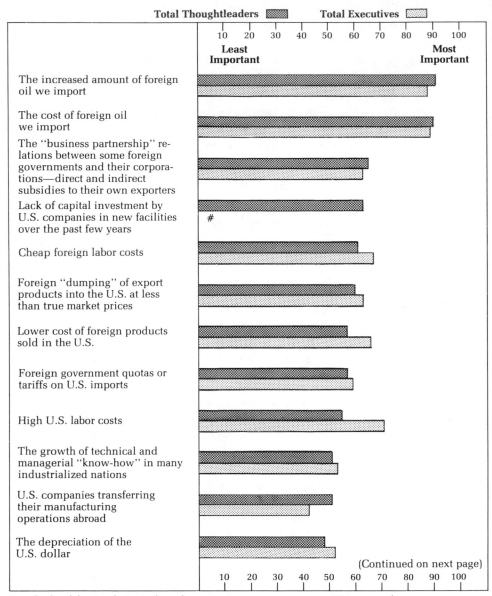

Length of each bar in relation to the scale represents a mean score #Not measured

1¹"Different people have different reasons for our current international trade deficit and trading problems. Please read through this list and, for each item, circle the number that best describes how important you think that item is as a cause of our trading deficit." (For each item, the respondent could select a numerical score ranging from a low of "Least Important" [zero on the above chart] to a high of¹"Most Important" [100 on the above chart].)

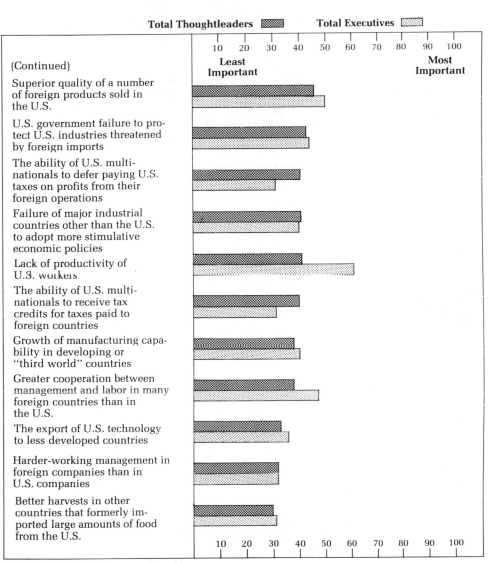

Length of each bar in relation to the scale represents a mean score

[1]"Different people have different reasons for our current international trade deficit and trading problems. Please read through this list and, for each item, circle the number that best describes how important you think that item is as a cause of our trading deficit." (For each item, the respondent could select a numerical score ranging from a low of "Least Important" [zero on the above chart] to a high of "Most Important" [100 on the above chart].)

Figure 11-7. Importance of Various Factors as Causes for U.S. Trade Deficit and Trading Problems.[1]

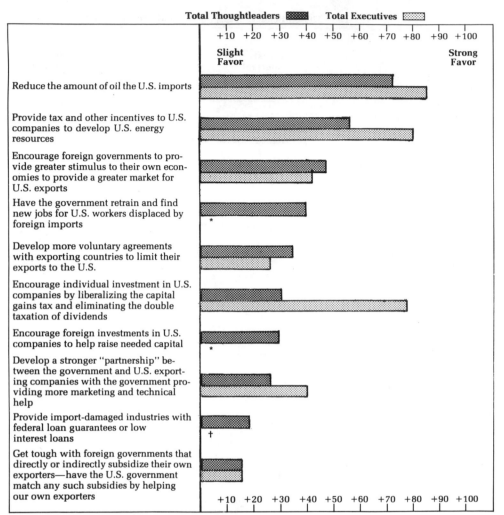

Length of each bar in relation to the scale represents a mean score
*Mean rating by executives falls between "Slight Favor" and "Slight Opposition"
†Executives are slightly opposed to this proposal

Figure 11-8. Attitudes toward Different Proposals for Reducing U.S. Trade Deficit and Accompanying Problems.

and gas through various means. Conversion to and gasification of coal; development of nuclear, solar, geothermal, and other exotic sources of energy [Senate aide].

A stronger energy conservation program. A stronger program to develop nonpolluting, alternative sources of energy, and a strong solar energy program. A much stronger and improved public transportation program [union leader].

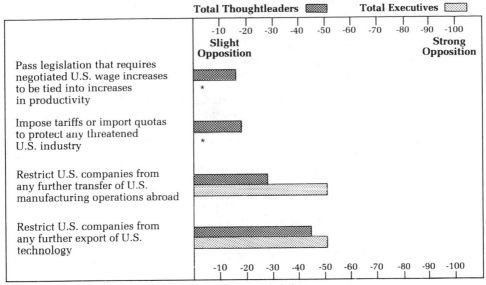

*Mean rating by executives falls between "Slight Favor" and "Slight Opposition"

Figure 11-9. Attitudes toward Different Proposals for Reducing U.S. Trade Deficit and Accompanying Problems.

Many thoughtleaders believe that the solution lies in promoting the export of American products, either by providing incentives for U.S. industry to market abroad or by adopting more aggressive marketing strategies. They suggested the following:

> More aggressive marketing of American products abroad. Agricultural products, which are the cornerstone of our international trade, should receive the greatest emphasis in promoting American goods [congressional aide].

> Do everything to improve our export trade and to educate the business community to selling abroad [executive department official].

> We should improve the DISC—domestic international sales corporation—which gives incentives to domestic corporations to sell abroad. This would enable us to compete with Japan, for instance, which gives incentives to its sales force [congressman].

> Greater incentives for private industry to market overseas—tax credits, etc. [press/media representative].

Thoughtleaders' positions regarding U.S. trade policy run the full gamut from support for a reduction in trade barriers to favor for negotiated or voluntary trade arrangements to approval of more protectionist trade policies. A few emphasize the need to enforce existing trade rules or to coordinate government trade policies. Among their recommendations:

> Negotiate better trade agreements with countries like Japan and the European community so as to reduce trade barriers which prevent more U.S. exports going into these countries [executive department official].

> Be more protectionist in areas such as steel and textiles, where there is a need because of dumping by other nations [congressional aide].

> We need to create a cabinet-level Department of International Trade and Investment to coordinate an overall policy to ensure maximum benefits for U.S. interests. At the moment, our governmental mechanism is chaotic and duplicative, oftentimes fighting with other parts of the federal government rather than trying to solve our international trade and development problems. This is the most urgently needed change I see [regulatory agency official].

Improved productivity or increased production efficiency are emphasized by some thoughtleaders in comments such as these:

> Modernization of industries like the American steel industry so that we can more advantageously compete with foreign producers [congressional aide].

> Increase the productivity of American workers. American workers used to be highly productive. Our rates of productivity are lower than most countries' so we have to make ourselves competitive—improve the training of American workers, update capital facilities and management techniques [executive department official].

Rather than simply encouraging our trading partners to stimulate their economies, other thoughtleaders believe that we should focus on solving our own domestic economic problems, principally by increasing or stimulating U.S. business investment, controlling inflation, or working toward a balanced federal budget at home. As one public interest group leader put it,

> The U.S. must first put its own economic house in order. It would help the deficit enormously. We need to restore integrity to the currency, develop alternative sources of energy, and deregulate the energy industry. We also have to increase production and decrease our dependence on foreign sources of energy. The first thing to do is balance the budget and return to a system of backing gold and silver for the currency.

Only a few would curtail multinational expansion overseas as a means of solving our trading problems. Suggested one congressional aide, "Put tariffs on some products to discourage U.S. corporations from going abroad to take advantage of cheap labor."

Summary and Implications for Management

Findings in this study underscore the absence of (and need for) a national consensus about the establishment of a uniform, coordinated approach to dealing with the nation's trading problems and developing a positive foreign economic policy. This lack of general agreement exists not only between those in Washington and those in the business community, but also among Washington thoughtleaders themselves.

On the positive side, Washington thoughtleaders in all key subgroups share with business executives a strong commitment to this nation's continued and growing participation in world trade. In fact, Washington thoughtleaders, including those in Congress, attach an even greater importance than do business executives to the relationship of international trade to the total U.S. economy. Both groups also believe that the U.S. trade deficit is very serious. And both consider the cost and increased amount of foreign oil we import to be the primary causes of our trade deficit.

However, while they generally agree on the causes of the trade deficit, thoughtleaders and executives differ sharply in specific proposals for doing something about it. The most striking differences relate to proposals involving incentives for business to develop domestic energy sources and tax incentives to encourage investment in U.S. business.

Although thoughtleaders consider oil imports to be the prime cause of our trade deficit, they are far less likely than executives to favor providing tax and other incentives to U.S. companies to develop domestic energy sources. Such is the case among all thoughtleader subgroups.

Similarly, thoughtleaders give a much lower priority than do executives to encouraging individual investment in U.S. companies by liberalizing the capital gains tax and eliminating the double taxation of dividends. Although thought-leaders place a great deal of importance on the lack of capital investment by U.S. companies in new facilities as a *cause* of our trade problems, they are not very enthusiastic about encouraging individual investment in U.S. companies through tax incentives; they would just as soon encourage foreign investment in U.S. companies to help raise needed capital. Such an attitude on the part of thoughtleaders may indicate a hesitancy in some quarters to accept the relationship between U.S. government tax and economic policies and the problems of business capital investment.

Perhaps one of the most significant findings to emerge from this study is the *lack* of support among Washington thoughtleaders for more protectionist trade policies. Only union leaders believe that the United States should become more protectionist. Fully half of those in Congress (51 percent), those in the executive/regulatory official subgroup (52 percent), and public interest group leaders (54 percent) would prefer the continuation of our current trade policies. With some exceptions, such as among union leaders, support for such negative measures as tariff barriers across the board have not as yet solidified.

In general, there seems to be a growing awareness among Washington thoughtleaders that the role of the United States in the global economy has changed radically and that this country will simply have to become more export minded to pay for the oil it imports and reduce its trade deficit. This seems clear from the comments of those who are optimistic about the competitive outlook for U.S. products over the next 5 years. They believe that this nation has many opportunities for significantly increasing its exports, especially in view of a growing world market for agricultural exports and high-technology products.

Indeed, the idea of *restricting* any further export of U.S. technology is a proposal most likely to be opposed by opinion leaders in Washington. Only labor leaders seem to fear that the United States will lose its competitive edge in the world by the sale of American technologies to other countries.

Overall, while many thoughtleaders seem to realize that the United States may have reached a major turning point, a watershed if you will, in its trading and economic relationships with the rest of the world, their thinking still has not crystallized in terms of what steps to take in the development of strong federal policies which would help, rather than hinder, exports.

Thoughtleaders, for example, believe that one of the major causes of the current trade deficit and trading problems is the advantage other countries have because of the close cooperation between government and business when it comes to their export policies. However, opinion leaders in Washington, especially executive/regulatory officials, do not seem ready to commit themselves to such cooperation between government and business at home.

Clearly, internationally minded businessmen have their work cut out for them in Washington. They are going to have to press, and press hard, to get the kind of stimulative moves, especially on the tax front, which would aid U.S. corporations in their efforts to compete worldwide. In sum, the thinking on trade in many U.S. companies, as well as that in government, may well have to undergo basic changes before this country can achieve a coordinated foreign economic policy based on maintaining its place in international markets and creating business for its industries and communities.

Part III
The Changing
Consumer

12 Some Alternative Scenarios

Gary A. Marple

America is a consumer-oriented economy. Alistair Cooke, in his famous *America* series, pointed out that following World War II, the average consumer in the United States had a lifestyle and a material comfort which, before the first half of this century, would have been enjoyed only by royalty. Some people are concerned that our consumer society may be faltering or failing to go forward. Furthermore, there is controversy as to whether it *can* go forward. To understand the controversy, one must first examine what the future of our consumer-oriented economy might be like. The future has many possibilities, but what we need is a baseline or "most likely" future, from which we can subsequently examine plausible alternatives which might occur and see what consequences might result.

First, let us examine some critical issues which affect consumers. Two such issues are inflation and unemployment—they hit us all in the pocketbook. They also have important psychological effects on our behavior as consumers. Most people are familiar with the idea of inflation psychology or depression psychology. Finally, these two issues are critical because they are manageable, in the fiscal and monetary senses, by the federal government.

Begin by imagining a map of these two items, inflation and unemployment, shown in figure 12-1. If we go from the bottom to the top of the map, we move from low unemployment to high unemployment. Similarly, if we go from left to right, we go from low inflation to high inflation. For thinking purposes, we have centered our baseline or "most likely" case. While the baseline will be the setting for the subsequent chapters, it is the point of departure for examining alternatives which might occur—the subject of this chapter.

In terms of the base case, we foresee inflation continuing at an average of about 6 to 7 percent annually through 1990. Remember in the 1950s when economists talked about 3 or 4 percent inflation to stimulate growth? Those days will not likely return during the next decade and a half. We also estimate that our baseline of unemployment will be in the range of 6 to 7 percent throughout this period. *Unemployment* is defined as the percentage of all those who are working plus those available and seeking work who cannot find a job. Unemployment will, of course, be higher among the young and minorities.

Inflation compounds; a 6 percent inflation last year is included in the basis on which this year's inflation is calculated, so that by 1990, the cost of living will be up 100 percent, or double today's cost of living. Unemployment, on the

CRITICAL ISSUES:

- Inflation
- Unemployment

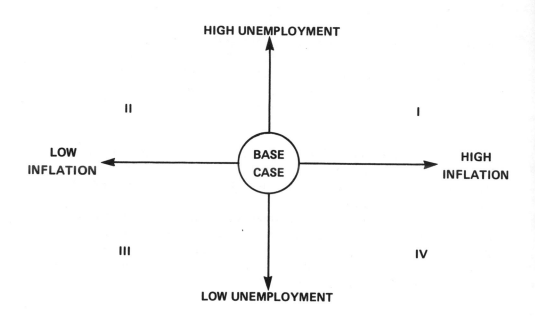

BASE CASE:

Inflation Rate:	6-7%
Unemployment:	6-7%
Cost of Living:	Up 100% by 1990

Figure 12-1. The Relationship between Inflation and Unemployment.

other hand, merely expresses the percent of the workforce that cannot find employment at a given point in time; thus it does not compound. In spite of inflation and unemployment at these baseline levels, real incomes and real productivity will nevertheless increase throughout the period, although their increase will not be as rapid as we have seen in the past.

These baseline values for unemployment and inflation can be viewed as forces having some important effects on consumers, such as an encouragement to greater debt, an increase in the value of positional goods, a reduction in savings rates, and a trend toward higher-quality consumer goods. First, consumer debt. In a world of inflation psychology, one is obviously better off to buy now and pay later, with cheaper dollars. This has an important effect on positional goods. *Positional goods* are those goods which, if one person owns them, no one else (or very few) can own them, because the supply is fixed, for example, a specific waterfront property, genuine rare antiques, or rare stamp collections. Positional goods tend to increase in value more rapidly than inflation. Consumer savings rates are reduced, both because of inflation and because of unemployment. Inflation psychology, by encouraging one to go into debt to buy now, reduces one's current savings. Unemployment also reduces savings, since unemployment benefits and welfare costs must be borne through taxes.

The prices of some products do not rise as fast as inflation because of their productivity changes or because of scale economies. These products are favored as they become, in a relative sense, less expensive than products for which prices rise with or faster than inflation. And finally, a trend toward higher-quality consumer goods occurs—quality in terms of durability, reliability, and operating costs. The preceding effects of inflation and unemployment on consumers have important consequences for certain categories of consumer demand. Table 12-1

Table 12-1
Impact on Consumer Market

Some Items "Win"
    Housing
    Automobiles
    Consumer electronics
    Recreation and travel

Some Items "Lose"
    Clothing
    Services
    Restaurants
    Food

Serious Stress
    Fixed incomes
    Unemployed
    Welfare

Higher Inflation, Lower Employment
Higher Inflation, Lower Employment,
Unemployment
    Same "winners" and "losers"
    Unemployed stress reduced
    Other stresses increased

Lower Inflation, Higher Unemployment
    Even "winners" lose
    Fixed-income stress reduced
    Other stresses increased

portrays a few of the consumer product categories which are expected to be "winners" and "losers" in the baseline or most likely future. Automobiles, which are examined in more depth in a subsequent chapter, are expected to gain relative to consumer products in general, because new auto prices are likely to increase more slowly than inflation, and because the preferences for quality (durability, reliability, and lower operating costs) will result in more of the higher-priced vehicles being demanded.

Similarly, some items will lose relative to consumer products in general. Table 12-2 shows some of those, two of which are discussed in chapter 14. One is restaurants—not fast-food restaurants, but full-service restaurants where wage costs tend to increase with or faster than inflation, so consumers reduce the share of their discretionary dollars for eating out in full-service restaurants. A second is food purchased at the supermarket, which tends to decline as a share of consumer incomes as real incomes increase and which is one of the "manageable" expenditures in the event that one's income does not rise (that is, welfare recipients and unemployed persons). There are, of course, some important shifts in demand for products within both restaurant and food categories which are discussed in chapters 13 and 14.

The combination of inflation and unemployment causes some serious stresses. These stresses affect three different categories of consumer: people on fixed incomes, mainly the elderly on retirement pensions; unemployed people; and welfare recipients. All three of these groups tend to lose in real income terms, thus the fraction of the population which is unemployed, on welfare, and on fixed incomes becomes critical in evaluating the effects of a given rate of inflation or level of unemployment.

These stresses cause political pressures to raise or supplement pensions, raise social security benefits, increase unemployment benefits, and/or increase welfare payments. This again leads to higher taxes and, of course, further social tension.

In the base of 6 to 7 percent annual inflation and 6 to 7 percent unemployment, consumers can live with the taxes, the tensions, and the changes. However, let us consider an alternative scenario. Returning to our map (figure 12-1), consider an increase in the inflation rate and a reduction in unemployment. Relative to our baseline, this would be downward toward the right. This alternative is relatively easy to achieve by increasing the money supply, lowering the interest rate, and deficit spending so as to increase jobs. For this alternative you get the same winners and the same losers among consumer products as shown before in table 12-1. Unemployment is reduced, which is clearly a benefit. However, there are serious tradeoffs: those remaining unemployed, along with those on fixed incomes and welfare recipients, are worse off than in the baseline because of higher inflation. This causes more tension and more taxes than in the baseline. This easily achieved solution worked in the past. However, in the future, there will be a larger proportion of the citizenry who are elderly, unemployed minorities, and/or welfare recipients. Thus, what was politically feasible in the past is probably going to be precluded in the future. Therefore, we do not envision this alternative as a very practical scenario to pursue. If, through some quirk of fate, it were to happen, there would be important consequences.

Let us review our map and examine the alternative of reducing inflation and increasing unemployment. Relative to our baseline, this would be upward to the left. Again, this is a pretty easily achieved alternative: reduce the money supply, raise interest rates, and run a budgetary surplus so the number of jobs is reduced and the inflation rate diminishes as demand is reduced. This alternative results in chaos, where even the baseline "winners" would lose. Aggregate real income would diminish; housing, autos, consumer electronics, and recreational products would receive reduced amounts of expenditures. This scenario is really a depression scenario. Fixed incomes would be much better off, but the unemployed and unemployed minorities would pose serious problems and political stress. The relative as well as the absolute tax level would have to increase to cover unemployment benefits and welfare costs.

These two alternatives are easily achievable by government policy, but they are less livable than our base rate—they have substantial effects on consumers in our society and they are politically unstable. To improve on the base case, we would have to reduce unemployment *and* reduce inflation simultaneously. This is difficult to achieve politically and managerially, for it requires restructuring government expenditures, increasing productivity, increasing consumer goods and services production, and selectively restructuring the tax laws. Thus it is apparent why the base case was selected. Chapters 13 and 14 are important analyses of base-case conditions, highlighting some important implications of our base case for lifestyles and the consumption of food and autos.

13 Changes in Demographics and Lifestyles

Linsay R. Clark and
Ellen I. Metcalf

The Demographic Outlook
Linsay R. Clark

In 1974 the *Wall Street Journal* published an article that envisioned slower economic growth through the mid-1980s.[1] Key product areas cited to experience this slowdown were automobiles, household appliances, furniture, clothing, and food. In addition, the forecasts quoted in the article postulated a major shift from single-family to multifamily housing. This less than encouraging perspective was tied almost entirely to the continuing slowdown in the overall rate of population growth, and labeled *demographics*.

Demographics, however, is more than total population growth. Forecasters who fail to identify the discrete demographic segments active in a particular market are overlooking valuable data. While some of the nondurable goods are amenable to a per-capita consumption analysis, other products, especially durable goods, respond more acutely to household formation and general lifecycle analysis. Had these earlier forecasters sliced the demographic pie to observe market behavior for each of the composite age groups, the forecasts just cited would not have been made.

It is important for planners to dig below the surface. The slowdown in population growth is a reality. Year-to-year changes will average 0.9 percent from 1977 to 1990 versus the 1.0 percent experienced from 1963 to 1977. But within the population mix, there will be a decline principally in the youth sector, as shown in figure 13-1. Consequently, the market place will likely experience a slowdown in many products associated singularly with that market—soft drinks, comic books, blue jeans, transistor radios, and records. The slowdown will be modified by the extent to which the population carries forward tastes developed during teenage years.

Although all forecasters recognized the end of the baby boom, many have failed to carry forward the impact of this shift into each market segment it is destined to affect. The number of people 25 to 44 years old will constitute nearly 32 percent of the population in 1990, versus only 26 percent in 1977. In terms of absolute numbers, total population will increase by 27 million between 1977 and 1990. When looking at the population breakdown by age, 80 percent of this increase will appear in the age group of 25 to 44 years old. Conversely, 14- to 24-year-olds will show actual declines.

113

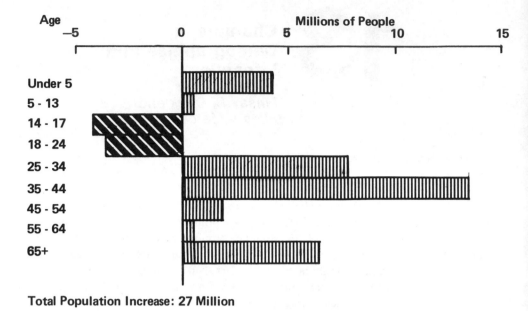

Figure 13-1. Age Distribution of Population Increase, 1977-1990.

Had the household/age/lifecycle approach been adopted in the forecast cited above, the conclusions would have been quite different. Single-family housing, household appliances, furniture, and consumer entertainment products would have been assigned stronger market potential than under the simplistic approach that used only total population growth as a guideline.

In 1973, the Bureau of Labor Statistics (BLS) conducted a consumer expenditure survey in conjunction with its consumer price index effort. This survey has shed some light on the importance of viewing the expenditure patterns which are characteristic of each population segment. Specifically, how do the household budgets of the various age groups compare?

For total expenditures, households headed by people in two of the age groups—25 to 34 and 35 to 44—spend more than the average household (as shown in table 13-1). Because of the timing of the baby boom peak, growth in the 25- to 34-year-old group will be the driving force in the marketplace until the mid-1980s, with the 35- to 44-year-old group becoming dominant thereafter. What does this mean in terms of individual purchase categories? While the BLS survey details several areas in the household budget, these can be easily summarized—home ownership, furniture, appliances, sports equipment, consumer electronics, alcohol, and food away from home. In addition, the 25- to 44-year-old group is the age segment that typically includes first-time home

Table 13-1
Index of Average Family Expenditures, 1972-1973
(Typical Household = 100.0)

Buying Category	Under 25	25-34	35-44
Food away from home	86.4	113.7	137.6
Alcoholic beverages	93.6	125.7	125.0
Owned dwellings	18.6	102.1	150.3
Home furnishings	78.4	127.8	137.5
Clothing	72.8	110.9	139.7
Sports equipment	102.4	142.5	156.9
Television	110.6	119.2	111.7

Source: Bureau of Labor Statistics.

buyers who are likely to continue preferring single-family living to multifamily structures. The 1974 forecasts were made when federal housing programs were extremely active and therefore overstated the likelihood of shifting to multi-family units.

Even with the kingpin in the marketplace the 25- to 44-year-olds, other age segments can still be expected to exert their influence on product demand. With the recent turnaround in the birth rate, we can expect to see a revitalization in certain baby product markets—food, baby durables, and clothing. Also, the much heralded graying of the population will increase the market importance carried by the older groups as well, most visibly the 65-year-olds and over. While the real impact will hit in the late 1980s, we can expect to see increasing attention to this market in terms of housing, health care, and transportation. We are already seeing it in the move against mandatory retirement, concern over the financial position of Social Security, investigations into nursing home practices, and other health care legislation. One indication of the likely impact on the health industries comes from earlier analysis that has shown that people over 65 are four times as likely to be disabled by chronic illness than people under 65.

Other factors which come under the heading *demographics* include income, employment status, social characteristics, geographic distribution, and immigration. Possibly the most important are the economic factors of income and employment status and the social factor of family status. The key trends here are female participation in the labor force and its adjuncts: the dual wage-earner family, the shift in the mix of households toward single individuals rather than families, and smaller-sized families.

The emergence of the dual wage-earner family and the career orientation of the female will boost total family income and certainly bolster discretionary income and its disposition. Product sectors likely to experience growth due to the dual wage-earner family will include convenience and time-saving products in both goods and services. Food and household maintenance are likely candidates, as illustrated by the rapid acceptance of microwave cooking and food away from home. Home ownership and its aftermarket are also likely to benefit from this trend. Present research into home-buying practices shows that dual-income households already account for over 40 percent of all homes purchased.

The trend toward singles households rather than family households will likely be maintained through the entire forecast period, affecting home ownership and the home aftermarket and also impacting recreation and leisure time. However, product-size considerations will likely induce some adjustments peculiar to servicing this market—smaller-sized housing units, smaller appliances, and the elimination of the need for the two-car garage. Obviously, the market responds to more than demographic shifts as reflected in lifestyle trends, technological developments, the underlying economic conditions, and the political environment.

In review, it will become increasingly important for market planners to search beyond summary statistics—total population has slowed but certain age segments within the total will be experiencing rapid growth while others decline. Total income will continue to grow moderately, but the spenders of the income will change. Average family size will continue to shrink, but the number of families with first-born babies will increase. It is in the slicing of the demographic pie that planners will more effectively identify their potential markets and the needs of those markets between now and 1990.

Consumer Lifestyles and Social Values
Ellen I. Metcalf

For many years, we have been tracking lifestyles and social values in the United States and we have been looking forward—to the 1980s and early 1990s. Most of what we foresee is evolutionary, not revolutionary (little change is). Seeds of impending changes are already shown in present behavior patterns.

A major trend which must be emphasized is that the United States is becoming increasingly segmented in terms of behavior and interests due in part to the breakdown of socially prescribed norms. This means that we have been and will be less able to predict what people will buy based solely on income, education, and age.

The U.S. population has been segmented in a variety of ways, for example, by size of household, psychographics, age, income, and marital status. We have attempted to combine some characteristics in a few household groups. Some groups are not covered explicitly, since they are a small portion within the larger group. Therefore, we have divided households into three major groups. The first is the much-discussed one- to two-person household—the majority of households today and in 1990. But it is comprised of three distinctly different major subsegments: young adults, the middle-aged, and the elderly. The second group is husband-wife families with at least one child. This group can be subdivided into households where the wife works and those where she does not. The last group consists of those who are single parents.

We will highlight some characteristics of three subgroups which should be of interest to consumer industries in general and to the food and auto industries in particular: young singles and marrieds without children, working husband-working wife families with at least one child, and the middle-aged "empty nesters."

Young Singles and Marrieds without Children

The number of households in this group will be stable to declining over this time period. However, this group is nonetheless of interest for its distinctiveness.

This group has comparatively lower incomes, since its members are near the beginning of their working lives. But these people have a high *discretionary* income—they have few obligations and maximum choice on how they spend their incomes. Furthermore, both members of a two-person household are likely to be working.

They are a highly social group, who look to activities outside the home for self-fulfillment. They are the heavy moviegoers; they like to travel; they go to local events of interest; and they eat out often. Home-maintenance activities get short shrift.

Self-indulgence is an underlying theme of this group—the search for activities which are self-rewarding. Interests change frequently—the activity that is self-rewarding today may not be of interest tomorrow, the brand that is hot today may be dead tomorrow. An example of a forerunner of this 1980s group is a car freak who bought an MGB, which he quickly traded for a Jaguar XJ12. Within a year he had traded his Jag for a Cadillac. Now he is planning to sell his Cadillac and walk so he can buy a house.

Behavior also tends to be nontraditional, according to whim. Meals, for example, are not planned activities but consist of food eaten when and where the mood strikes. The food itself is whatever is of interest, rather than foods associated with a given time of day; for example, cereal in the afternoon, eggs for a late evening snack, and a hamburger for breakfast.

The group's interests can be discovered by noting the types of products they buy, since products in areas of interest are likely to be of high quality. For some, this means an expensive stereo set; for others, a sporty car.

Working Husband—Working Wife Families
with at least One Child

This group is increasing in numbers between now and 1990. They tend to have somewhat fewer children and to be upscale in both income and education.

Having two incomes means that this group has a high disposable income. These people tend to spend more money on products and services which buy them time, like microwave ovens, dishwashers, and yard services. Both adults tend to be highly active people who are heavily oriented outside the home. Home-maintenance activities are generally given low priority and are shared to some extent by all family members.

These people are active sports participants; they frequently attend sports and entertainment events, and they tend to eat out often. Both adults pursue individual interests, however, as do their offspring, so the family tends to be together rarely. Each member tends to treat the home as a hotel, restaurant, and storage depot. Meals are often eaten by each individual as his or her schedule allows, and "convenience" is a key theme for foods in this household. Convenience can be in the time to prepare, cook, or clean up meals. Frozen pizza, steak and frozen french fries, canned chili, or microwave baked potatoes and a casserole could all fit the bill at different times.

The Middle-Aged "Empty Nesters"

A "sleeper" group, one that is getting little attention, is the husband-wife family whose children have left home. This group will increase in numbers between now and 1990, but its growth will be a little slower than population growth.

Despite later marriages, the "empty nest" period comes earlier than ever before, because fewer children are born and children leave home at an earlier age to be on their own. By the mid-1980s, a potential trend away from early retirement, even retirement at 65, may prolong this period of time.

Both husband and wife are likely to be working in a majority of these households, and earnings potential is at its peak. Thus disposable income is likely to be high. This group tends to have an awakening desire for self-indulgence, an attitude of "I've done my sacrificing, now it's my turn."

However, this group is also likely to be overcommitted to material possessions acquired during the years of child rearing. For some this means second homes; for others, recreational vehicles; for still others, too many cars or too large a house. This excess of possessions tends to eat up operating capital. However, if they begin the process of dispossessing, this group has considerable discretionary income to spend.

We expect the 1980s will be a time of change for this group—a period of evolving lifestyles. Although we are not sure whether this group, which has tended to be somewhat home and family focused, will remain home focused or will begin to spend time and money in travel and out-of-the-home leisure and entertainment, we expect this group will provide an important market opportunity for high-quality luxury products.

Note

1. "The Long Run—Analysts See Growth of Economy Slowing Over Next 10 Years," *Wall Street Journal*, August 8, 1974.

14 Impact on the Food and Automotive Industries

James F. Fleming and Donald A. Hurter

Implications for Eating Patterns
James F. Fleming

The continuing changes in demographic patterns and consumer lifestyles, as well as the recent trend toward increased scrutiny of the health/nutritional content of food products, have stimulated widespread changes in the food industries. The changing demographic profile and lifestyles of the U.S. population, discussed in chapter 13, are reflected in where people eat, when people eat, and what they eat. Growth in fast-food and other away-from-home eating establishments in general has been rapid. Retail grocery stores have developed new merchandising activities to meet the consumer's growing demand for total convenience. Food processors have modified their traditional technologies and developed new types of products for both markets. We expect these trends to continue through 1990.

An excellent example of the fundamental change is the continued growth in the away-from-home food service industry. Today's smaller families with lower food volume needs can afford to eat out more often. Families with higher incomes because of a second breadwinner—working wives—also eat away from home more frequently. In these households, family members not only eat lunch away from home (for example, at work or at school) because the wife/mother is away at work, but they also tend to eat other meals away from home more frequently because of time pressures (conflicting schedules of individual family members, the need for time to perform other household tasks, the desire to participate in recreational activities, etc.). Not surprisingly, studies show a significant correlation between dollars spent eating away from home and the growth in per-household discretionary income since the mid-1960s. Women's per-capita salaries and wages are still less than two-thirds those of men, but we expect continuing pressure from the government to enforce equal opportunity to close this gap. We expect continued growth in the away-from-home eating industry as women's incomes continue to increase.

Aging of the population will also impact the away-from-home eating industry. Studies show that as people move out of the teenage and early twenties age group, they seek restaurants which provide more services than does the average fast-food chain. Also, as people eat out more frequently, they demand greater variety. Thus we expect to see increased variety of menu per restaurant as well as expansion of the variety of eating establishments.

In terms of the amount of food sold (excluding cost of services), the retail sector continues to be the largest market by a factor of three to one. Although the retailers' market share has been declining, they have made a strong response to the encroachment of fast-food and other chains on their business. They have already incorporated within their own operations fast-food counters, instore bakeries, delicatessens, and faster checkout systems. We expect their attempts to meet consumers' demands for increased convenience to continue.

Food processors have responded to changes in the restaurant and retail grocery business. Some have developed new products especially designed to meet the needs of the food service business. Some have directly entered the away-from-home food business by acquisition or merger, and others participate as distributors. An equally important move has been to improve the quality of the convenience food products marketed through supermarkets by upgrading flavor, texture, and level of convenience. For example, recently introduced cake mixes include the pan as well as the ingredients in the package.

Food processors are also cognizant of the development of consumer appliances to meet changing lifestyles. The microwave oven is a case in point. Traditional ovens make a significant contribution to the development of flavor in the cooking process not provided by microwave ovens. Thus processors are developing unique products for reconstitution in microwave ovens. These products incorporate different flavor-development systems as well as special packaging materials. Only a few such products are now on the market (for example, the Green Giant line), but others are in the wings now that the number of microwave ovens in homes is approaching significant levels in some areas, e.g., California.

A parallel trend is increased consumer and government interest in health/ nutrition and body consciousness. New government definitions of food product safety go beyond freedom from toxic substances and pathogenic organisms. In line with the trend toward preventive medicine, the emphasis has moved to reduction of adverse environmental factors. Thus the consumer movement and some regulators are questioning food products that could be harmful (for example, by causing dental caries or obesity). Advertising and serving in the schools of presweetened and junk food has become a controversial issue. A recent U.S. Senate Select Committee on Nutrition set dietary goals for the United States. For example, this report points out that six of the ten leading causes of death in the United States are related to fat-consumption patterns.

We expect processors increasingly to respond to these health/nutrition trends. Procter & Gamble introduced Puritan brand salad oil, which contains polyunsaturated sunflower seed oil, in a move to capitalize on concerns about fat in the diet. Heinz acquired Weight Watchers to enter the market generated by consumers' growing body consciousness. Another example of the health/

nutrition trend is the growth in sales of yogurt and high-fiber bread. The nutritional benefits of these products as compared with conventional foods is questionable. However, consumers obviously accept yogurt's image as a very healthy food and high-fiber bread's image as a means of preventing colonic cancer.

In the future, we expect consumers to continue to demand much more of food suppliers than they do today. Furthermore, we expect all levels of the food industry—away-from-home, retail grocers, and food processors—to respond to these demands with increasing sophistication. In addition to meeting demands for increased convenience, they will respond to consumers' desires for greater variety and the chance to experiment with new flavors and forms of food, and they will generally seek to provide consumers with foods which mesh with their changing eating patterns during recreation and work.

The Impact of Federal Regulations on the Automotive Industry
Donald A. Hurter

This section addresses some of the major factors that will affect the 1980-1990 automotive market, such as government regulations, responding to societal and economic pressures and the technological innovations resulting as a response to the regulations. In addition we will look at possible segmentation of the market choices for automobiles caused by demographic changes and the influence of such segmentation on the ability of industry to meet the regulations.

Since the late 1960s, the automotive industry has been increasingly influenced and controlled by government regulations and directives resulting from growing societal needs for emissions and noise control, safety, and fuel economy. In addition, consumer groups have brought pressure to bear for improved product quality, reliability, and lower maintenance and repair costs. These concerns have resulted in a foreign-competition response with innovatively designed vehicles corresponding to each of the areas mentioned. Figure 14-1 diagramatically shows the interaction, responses, and pressures placed on this industry.

Areas of Regulatory Activity

Fuel economy regulations are perhaps receiving the major emphasis of the policymakers. Automobiles and trucks are major users of petroleum, consuming about 95 billion gallons per year. Because of the administration's desire to reduce the nation's dependence on foreign sources of oil and improve the balance of payments, the President has focused on the automobile as a principal

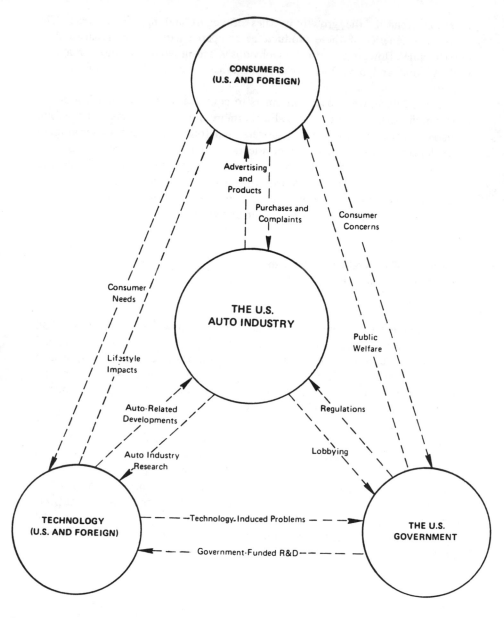

Source: Arthur D. Little, Inc.

Figure 14-1. Interaction between the U.S. Automobile Industry, the U.S. Government, Technology, and Consumers.

means of making the American public conscious of energy conservation goals. On the basis of a continual study of regulatory policy and corresponding actions taken to meet these policies, we judge that fuel economy requirements now in effect will remain and, in fact, become more severe in the future, possibly increasing from the present requirement of 27.5 miles per gallon for a corporate average fuel economy (CAFE) for the fleet produced in any given year after 1985 to levels approaching 35 miles per gallon.

Although the control of emissions tends to be counterproductive to the desire to improve fuel economy, the auto industry has developed techniques and equipment which effectively solve the compromise between emission control and fuel economy improvement. However, there remains a concern regarding one of the major technological approaches for fuel economy improvement, that is, the emissions from a diesel engine. The diesel engine under average usage can improve fuel economy of a vehicle by approximately 25 percent. However, not only are the emissions from a diesel noxious to the driver/passengers and man on the street, but there may also be possible long-term effects which could be deleterious to the public's health. The near-term effects relate to the irritation caused by diesel emissions to the eyes and skin, coupled with the odor problem associated with heavy-duty truck and bus engines. In addition, if the diesel is not maintained carefully, smoke and particulate pollution occurs, which is not acceptable in crowded urban conditions. Of major concern is the long-term effect of the currently unregulated emissions which are possibly carcinogenic.

Noise created by heavy-duty vehicle operation has been given a great deal of attention by regulators. One goal is to improve driver safety by reducing the noise in the driving compartment, which causes fatigue and sleepiness. The public is considered as well, and in the near future heavy-duty trucks and buses will be designed to reduce outward noise, particularly in vehicles used primarily in urban locations, such as garbage trucks and delivery trucks. A great deal of effort has been directed toward improving the safety of the automobile in terms of crash avoidance and occupant protection. Public awareness of occupant protection will grow throughout the years as the process of reducing car size is accomplished. Traditionally, the larger the car, the safer the car was considered by the public. In the future, with the development of small, fuel-efficient automobiles, manufacturers will have to develop marketing strategies that will convince the public that small cars can be equally safe, if not safer, compared to the large cars previously produced. Prototype automobiles of the four-passenger size have been produced which are in fact quite safe and provide occupants the assurance of emerging from crashes occurring at up to 40 miles per hour. However, to accomplish this result, the designers have had to rely on design techniques which manage the rate in which the energy is absorbed during the crash. This is done by having the vehicle collapse in a planned manner, which results in the energy of the crash being absorbed by the crushing of materials. This results in the protection of the passengers but quite likely the complete destruction of the car. Whether the public can be convinced that this approach results in a safe automobile will remain to be seen. However, it could have a major impact on the fleet mix of the manufacturer if the public does not choose to buy a small car because of safety concerns. We think that a great deal of emphasis will have to be placed on the marketing of safety to the public in the future.

Technological Options for Improving
Emissions and Fuel Economy

The industry has applied itself vigorously to the problem of improving emissions and fuel economy. It is generally agreed between manufacturers and regulators that the goal for fuel economy and emissions through 1985 can be met. However, this achievement will not come without great modification to the automobile and to the manufacturing plants that produce the vehicles. The required vehicle and manufacturing plant changes are quite extensive.

To meet the challenge of fuel economy and emission regulations, the auto designers have used a number of approaches in the design of vehicles. The first and most widely used approach is weight reduction, principally in the downsizing of passenger vehicles. This simply means an overall reduction in the length of the car, while maintaining the interior passenger capacity. This is done by placing the passenger in a more upright position, which in turn reduces the overall length of the passenger compartment and hence the overall length of the car. The result is a reduction of about 40 to 50 pounds per foot length of automobile, or a total of some 600 to 700 pounds for a downsized six-passenger vehicle. Further weight reductions are accomplished through reduction in the weight of component parts by substitution of lighter-weight materials or more efficient use of the usual material.

The second major approach that designers are taking to improve the efficiency of the automobile is the better matching of the powerplant to the vehicle requirement and drivetrain components. This may be accomplished by using more efficient engines, such as the diesel, or engines which have optimally matched the total output power to the vehicle operation. Advanced transmissions, both automatic and manual, are being considered.

Lastly, the automotive engineer is beginning to use electronic control mechanisms to integrate the entire automotive system, consisting of fuel control, spark timing, transmission shift points, and vehicle exhaust control systems, through the use of microprocessors.

All these changes result in increased production costs for the vehicle and in many cases increased maintenance costs throughout the life of the vehicle. The risks in terms of engineering and marketing are moderate to low, and should not be a deterrent to their adoption by vehicle manufacturers. However, the increases of the cost of new vehicles and their maintenance costs could present a major deterrent to new auto sales, and it is for this reason that increased efforts will be taken to keep the initial cost and maintenance at a minimum through efficient design.

Effects of Technological Innovation on Vehicle Manufacturers and Automobile Component Manufacturers

Associated with any new technological innovations are risks related to whether or not the innovation will work as originally planned. Because of the extensive development and testing costs of new ideas, it is unlikely that a product that does not work properly under most conditions will be put on the market. However, the risk in the marketplace associated with recalls and reliability *is* a real one, since it is virtually impossible to test vehicles under *all* conditions experienced by the public. Associated with the regulations for improvement in emissions and fuel economy is a requirement that the automobile must operate as originally produced and designed for 50,000 miles. This requirement has resulted in a number of recalls by the manufacturers to correct design errors or operational components on vehicles, which leads to a very high cost to the manufacturers, plus the potential for lawsuits. The result is increased attention to high reliability and low service costs as part of the design specifications of the vehicle. This effort will increase markedly over the next few years.

In addition to the preceding as a design requirement, manufacturers are considering the conservation of material used during the manufacturing process, as well as designing vehicles so that they may be recycled after their useful life. Designs of the future will consider how the salvage operation can be improved so that materials of different types can be kept separate and fed back into the manufacturing process with a minimum of contamination resulting from mixing.

One of the major limitations facing the car manufacturers is resources in terms of skilled manpower for the design of future vehicles which meet the regulations and correspond to the factors just mentioned. This limitation in many cases is more severe than the cost of financing the changes; and in many instances, this is the pacing item for the development of new approaches. This lack of skilled manpower resources is made more severe by the minimal lead times given to develop an automobile to meet future regulations, not to mention the added problem of quick turnaround time required if a given innovation or design thrust does not work out.

The result is that the American automobile manufacturers are strained to make changes in their product lines and manufacturing capabilities, so that they cannot possibly supply vehicles to meet every slot in the market. However, there are cases where a given market requirement has been more than adequately covered by one or more producers. This market implication adds to the problem of the manufacturer with limited resources who must select and develop a vehicle to meet a given slot or niche in the marketplace as an answer to his lack of resources to produce a wider range of vehicles.

Implications of Market Segmentation

For a number of years, various members of Arthur D. Little have examined the potential makeup of future household groups and have developed characteristics relating to these groups. In turn, these characteristics have been applied to project choices in automobiles and possible implications for the meeting of regulations.

Probable automobile choices tend to follow four major household groupings (table 14-1). The first may be characterized as the young single person or young married couple without children, which is projected to account for approximately 18 percent of the households in 1990. This group has a high discretionary income which is used to satisfy a desire for self-gratification in terms of the products they buy and the behavior patterns they follow. The behavior patterns are not traditional and are quite free-form in their expression, resulting

Table 14-1
1990 Households and Their Cars

Household Groupings	Percent Distribution	Probable Automobile Choices
One or two young persons Childless	18	Sports car, recreational pickup, van or utility vehicle No brand loyalty
Middle-aged couples with No children Husband/working wife/ child families	18 34 16	Luxury car, spacious With maximum maintenance and operating reliability and minimum downtime First cost and operating cost not important
Single parent Elderly	12 34 22	Low cost or used car With perceived minimum bare-bones transportation Low first cost and operating cost very important
Husband/nonworking wife/ child families	14	Basic car, spacious Moderately important maintenance and operating reliability First cost and operating cost moderately important (at lower income levels, first cost very important)

in a much lower degree of brand loyalty. The principal social activities of this group are oriented away from the home and result in the purchase of products which meet these desires. The products purchased are usually of high quality with unique characteristics. This group is seen as the one that purchases sports cars, recreational pickups, vans, or utility vehicles.

The next groups, which have similar probable automobile choices, consist of the middle-aged couples without children, affectionately called the "empty nesters," and the husbands and working wives with perhaps one child. The "empty nesters" represent about 18 percent of the households and the husbands and working wives with one child represent 16 percent. Grouped together they account for 34 percent of the household groups.

The "empty nesters" are increasing in numbers. They are characterized as being at a level of peak earning power and thus having a high discretionary income. They are overcommitted to material possessions, resulting from a collection of houses, boats, cars, and recreational devices throughout their lives. Because of this they focus on ways to save time, whether it be by eating out or by reducing the amount of time spent maintaining their possessions. Their lifestyles are changing, and again, similar to the young single people and married couples, they show a high degree of self-indulgence. Moreover, they are relatively insensitive to price, particularly in automobiles if the automobile provides them with luxury and a reduction in nuisance caused by unreliability or repairs. The husbands and working wives with one or two children are much the same as the "empty nesters"—very interested in buying services because of their outside activities and lack of available time. They, too, want a spacious car that is reliable and offers minimum operating inconvenience, and they are not as much concerned about first cost or operating cost, providing maintenance does not distract from the time needed for their outside activities.

The next group consists of single parents, who are perhaps overcommitted financially and most certainly overcommitted in time, coupled with a certain amount of guilt feeling related to the position they find themselves in and concerned about the problems of inflation. This group constitutes about 12 percent of the total households, and when coupled with elderly retired people, who have much the same constraints as single parents, the total is 34 percent. This group is interested in a low-cost car, whether it be new or used, with a perceived minimum transportation cost, both in terms of operating cost, repair costs, and first cost.

The final group, which accounts for 14 percent of households, consists of husbands and nonworking wives with children. This is the typical American family, or *thought* to be the typical American family. They are relatively conservative in their pace, and they have little discretionary income to spend on necessary transportation. They are very price sensitive toward first costs and operating costs. Maintenance is a factor, and frequently a car that can be maintained by the owner is most attractive to this group. The car itself must be available for vacation, with the spaciousness necessary to accommodate three, four, or five people, as well as luggage and traveling materials.

When one considers the manner in which the market is segmented, four types of vehicle choices emerge. First is the special-purpose vehicle, such as a sports car, recreational pickup, van, or utility vehicle. The second type is the luxurious, spacious vehicle, for which first costs are not important, but minimum maintenance and downtime is. The third type is the bare-bones fuel-efficient, low-cost vehicle, not necessarily small, but low in operating costs. The final vehicle is a reliable bare-bones, minimum-first-cost, spacious vehicle that can serve a number of different purposes.

The interesting aspect of these projections is that while the government can cause realistic tight regulations for improving emissions and reducing the use of petroleum fuels for automobiles and the manufacturers can respond with fuel-efficient clean automobiles, it is really the buying public that will determine the success of these regulations. If the individual family group decides to buy a spacious luxury car or a spacious moderate-cost car, or if single people elect to buy vans and sports cars, perhaps the ultimate goal of reduced fuel consumption will not be reached as planned. The question, therefore, is: Will the fuel economy regulations become tighter for larger cars, pickup trucks, and vans, or will they restrict the public as to what automobiles they may purchase?

**Part IV
Meeting Energy Needs**

15 International and Domestic Oil

Howard E. Harris

Introduction

We would like to focus this chapter on two topics: the outlook for the supply and price of foreign oil and of domestic oil. Oil will be the balancing energy source throughout the world through 1990 and beyond.

The foreign and domestic oil topics are closely interrelated in two ways. First, in 1977 imports of crude oil and refined products into the United States reached 8.7 million barrels per day and supplied 47 percent of total domestic consumption. This situation of import dependency, with a minor exception over the next few years resulting from Alaskan oil, will certainly continue and might even increase toward the end of the decade of the 1980s. Therefore, contrary to any political rhetoric you might have heard, oil imports are here to stay; our dependency on foreign oil is a very real and permanent phenomenon. Second, domestic oil prices may be linked even more directly in the future to foreign oil prices. Under any of several possible oil-price scenarios under consideration by the Carter administration, the domestic price of oil to refiners would be tied to the foreign price. Thus both in terms of our physical need and the financial conditions under which oil will be available to supply that need, the domestic and foreign oil pictures will remain very closely interrelated.

Foreign Oil

Let us turn first to the outlook for foreign oil, commencing with a very brief review of trends to date. Until the late 1960s, the supply, and by and large the price, of foreign oil was under the dominance of the international oil companies, both the majors and, to an increasingly significant extent, the independent oil companies. Toward the end of the 1960s and into the 1970s, the balance of power in setting oil prices passed gradually into the hands of the OPEC cartel. This was particularly emphasized by the rapid increases in price and by the temporary embargoes in supply following the 1973 Arab-Israeli war. There was no physical resource-base-imposed shortage of supply, even at the time of supposed "energy crisis." The crisis was, in fact, a politically imposed control upon supply to primarily two destinations, the United States and Holland. The culmination of these actions was a significant temporary physical shortage of supply. The antecedents of that shortage were not related to the physical resource base, but to a series of political decisions.

Until late in 1978, foreign oil prices were relatively soft and discounts off official prices were available. There was a surplus of productive capacity over demand. This reflected, in part, the impact on demand and the world economy of the significant oil price increases of late 1973 and early 1974. Only recently did U.S. and foreign total consumption levels reach pre-1973 crisis levels. The real price (expressed in constant 1974 dollars) has fallen. This situation was dramatically reversed in late 1978 and early 1979 when over 5 million barrels per day of Iranian exports were removed from the world market, causing a shortage of production versus demand and temporarily causing spot prices to skyrocket. If Iranian production and exports are restored to anything approaching previous levels, the situation of a temporary surplus in productive capacity will return. If not, then the tight supply/demand situation described below will materialize at an earlier date, leading to permanently higher prices. In any event, OPEC as a cartel and as the dominant force in the setting of world oil prices is here to stay. We believe this has been demonstrated by OPEC's ability to maintain internal coherence in the face of falling real demand for its oil—a most difficult situation for any cartel to negotiate.

As the temporary surplus of oil-productive capacity versus demand is worked off by the mid to late 1980s, there will be increasing pressure on the perceived amount of supply of oil available from the existing resource base and the development of productive capacity of that base versus likely levels of demand, and at that particular time the policies of Saudi Arabia will become particularly crucial. Let us briefly describe some scenarios for the late 1980s or even 1990s (figure 15-1). Total world oil-production capacity could be approximately 70 million barrels per day, of which 45 million comes from OPEC countries. Of that OPEC capacity, approximately 17 million could be in Saudi Arabia alone. Demand, if it were severely depressed, could be as low as 53 million or 55 million barrels per day, which would be equivalent to only a very small fraction of OPEC, including Saudi Arabia. More likely demand will be in the 65 million to 70 million barrel a day range, that is, right at the limit of the OPEC productive capacity. If demand trends prior to 1973 were extrapolated to 1985 or 1990, demand could be well above 80 million barrels a day and well above the theoretical capacity to produce oil to meet that demand. Therefore, even with conservation efforts and a continuation of exploratory efforts in OPEC and in particular non-OPEC countries, the outlook is for an increasingly tight supply/demand balance for foreign oil supplies by the late 1980s. If Iranian crude oil exports are significantly reduced on a continuing basis, this will merely bring forward in time the point at which oil demand begins to approach the limits of productive capacity. As perception of that tightening balance develops, there is every probability that the OPEC cartel will indeed extract very real and very significant increases in the price of foreign oil. Whether this comes about

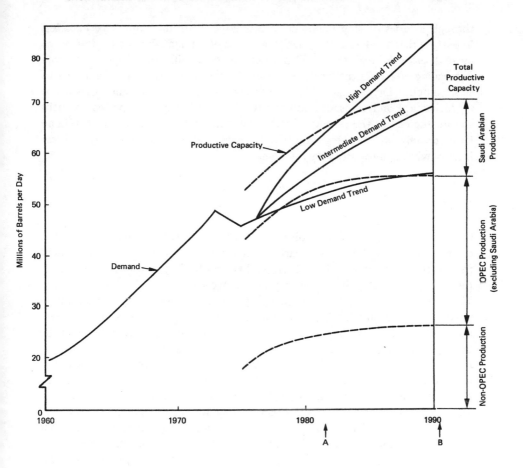

Source: Arthur D. Little, Inc., estimates.
A. If high demand, then supply limited in early 1980s.
B. If intermediate demand, then supply limited in early 1990s.
C. If low demand, then no limitations before 2000.

Figure 15-1. Comparison of World Oil Demand and Productive Capacity, 1960-1990.

through a series of step jumps or in one large quantum jump is perhaps less important than the fact that by 1990 the price of foreign oil could be double the current price in real terms. This price increase will then have a renewed dampening effect on the world economy. Price is obviously a great rationer of short supplies; increasingly oil will be forced into higher form/value uses in the petrochemical and transportation fields only. Following this period, perhaps toward the end of the century, we may move into a transition phase wherein oil is used only in very high form/value uses and renewable energy sources increasingly begin to satisfy energy demand.

U.S. Oil

Given this outlook for foreign oil prices, what is likely to be the impact on the domestic oil supply? As we said earlier, domestic oil supplies could be equivalent to as little as 50 percent of our total oil demand. It is frequently said these days that the United States has no energy policy. We submit that this is not the case. The United States does have an energy policy; it is, in fact, very implicit in the differences between what happens now versus what would happen if there were no government at all. The U.S. energy policy for the past 25 years may be briefly summarized as favoring consumption, discouraging production, inducing through regulation demand for those energy sources in the shortest supply, and increasingly placing a number of regulatory roadblocks to conversion to energy resources which are in potentially greater supply. In view of these policies, the U.S. credibility when we exhort other nations to conserve energy is very low. Very recent U.S. efforts to discourage the building and adoption of the breeder reactor and similar technologies due to concern about the proliferation of nuclear weapons rings very false on the ears of many European and Japanese policymakers. To them it sounds very much like the country with the greatest energy resources trying to discourage them from converting to the one energy resource that could reduce their dependency on oil. Thus they are suspicious that U.S. energy policy may have as one of its objectives the enhancement of our competitive position in the international market.

The situation today is a very gradual moving away from the U.S. policy of the past 25 years through the initiatives proposed by the Carter administration. The centerpiece of that legislation as it reflects upon oil is a proposed crude oil equalization tax that would gradually by 1980 or 1981 increase the tax-paid cost of domestically produced oil to its foreign oil equivalent and theoretically thereafter allow U.S. and foreign oil prices to increase together. Clearly the objectives of this policy are to utilize the pricing mechanism as the means of controlling demand and inducing conservation while preventing windfall profits to the producers through the confiscation of the economic rent represented by the difference between current domestic prices and foreign oil prices. The crude oil equalization tax or similar legislation that would have the same effect is likely to become enacted in one form or another. Increasing oil prices will provide additional incentives for conservation. In fact, as Dick Messing reported in chapter 3, the oil price increases to date have already induced notable conservation in the industrial sector.

Nevertheless, increasing domestic oil prices is a very difficult political decision, especially for members of the House of Representatives, who must face election every 2 years. The energy crisis is in many ways a hidden crisis. The public sees only the tip of the iceberg—and that is sinking quickly. Long lines of cars at gasoline pumps are but a fading memory. There were no significant gas curtailments last winter. There has been price competition on almost all products. Real foreign oil prices (adjusted for inflation) have fallen. Thus it is very difficult at the present time for politicians to embrace policies which are, or seem to be, unfriendly toward the consumers who elect them. However, the present period can only be considered the lull before the storm and the Iranian crisis has highlighted this fact. Unless action is initiated now, very severe dislocations could take place if foreign oil prices rise dramatically and suddenly in the mid to late 1980s (or sooner). These potential dislocations include slower economic growth, greater unemployment, possible reductions in Western standards of living, and disruptions of the international monetary and trade systems. To avoid these very significant dislocations later, much smaller dislocations such as increased domestic oil prices are required now.

16 Natural Gas and Coal: Utilization and the Environment

Richard F. Messing and
Charles R. LaMantia

Natural Gas and Coal
Richard F. Messing

Natural Gas

The uncertainties relating to the supply and demand for natural gas in future years are probably greater than for any other energy form. The availability of natural gas has a tremendous leveraging effect on energy demand, since curtailment of gas supplies will force users to convert to oil, coal, or electricity, and will thereby add significantly to requirements for these other energy forms.

The uncertainties in the natural gas industry are highlighted by the adoption of new pricing legislation as a part of the National Energy Plan proposed by the Carter administration. The Natural Gas Policy Act contains the following principal elements:

> A price for new gas of $2.07 per thousand cubic feet as of December 1978, escalated by 3.7 percent above inflation to 1981 and by 4.2 percent between 1981 and 1985. Depending on the inflation assumptions used, this would bring the wellhead price for new gas by 1985 to about $3.75 to $4.00 per thousand cubic feet. Other pricing levels are allowed for stripper gas, for rollover of old contracts, for incentive gas, and for difficult-to-obtain gas. In all there are at least seventeen different pricing levels which will be applicable to natural gas sales.
>
> Pricing regulations will apply to gas sold in both interstate and intrastate markets.
>
> All higher-priced new gas and supplemental gas must be incrementally priced to large users under rules to be promulgated by the Department of Energy by late 1979.

Much of the controversy over the adoption of these pricing standards has concerned the supply response which might be anticipated. Various supply models which reflect the pace of drilling activity in relation to the financial incentives show that there should be a reasonably high level of drilling activity and hopefully a pace of reserve additions which will more nearly parallel current withdrawals. Many have been heartened to see that, even under the previous pricing standards for new gas at $1.49 per thousand cubic feet, drilling activity was stepped up considerably and current production levels have increased. Perhaps the greatest benefit from adoption of the legislation will be the enhanced ability for operators to plan their future drilling commitments with more certainty than has been true in recent years.

The feature of the legislation which has not drawn as much attention, but which may have more profound implications for industrial users, is the incremental pricing. These provisions are quite complex and apply only to gas moving in the interstate market. In Phase I, incremental pricing applies only to large boiler fuel users, with exemptions for those using less than 300 million cubic feet per year, for agricultural users, for essential human needs, and for electric generation. In Phase II, other large users would be included, and exemptions for small boiler fuel users would be limited to 5 percent of the boiler fuel market for gas. A limit is placed on the amount of the incremental price passthrough so that the maximum price of gas corresponds to the regional price level for distillate fuel oil.

The implications of these provisions to large users depend on one's estimates of the decay rates for the production of committed gas under old contracts, the rate at which new gas will be marketed, and the pace at which higher-priced supplements will become part of the sendout. Most of the estimates of the decline rate in existing production indicate that by 1985 old gas will be sufficient to supply only the high-priority sector of the market, that is, the small users. Thus industrial users will be virtually entirely dependent on new and supplemental gas, all incrementally priced. A weighted average of new and supplemental gas prices at that time appears to be about $4.25 per thousand cubic feet at the source, or $5.50 per thousand cubic feet delivered (about a threefold increase over current levels). In real terms, the price of gas to large users will be escalating at an annual rate of about 7 percent. Whether the limit of equivalence with the distillate oil price will be reached by 1985 is debatable, depending on the price progression assumed for oil, but a recent Arthur D. Little survey of comparative energy values showed a likely current-dollar price for fuel oil delivered to a large industrial user at close to $6.00 per million BTUs in 1985 (see table 16-1), hence the prices for gas and oil would tend to approach equivalence. Coal should become an even more attractive fuel for large boiler users where logistics and siting allow conversion to coal firing, although many companies are reluctant to make the capital commitment in light of the environmental and economic uncertainties associated with this type of investment.

Coal

The coal industry faces its own set of problems, which in many respects are quite different from those of other sectors of the energy industries. Unlike oil

Table 16-1
Forecast of Energy Prices for Industry

	1976	1985	Percent per Year Increase
Oil (no. 6, 0.5% sulfur)	2.00[a]	5.97[a]	13
Gas	1.73	5.50	14
Coal (without scrubber)	0.95	1.72	7
Coal (with scrubber)	1.40	2.47	7
Electricity	8.29	14.36	6
Electricity (cents/kwh)	2.83	4.90	6

[a]Current dollars per million BTUs.

and gas, the resource base of the coal industry is large in relation to the current pace of production, with the recoverable reserves estimated to have a life index of at least 300 years. Because coal mining is more labor intensive, however, the industry has been confronted with escalating labor costs, reduced productivity, and intermittent interruptions of production by strikes. Some have expressed the view that the 1977 strike and wage settlement were a real setback to the ambitious growth plans of the industry. Whether this portrayal is accurate remains to be seen, but meanwhile the industry is proceeding with a rapid pace of expansion to accommodate future requirements, and many companies active in the oil and gas industries are looking to coal as an attractive means of energy diversification.

The United Mine Workers (UMW) contract contains provisions which are expected to increase the wage-related costs of coal mining by 20.5 percent in 1978, 7.5 percent in 1979, and 6.2 percent in 1980, or a cumulative total of 37.5 percent over the three years. For an Eastern underground mine, this would mean that labor-related costs would increase from about $9.40 per ton in 1977 to about $13.60 per ton in 1980. Based on the cost passthrough provisions of most contracts, the users will in most cases bear these costs directly. Some productivity improvement may be forthcoming if the production-incentive provisions allowed in the contract become effective at the local level.

One offset to the added burden of wage costs will be the expected higher proportion of coal produced by strip-mining methods, which are not so labor intensive. The development of the industry in the Powder River Basin area of Wyoming is proceeding rapidly, and over 500 million tons of capacity per year have been announced for that area, although it is questionable whether all this will be installed in light of delays in construction of user facilities. Some producers in that area have been surprised to find that available capacities substantially exceed current requirements, with the result that prices for new contracts have generally been rather soft, about in the range of $6.00 per ton, which corresponds to only about 37 cents per million BTUs at the mine mouth. Transport costs are an important component of user costs in this case, however, since most large consuming destinations involve hauling costs that are as large or larger than the mine-mouth cost. One area of the country where this factor will be increasingly critical is on the Gulf Coast, where interest has been shown both by utilities and industrial companies in use of coal as boiler fuel, and where the subbituminous coals from the Powder River Basin will presumably compete head on with the lignite reserves which are indigenous to the area. We believe that lignite will in fact become an important fuel for both power generation and industrial boiler applications in the Southwest, and we expect that its tonnage will contribute substantially to the national supplies.

While problems at the production level are evident in the coal industry, they are accompanied by equal or greater uncertainties at the user level. The question of when to commit to conversion of existing oil- and gas-fired boilers to coal remains a key issue with many large users, as does the question of whether a cogeneration plant providing both electricity and steam service may be the most practicable approach. Cogeneration offers much higher heat efficiencies than a typical electric generating plant, and can also offer advantages of larger scale when the unit is designed to serve a number of adjacent customers.

As noted in the discussion on natural gas, one of the key factors influencing fuel conversion will be the availability of natural gas and the pricing standards that will apply to its use for industrial purposes. Our analyses show that the likely higher rates of price escalation for oil and gas will widen the advantage of coal with time and that, in instances where the logistics and environmental standards permit burning of coal, it will be attractive to invest in a conversion facility. Use of low-BTU gas continues to be investigated as an alternative, but until new cost breakthroughs become apparent, it appears more economic to invest in complete boiler replacement and stack gas scrubbing facilities than in a gasification facility which would allow continued use of the existing boilers.

Coal Utilization and the Environment
Charles R. LaMantia

There are several pieces of federal legislation which could influence or constrain the utilization of coal by both utility and industrial users. These involve air, water, solids, and hazardous and toxic wastes control legislation. But the legislation which has been most formally reduced to enforceable regulations at this time are the air pollution regulations. These regulations, which will probably have the most immediate and far-reaching impact on coal utilization and which are being modified frequently, will be described briefly.

The Clean Air Act was originally passed in 1967 with the first set of amendments in 1970. This legislation set the framework for the definition of what are now six criteria pollutants: particulate, sulfur dioxide, nitrogen oxides, carbon monoxide, hydrocarbons, and photochemical oxidants. The first two, particulate and sulfur dioxide, are generated on combustion of coal. The last three are generated, primarily, by the automobile; and nitrogen oxides are common to all combustion sources, stationary fuel combustion as well as automotive sources.

Ambient Air Quality Standards, set by the federal Environmental Protection Agency (EPA), define the quality of the environment relative to these pollutants—the maximum concentration of each one of these criteria pollutants which is allowable any place in the United States. These are minimum air quality standards.

The Clean Air Act, the amendments, and the regulations required each state to develop a set of implementation plans consisting of local codes and emission limitations to achieve the air quality standards throughout the United States. The Primary Ambient Air Quality Standards were to be achieved by July 1975 for each of the criteria pollutants.

Progress has been made. There has been a general reduction in the atmospheric concentration of most of these pollutants in most places. However, there are many areas in the country which are not in compliance with Ambient Air Quality Standards for one or more of these criteria pollutants.

With regard to utilization of coal, total suspended particulate is a problem in many parts of the United States. Sulfur dioxide concentrations also remain a problem in some locations, but are not as widespread as the particulate problem.

We are now into the second iteration of attempts to improve the environment. The second set of Clean Air Act amendments was passed in August 1977. They were enacted in the face of a strong lobbying effort on the part of utilities and represent a very tough set of amendments, with no softening apparent in the federal posture with regard to air pollution control. We have a new time frame for achieving compliance with the Primary Ambient Air Quality Standards, until December 1982. Also, we are taking a second pass at development of state implementation plans and resulting local codes. The implementation plans are to be developed and approved by EPA by July 1979. There could be delays in approval. There remains a question as to whether or not we will achieve compliance by 1982, but we will get much closer than we did the first time.

The 1977 amendments dealt with nonattainment areas, areas that are not in compliance with particulate and sulfur dioxide, especially. Furthermore, the amendments provided for prevention of significant deterioration in locations where the air quality is far superior to the minimum federal standards. There is also a requirement in the amendments for development of much tougher emission standards for new stationary sources, especially coal-fired boilers, both utility and industrial scale.

Through July 1979, to enable construction of a new emissions source in a nonattainment area, an equivalent emission reduction must be achieved from the existing sources in that area. After July 1979, the revised state implementation plans would deal with new sources in each nonattainment area.

Prevention of significant deterioration allows for three air quality classes:

class I, pristine areas, where very little industrial growth would be possible; class II, where moderate growth would be allowed; and class III, where intensive growth would be allowed. All areas in the United States would be initially class II, except national parks (class I). Each state has options to reclassify areas as either class I or class III. In no case would a state be allowed to let the environment deteriorate below any federal air quality standards. These provisions for prevention of significant deterioration will affect plant sitings, in terms of location, and will also affect the size of plants that may be put at certain locations. With regard to nonattainment and prevention of significant deterioration, we can expect to see requirements for the best available control technology for any new boilers in these types of locations.

Finally, the 1977 amendments required revision of New Source Performance Standards (NSPS) for coal-fired boilers. The current NSPS for utility boilers firing coal are given in table 16-2. Revisions of NSPS are to reflect improvements in technology which have occurred since the current standards were promulgated by EPA in 1971. These federal standards apply to all new utility boilers, regardless of where they are built in the country. Local standards, for example, in nonattainment or prevention of significant deterioration areas, could be even tighter than these federal standards.

The revised NSPS were due to be promulgated in August 1978 but are late because of detailed review and debate regarding their ultimate impact. The revised NSPS will probably require 85 percent removal of sulfur dioxide down to as low as 0.2 pound of sulfur dioxide per million BTUs; other probable 1985 limits are 0.03 pound of particulate and 0.6 pound of nitrogen oxides (table 16-2).

What will be the impact of these revisions? In regard to particulate removal, electrostatic precipitators, which traditionally are used by utilities for particulate control, will be very much more expensive and probably very difficult to build to meet the standards for boilers burning low-sulfur western coals. Scrubbers probably will not be used for particulate control because of the high energy requirements to meet the 0.03 pound standard. Fabric filters, or baghouses, which traditionally have not been used by utilities, will be used on utility boilers

Table 16-2
New Source Performance Standards, New Utility/Coal

	Allowable Emissions (lb/MMBTU)	
	Current	Probable Future
Sulfur dioxide	1.2	85-90% Removal (0.2)
Particulate	0.1	0.03-0.05
Nitrogen oxides	0.7	0.6

for particulate control. The standards for nitrogen oxides have been set by the EPA so that they can be met by design of the boiler as opposed to requiring an add-on system for nitrogen oxides removal from flue gas.

These revised NSPS are for utility boilers, 25 megawatts and up, which generate electricity for sale. The larger industrial boilers (25 megawatts equivalent and larger) would still be subject to the current NSPS. The industrial boiler standards also are being reviewed by EPA for revision. The revised industrial boiler standards will cover smaller boilers and will probably be developed by EPA over the next 2 or 3 years. Existing industrial boilers, as any existing boilers, would be regulated by local requirements, as would smaller, new boilers until covered by revised industrial boiler standards.

Table 16-3 gives an indication of the cost impact of the tightening sulfur dioxide standards for new utility boilers (400 to 800 megawatts). The current NSPS results in sulfur dioxide control costs in the range of 40 to 50 cents per million BTUs of high-sulfur coal fired (including capital charges). For low-sulfur coal, costs range from zero (for compliance coal) up to about 25 cents per million BTUs. For the higher removal required by revised NSPS, we expect roughly 20 to 25 percent cost increases in the total annual cost for high-sulfur coal. For low-sulfur coal, we expect a more substantial percentage increase; there will no longer be compliance coal which can be used without sulfur dioxide removal. The overall impact is a lower air pollution control cost differential between low- and high-sulfur coal. If the industrial standards for this kind of control are as tough, the industrial-scale costs comparable to these utility costs might be about twice as high, roughly a dollar per million BTUs.

Very briefly, what are the alternatives to flue-gas desulfurization? One alternative for new units would be fluidized-bed combustion (table 16-4). Here the economics are potentially competitive or more favorable than those of conventional combustion with flue-gas desulfurization. Combustion occurs at a lower temperature so that generation of nitrogen oxide is much lower. However, it becomes more and more difficult to meet higher sulfur dioxide removal requirements at reasonable limestone consumption (limestone is added to the bed for sulfur dioxide removal). At any rate, this technology is yet to be demonstrated on a large scale and cannot be expected to have any significant impact, if indeed the economics prove out, for 5 to 10 years.

Table 16-3
Sulfur Dioxide Removal Costs, New Utility

	Annual Cost (cents/MMBTU)	
	Current NSPS	85-90% Removal
3-4%-Sulfur Coal	40-50	50-60
0.3-1.5%-sulfur Coal	0-25	30-60

Table 16-4
Alternate Technologies

Fluidized-bed combustion

Solvent-refined coal
$2.50-4.00/MMBTU

Low-BTU gas
$2.50-3.50/MMBTU

Another alternative is to process the coal for sulfur removal. One process involves producing a solvent-refined, semiliquid product. These costs, which are shown very roughly, are for conversion of the coal to the solvent-refined product, but do not include the cost of the coal. These costs would be directly comparable to the flue-gas desulfurization costs given in table 16-3. The economics are for a large-scale facility with a fuel output comparable to that required for a 500-megawatt boiler; a small plant would not be built to service an industrial facility. There is some question regarding the sulfur removal capability of the process—its ability to remove 85 to 90 percent of the sulfur from a variety of coals. It is possible that additional hydrodesulfurization or possibly flue-gas desulfurization would be required for the solvent-refined product, adding to the costs shown here. If demonstrated in the next 5 years or so, the economics for this technology may not be favorable for new base-loaded units.

The last alternative involves producing low-BTU gas, a technology currently available for use even on the industrial scale. However, low-BTU gas is a premium fuel that has considerable form value for process uses. On the utility scale, economics would require use of a combined cycle or some approach to improving the overall utilization of the energy to reduce costs. It is unlikely that we will see much low-BTU gas going into boiler fuel.

For the near to medium term, it appears that conventional combustion with flue-gas desulfurization, together with baghouses for particulate control, are the options for burning coal in large boiler facilities. The use of new technologies appears to be restricted to the longer term.

17 The Potential for Solar Energy Development

Peter E. Glaser

Introduction

The use of energy has been the key to the social development of man and an essential component in improving the quality of life beyond the basic activities necessary for survival. The striking feature of the history of exploitation of energy resources has been the sustained growth of energy consumption during the last century. Meeting this demand for energy has been the primary driving force in the development of technology to mine coal, dam rivers, drill for oil and gas, and extract uranium. Furthermore, the conversion of the various energy resources into power has been and will continue to be essential to the growth of industrial activities, with the amount of energy and the changes in the mix of resources used for power generation dictated by economic, environmental, and political considerations.

The recognition that no one energy source will, by itself, meet all future energy demands, that the search for new sources of nonrenewable fuels can only put off the day of their ultimate exhaustion, and that uncertainties inherent in achieving the potential of known energy conversion methods are large when applied on a global scale has led to renewed emphasis on solar energy applications. Solar energy, the primary source of energy for the global ecosystem, drives the hydrologic and atmospheric cycles and is the basis for photosynthesis, which sustains life in all its varied forms. It is by far the largest source of energy available to the earth, with about 1.7×10^{14} kilowatts intercepted by the earth. The sun contributes 5,000 times the total energy input from all other sources and its availability is assured for eons to come.

For more than 100 years, the potential of solar energy as a source of power has been recognized and evaluated. Efforts to harness solar energy were accelerated during the last half of the nineteenth century and the beginning of the twentieth century as the world's energy needs grew as a result of the industrial revolution. These efforts subsided with the successful development of energy economies based on the use of liquid petroleum fuels. It was not until the early 1970s that the development of solar energy technology was again being pursued seriously.

The degree to which the application of solar energy technology will be successful will to a large extent depend on its economic feasibility and the reduced availability of nonrenewable fuels and their future cost escalation.

147

Although solar energy is a widely distributed resource—each square meter of earth's surface exposed to direct sunlight at noon receives the equivalent of 1 kilowatt—the conversion technology is capital intensive.

The successful and widespread introduction of solar energy technology will require considerable development to strike the appropriate balance among conflicting requirements presented by economics, the environment, and society's needs. Current solar energy research and development is directed toward a search for new technology and approaches to reduce the cost of conversion and for designs and processes to permit low-cost mass production. Although expectations for significant benefits are high, results on the desired scale are unlikely to be achieved quickly—not because of the lack of appropriate technology, but because of limited experience with such technology and, until very recently, the lack of appreciation of the potential of solar energy.

Industry and governments in many nations have recognized that solar energy has the potential to supply a major portion of future energy needs if effective ways can be found to convert solar energy into heat, power, electricity, or other fuels economically and efficiently. They are devoting efforts to finding out which solar energy applications are most likely to be successful, what products should be developed, how big the solar energy market will be, how to plan entry into the market, what the role of government should be, and when the potential of solar energy will be realized on a significant scale.

Water, Space, and Process Heat

One application—solar water heaters—is already contributing to energy conservation in Australia, Japan, and Israel, and is beginning to do so in the United States. Heating water with solar energy is particularly attractive because of the year-round need for hot water in residences, schools, hospitals, hotels, and some industrial processes, such as textile dyeing and finishing and food processing, and because of the established technology based on the use of flat-plate solar collectors—the main components of hot water systems. Furthermore, the cost, including installation, of residential solar water heaters with a typical solar collector area (5 square meters) ranges from $1500 to $2500 in the United States, and this cost can be amortized over 7 to 10 years. Also, solar water heaters can be installed in existing and new buildings, which opens up a substantial retrofit market. And finally, government incentives and subsidies in several countries make the purchase price of solar water heaters attractive to consumers.

Another application—solar space heating systems—requires a larger solar collector area (typically about 30 square meters) and provides, depending on location, from 30 to 70 percent of a residence's heating needs. The required capital investment, about $10,000 to $15,000, is substantial and, for a new residence, may have to be included as part of the mortgage. If it is, the monthly payments for heating could be lower than those in a conventionally heated residence. For existing residences, however, space heating systems are unlikely to be economical, because of the cost of custom installations, but the economics for commercial and industrial buildings are promising.

Related to solar heating is a not yet widely used application—solar cooling—which involves the use of heat-actuated air conditioners. Such an application may grow significantly in locations with extended hot seasons, although improved heat pumps may prove to be competitive.

In the United States, the solar energy industry has doubled the output of solar collectors every year for the past 5 years. In 1977, 430,000 square meters of solar collectors for solar heating systems, including swimming pool heaters, with an installed value of almost $100 million, were sold in the United States. The value of solar installations approached $200 million in 1978 and is projected to reach $1 billion per year in the early 1980s and $1.5 billion per year by 1985.[1] Depending on the degree of public acceptance, the United States market for solar heating and cooling equipment could increase to $5 billion to $10 billion per year by the year 2000.

To stimulate purchases of solar heating systems, incentives are being devised, among them low-interest loans, an income tax credit for space heating, and grants for solar water heaters.[2] With such incentives available to the buyers, it is conceivable that 2.5 million buildings in the United States could be equipped with solar heating systems by 1987, using products which are now undergoing demonstration tests.

The use of solar energy to displace fossil fuels and electricity for supplying process heat in agricultural and industrial applications will require heating systems based on either more efficient high-temperature flat-plate solar collectors or solar concentrators. Such systems will be able to heat water and produce steam and hot air over a temperature range from 50 to 200°C. Investments in solar process heat systems in the United States are projected to reach a total of $100 billion by the year 2000, particularly as the process heat demand is expected to increase from 6 quads (1 quad is 10^{15} BTU) per year in 1975 at a rate of 3.5 percent per year. The solar process heat systems are expected to displace oil, gas, and electric usage so that by 2000, solar process heat systems will supply about 2 quads per year.

Thermal Conversion Systems

Every schoolboy knows that a lens can concentrate sunlight to burn a hole in paper. This principle is the basis for applications in which solar energy is concentrated with parabolically shaped mirrors for such prosaic purposes as pumping irrigating water and generating electricity for communities. In these solar thermal conversion systems, engines operating on solar heat drive either pumps or generators. Production of enough electrical power to meet the needs of a small community (about 10 kilowatts) would require a solar concentrator area of about 100 square meters. Although several times as costly as electricity supplied by large power generating plants, the power produced by these solar power conversion units is expected to have wide application, particularly in remote areas of developing countries where electricity is not available and where engine generators will not be cost effective.

Solar thermal conversion systems are being designed to operate in conjunction with conventional large power plants.[3] In this application, large flat mirrors (heliostats) are arranged to follow the sun and to direct the reflected radiation onto a boiler atop a tall tower. Such a tower would be about 260 meters tall; to generate steam to provide about 100,000 kilowatts, the boiler would have to receive, while the sun shines, radiation from mirrors with a total area of about 3.5 square kilometers. Thermal storage would be required to keep the system operating during the time when the sun does not shine. Because it is economically impractical to provide enough thermal storage to operate continuously 24 hours per day, this method for large-scale conversion of solar energy to power would most likely be used to generate electricity only during peak consumption (including evening) periods, in which case 2 to 4 hours of thermal storage would suffice.

With present technology, about 8 square meters of mirror surface would be required to generate about one kilowatt of electrical power. Each heliostat would have to be mounted so that it would track the sun as it moves across the sky and be designed to withstand extreme weather conditions. Thus, a 100,000-kilowatt plant would require about 800,000 square meters of mirrors. If each heliostat comprised 40 square meters of mirror area, 200,000 individual heliostats would have to be erected in the field. The capital costs for a mass-produced 100,000-kilowatt solar power plant would be about $1,700 per kilowatt.

To reduce the uncertainties, two solar power plants are under construction, with a 5,000-kilowatt plant being completed in Albuquerque, New Mexico, and a 10,000-kilowatt plant to be constructed in Barstow, California, at costs of about $10,000 per kilowatt. The experience obtained during the construction of these demonstration plants will indicate whether the costs of large solar thermal conversion systems are competitive enough to provide peak or intermediate power to merit commercial development.

An alternative would be to combine solar thermal conversion with fossil-fuel-fired power plants—particularly an oil-fired plant. In such a hybrid power plant, there would be no loss of capacity when solar energy is not available.

Photovoltaic Systems

A very promising application of solar energy is to convert it directly into electricity by the photovoltaic process. In this process, as long as sunlight is available, solar cells exposed to the sunlight generate electricity without consuming any materials. Solar cells, invented in 1953 at the Bell Telephone Laboratories, are best known for applications in most satellites orbited during the past two decades. Such photovoltaic systems have reliably supplied power, ranging from a few watts to about 30 kilowatts, to navigational, meteorological, communication, and earth-resources satellites and instrumented deep-space probes.

More recently, solar cells have begun to be utilized for terrestrial applications,[4] for example, for unattended power supplies for use in remote areas where conventional engine/generators may not be feasible due to lack of accessibility and where electrical power transmission lines cannot be economically justified. Even at the current high prices, ranging from $15 to $25 for each peak watt generated at noon on a sunny day, photovoltaic systems are being used in such diverse applications as navigation aids, devices to protect pipelines against cathodic corrosion, consumer products such as calculators and watches, and battery chargers, and to power water pumps for irrigation.

Single-crystal silicon is the most widely used material for solar cells and is expected to remain in wide use in the future. Commercially available silicon solar cells have an efficiency of 12 to 15 percent, but in the laboratory, such solar cells already have achieved efficiencies of up to 18 percent.

In recognition of the potential contribution of photovoltaic systems, the U.S. Department of Energy has established a program to develop low-cost silicon solar cells and to stimulate the creation of a viable industrial and commercial capability to achieve production volumes at predictable and reasonable costs.[5] The cost goals (in 1975 dollars) are:

Reduction by 1982 of silicon solar cell array costs to $2 per peak watt

Reduction by 1986 of silicon solar cell array costs to 50 cents per peak watt

Achievement by the year 2000 of a photovoltaic industry technological capability to meet 3 percent of the U.S. electrical power demand, with solar cell arrays at a market price of 10 to 30 cents per peak watt

Major efforts are under way not only in the United States but also in Europe and Japan to develop new processes to produce solar cell materials which could drastically lower costs. Attention has been focused on the production of single-crystal silicon which would be grown either as ingots (up to 8 centimeters in diameter) or in the form of ribbons (up to 7 centimeters wide), and more recently, by casting silicon in polycrystalline blocks from which large square silicon solar cells (11 X 11 centimeters) can be produced. Near-term cost reductions are likely to be obtained by combining solar cells with solar concentrators to reduce the area of the more expensive solar cells.

The United States market for photovoltaic systems is projected to reach 1,000 kilowatts in 1978 and to double by 1979. Reduction of the silicon solar cell cost to $2 per peak watt is likely to be achieved when the market reaches about 4,000 kilowatts per year by 1982. Achievement of the cost goal of 50 cents per peak watt will require a significant technological advancement which can be justified only if the market continues to grow. Although at first the market will be stimulated primarily by government purchases, commercialization of the photovoltaic industry is expected to result in increased market growth; increasing industry volume will lead to further cost reductions.

In developing countries, photovoltaic systems could be used to power irrigation pumps. Because of the low maintenance costs and reduced need for skilled labor for installation and servicing, photovoltaic systems would be competitive with engine/generators when their costs reach about $2 per peak watt. With continued improvements to reduce processing costs and with the development of materials such as cadmium sulfide, amorphous silicon, and gallium arsenide for thin-film solar cells, the photovoltaic system market could reach 10 gigawatts by 2000 and up to 50 gigawatts in 40 years.

As solar cell costs decrease, photovoltaic systems could be used for dispersed onsite applications, such as for residential and commercial buildings, to augment the power supplied by electric utilities. The difficulty of developing low-cost energy storage to provide electricity continously for 24 hours places photovoltaic systms for central power plant applications at a disadvantage, although they may be used to meet peak power demands in sunny locations.

Indirect Processes

In two other conversion processes—the extraction of power from the winds and from sun-warmed ocean waters—solar energy is available in stored forms, that is, in the warmed atmosphere and in the ocean; thus, systems utilizing either wind or the ocean waters can operate even when the sun does not shine. In a third—the bioconversion of land and/or water products of photosynthesis—the solar energy is also available in a stored form, that is, in the various forms of plant life.

Wind Power

There is a great deal of experience in the use of wind power systems for generating electricity or producing mechanical power. Such systems are in use in remote areas not served by a transmission network and where operation of engine/generators is impractical. Wind turbine types include the multiblade horizontal-axis wind turbine, which operates at low speed and two- or three-blade horizontal-axis turbines that operate at high speeds. Commercial high-speed wind turbines with outputs of a few kilowatts to tenths of a kilowatt have blade diameters of 2 to 10 meters, with experimental units being designed with blade diameters of up to 100 meters for outputs of about 1,500 kilowatts. Wind turbines require a wind speed of 10 kilometers or greater and usually achieve rated output at wind speeds of about 35 kilometers. However, in areas with favorable winds, average wind speeds are about 20 kilometers, reducing the average output to about one-fifth to one-third of the rated output. Unit costs of medium-sized wind power systems, excluding the tower and energy storage, range between $1,300 and $1,800 per rated kilowatt. Typical cost of a small wind power system (4-meter diameter blade and rated capacity of 6 kilowatts) is about $2,300, but the cost per operational kilowatt (about 20-kilometer wind speed) is $9,500.

Wind power systems with outputs of 1,500 to 2,500 megawatts are expected to be used in an integrated electrical utility system in areas with winds averaging 20 kilometers or more. Such systems will be used primarily to save fuel and over their lifetime could displace up to four times their initial cost in fuel equivalent.

In the United States, about 100,000 sites have been identified as having the potential for installation of a wind power system with a total capacity of about 150 gigawatts. About 27,000 such systems, each with an output of 1,500 kilowatts, could be installed by 2000, resulting in a fuel savings of about 2 quads per year.

Ocean Thermal Energy

The use of ocean waters as a source of power has been an intriguing concept since the early 1900s. In the tropical and subtropical oceans temperature differences of about 20°C between the sun-warmed surface water and colder waters at depths of 600 to 1,500 meters offer a potential resource for ocean thermal energy conversion (OTEC).[6] In this conversion process, an appropriate heat transfer fluid, for example, ammonia, would be circulated through a conventional heat-engine cycle. The fluid would be vaporized by the warm surface waters and the vapor used to power a turbine-driven electric generator. The vaporized fluid would then be condensed by cold water pumped up from the lower depths and recycled. The conversion efficiency of an OTEC plant is expected to be, at best, 2.5 percent; however, such a plant could operate with a constant output of about 500 megawatts for 24 hours, and since it would require no energy storage system, it could be used for baseload power generation. The waters off Florida's coastlines and still within the 360-kilometer U.S. jurisdiction would be suitable for OTEC plants. Such a plant would require deep undersea transmission of power, at a cable cost of about $1 million per kilometer.

Many technical and material problems remain to be solved before an OTEC plant can be demonstrated to be commercially feasible. The development of

OTEC plants presents challenges in the design of effective heat exchangers which can withstand corrosion and biofouling during 30 years of exposure in the ocean. The OTEC plant has to be designed to operate in currents of up to 10 kilometers per hour with cold water intake pipes reaching to 1,500-meter depths. About 60 percent of the cost of an OTEC plant will be associated with the heat exchangers for the evaporator boiler. Titanium heat exchangers are being investigated, but development of aluminum heat exchangers could lead to significant cost reductions, for example, from $2,100 per kilowatt for titanium to $1,400 per kilowatt for OTEC plants with aluminum alloy heat exchangers. Biofouling and corrosion could lead to significant reductions in efficiency. An additional 0.5°C temperature drop across the heat exchanger surfaces of both the evaporator and condenser due to biofouling could reduce the net power output by 7 percent. Undersea cable costs to transmit the power from the OTEC plant to shore could result in doubling of the OTEC capital cost if the plant were located far offshore. Only a small capacity of OTEC is projected to be installed by 2000.

Bioconversion

Another indirect application of solar energy that has substantial potential is the conversion of products of photosynthesis (bioconversion), such as trees, algae, and ocean-grown kelp, into fuels. Bioconversion systems can utilize a variety of organic materials, which include products of farming, for the specific purpose of producing biomass feedstock, as well as residues from logging and mill operations and from agricultural wastes. Conversion processes include direct combustion and thermochemical (pyrolysis and gasification) and aqueous processes (hydrolysis and bacterial digestion). The challenges are to increase the efficiency with which plants convert solar energy into their constituent organic materials, to find the required large land areas on which to grow the products, and to develop methods for ocean farming.

The potential for biomass technologies has been recognized in other countries. Nearly 30 percent of Brazil's energy comes from burning of wood and sugarcane bagasse. In 1978, 1.5 billion liters of ethyl alcohol was produced from sugarcane. Brazil is also considering the economic feasibility of producing ethyl alcohol from the cassava root. Brazil has substantial sunny land areas and the manpower to cultivate the root; the alcohol extracted from it could be a substitute for imported gasoline. China has successfully introduced several million family-sized methane-producing units utilizing organic wastes, and similar efforts are under way in India and other developing countries. In tropical areas, palm oil could be used as a fuel for diesel engines. Although providing a long-term opportunity, improved management of hundreds of millions of acres of productive forest land in the United States for large-scale production of biomass to fuel power plants and for synthetic fuels is considered to be less appropriate for the U.S. energy economy.[7]

Bioconversion and wind power combined with small-scale solar thermal conversion and photovoltaic systems could be integrated in suitable combinations in a rural electrification system. Such combinations also show promise for applications in remote villages in developing countries where such systems could be competitive with engine/generators to provide drinking water, cold storage, lighting, irrigation, and light industrial facilities. Such a rural electrification system, although more capital intensive than an engine/generator, would permit greater use of renewable resources in developing countries. The market for such systems is represented by about 2 million villages worldwide. The constraints on this market will be the financing and the requirement to create an infrastructure to install the systems, train operators, and supply spare parts.

Solar-Power Satellites

Solar-power satellites (SPS) in geosynchronous earth orbit at a distance of 36,000 kilometers could obviate terrestrial obstacles to baseload solar-generated power to meet future global energy demands. Electricity produced by solar energy conversion at the SPS will be fed to microwave generators forming part of a transmitting antenna. This antenna is designed to direct a microwave beam of low-power density precisely to one or more receiving antennas on earth. At the receiving antenna, the microwave energy will be reconverted at high efficiency to generate electricity (from 1 to 5 gigawatts) for transmission to users.

The SPS will receive from four to eleven times the solar energy available on earth in areas that receive copious sunshine. It will be continuously illuminated by the sun, except for precisely predictable periods around the equinoxes, when it will be eclipsed for up to 72 minutes a day. These eclipses will occur near local midnight at the receiving antenna sites—at a time when power demands are at the lowest level. These interruptions can be accounted for in the load management of an electrical utility system.

Because conversion of microwaves to electricity at the receiving antenna will be more efficient than power generation based on thermodynamic cycles, thermal pollution will be greatly reduced. (Conversion at 83 percent efficiency was demonstrated in 1975.) The microwave transmission system will be designed to meet international guidelines regarding exposure to low-level microwaves.

The SPS concept was first proposed in 1968 as an extension of existing technology.[8] Current system studies are leading to increased confidence in technology and cost predictions.[9] The SPS development and evaluation program of the U.S. Department of Energy and NASA[10] is designed to assess technical, economic, and environmental issues in order to select the most promising systems for further development. The accelerated pace of space operations possible with the advent of the space shuttle in 1980 could lead to the introduction of the SPS after 1995.

Economic analyses based on probable distributions of component costs indicate a convergence of capital cost projections in the range of $1,600 to $3,000 per kilowatt, leading to electricity costs based on a 30-year lifetime and a 15 percent return on investments as low as 30 mills per kilowatt-hour, a nominal 60 mills per kilowatt-hour, and an upper bound of 120 mills per kilowatt-hour. These costs lie within the competitive range of the costs of future terrestrial power-generation methods.

The SPS is projected to be one of the most significant contributors to baseload electric power generation, which represents now about 65 percent of total U.S. electrical generating capacity. Assuming that each SPS will deliver 10 gigawatts to the electric utility system, then starting in 1995, fifty SPS could be constructed by 2020 with a total installed generating capacity of 500 gigawatts, which exceeds by at least a factor of five the total projected for OTEC and by a factor of two the combined electrical power output of terrestrial solar electric conversion systems, including baseload, intermediate, and peakload power (see table 17-1). The 500-gigawatt generating capacity would correspond to about 25 percent of the total U.S. electrical energy requirement projected to be required in 2020.

Although extensive SPS studies have confirmed that there are no known technical barriers to the SPS, there are technological and economic uncertainties. These include solar energy conversion technology, fabrication and assembly of large structures in space, cost of large-scale space transportation, cost of electric power produced by the SPS, and the constraints imposed by environmental effects such as microwave heating of the ionosphere, space vehicle emissions in the upper atmosphere, microwave biological effects, and radio frequency

Table 17-1
U.S. Electrical Generating Capacity Projections

Renewable Resource Conversion System	Year	
	2000	2020
Wind power	50[a]	140[a]
Solar thermal	10	100
Photovoltaics	10	30
Ocean thermal	4	100
Biomass	2	20
SPS	2	500
Total	78	890

Source: MITRE Corp., "Solar Energy, A Comparative Analysis to the Year 2020," ERDA ERHQ 12322-78/1, March 78.
[a]Gigawatts.

interference. Future space law developments are being assessed to establish the need for new international agreements on such aspects as suitable frequency assignments, microwave beam specifications, geosynchronous orbit positions, favorable launch sites for the space transportation system, and sites for the receiving antenna and international institutions to ensure that the benefits will be available worldwide.

The SPS represents one of the most promising power generation options which could significantly impact global energy demands by the beginning of the twenty-first century. Its successful implementation in conjunction with appropriate terrestrial solar technology could lead to the elimination of energy-related concerns. In a broader sense, the SPS represents a major and meaningful step toward extending human activities beyond the confines of the earth's surface.

Conclusions

Of the several energy sources that have the potential of meeting future energy requirements, none has the major potential of the inexhaustible resource represented by solar energy. But, with the exception of solar water and space heating, solar energy applications are still in various stages of development. Assessments of technical feasibility, economic competitiveness, environmental impacts, and social desirability are proceeding on the various solar energy applications, with significant efforts being undertaken in many countries.

Although it is too early to tell which solar energy applications will have the greatest potential and be of widespread benefit to society, it is already clear that even if only a few of the applications now being developed are successful, it should be possible to take a more optimistic view of the world's energy future. Furthermore, the decisions to implement the most promising solar energy applications, whether based on technology advancement, regional appropriateness, economic considerations, resource conservation, or environmental protection, will be based on quite different considerations over the next decades, particularly as costs of nonrenewable energy sources continue to escalate as a result of increasing demands on finite resources.

The magnitude of the challenge to convert energy economies to solar energy is beginning to be appreciated. Although the impact of solar energy applications over the next two decades will be limited, the development of promising solar energy applications has to proceed on a broad front so as to select those applications with the greatest promise. With increased efforts being devoted to the development of solar energy applications, it is conceivable that the inevitable transition to renewable energy resources could be well under way by the first quarter of the twenty-first century and be completed by the middle of that century. The challenge is to ensure that this transition takes place with the least adverse effects and in a harmonious relationship with conventional energy resources. The key to the successful development of solar energy will be international cooperation and a sharing of the knowledge gained so that the transition can be carried out on a global basis with the widest possible benefits for humanity.

Notes

1. Arthur D. Little, Inc., "Solar Climate Control Project," sponsored multiclient study 1973-1976.

2. Division of Solar Energy Applications, "Analysis of Policy Options for Accelerating Commercialization of Solar Heating and Cooling Systems," U.S. Department of Energy, Contract No. EX-76-G-01-2534.

3. A.F. Hildebrandt and L.L. Vant-Hull, "Power with Heliostats," *Science* 197, September 16, 1977, pp. 1139-1146.

4. H.J. Hovel, "Solar Cells for Terrestrial Applications," *Solar Energy* 19, 1977, pp. 605-615.

5. U.S. Department of Energy Photovoltaic Program Summary, Division of Solar Technology, Washington, D.C., January 1978.

6. G.L. Dugger, J.F. Evans, and W.H. Avery, "Technical and Economic Feasibility of Ocean Thermal Energy Conversion," *Proceedings of Sharing the Sun Conference*, Winnipeg, August 1976, Pergamon Press, Oxford, 1976, Vol. 5, pp. 9-45.

7. C.C. Burwell, "Solar Biomass Energy: An Overview of U.S. Potential," *Science* 199, March 10, 1978, pp. 1041-1048.

8. P.E. Glaser, "Power from the Sun: Its Future," *Science* 162, November 1968, pp. 857-886.

9. P.E. Glaser, "The Potential of Satellite Solar Power" *Proceedings of the IEEE* 65, No. 8, August 1977, pp. 1162-1176.

10. NASA and U.S. Department of Energy, "Satellite Power System Concept Development and Evaluation Program Plan July 1977 to August 1980," U.S. Government Printing Office, Washington, D.C. DOE/ET-0034, UC-13, February 1978.

11. MITRE Corp., "Solar Energy, A Comparative Analysis to the Year 2020," *ERDA, ERHQ* 12322-78/1, March 78.

**Part V
Development and
Funding of Corporate
Growth**

18 Strategic Planning: Developments and Impacts

John R. White and
Robert V.L. Wright

New Developments in Strategic Planning
John R. White

This section first comments briefly on the new developments or trends in the practice of strategic planning. First, there is a generally accepted set of ideas comprising strategic planning. Some of these are strategy centers, maturity curves, growth-share diagrams, and other business economic principles that have been sharpened and systematically applied during the last decade.

Second, many traditional business research activities are increasingly perceived in a strategic context. For example, a client in the fiber field asked Arthur D. Little to conduct, in the traditional mode, a worldwide technical-economic analysis of his business. A grim and challenging picture unfolded. We proceeded beyond the analysis to identify and appraise strategic alternatives. The traditional diagnosis was thus transformed into a constructive prescription.

Third, more and more, strategic planning engages industry technical and economic specialists. A client in the small industrial motor business asked Arthur D. Little to help find a diversifying acquisition to improve his profit growth. Before starting on that strategy, however, we recommended an analysis of his existing businesses with a review of all his strategy alternatives. It turned out that industry specialists helped find attractive opportunities in new markets for his present products.

Furthermore, technical specialists helped identify some new products for his present markets. Today, several years later, his earnings are still growing without recourse to acquisition.

Fourth, plans made by the managers who will use them are more effectively implemented than those laid on from above or outside. Six years ago, Arthur D. Little helped a multinational corporation with fifteen divisions in forty-seven industries build a corporate strategic plan. Unit management teams developed profiles of, and preferred strategies for, their businesses. They all took their plans into a "scrum" at headquarters and hammered out corporate strategy and the strategic role of each business. This process enabled every business manager to understand and commit to the plans. The company adapted and internalized the process. Today they profile and scrum annually.

Last, external forces grow more important. Top executives say they now spend half to two-thirds of their time coping with the environment. This brings us to the next section of this chapter: the impact of environmental change on strategic plans.

The Impact of Externalities on Content and
Design of a Corporate Strategy
Robert V.L. Wright

The corporate world of 1900 might be described as a closed box. This box might be defined as having known and controllable sides and being closed and secure at its corners. The sides might be labeled labor, markets, government, and technology. Little or nothing is able to intrude into this box. Labor is described as docile; markets are stable, government is "owned" or benign; and technology changes, but at a gradual and controlled rate.

In the last 80 years, each of the sides of this box has become a veritable sieve—allowing threats and options to intrude. The corners have split apart and the dimensions of the business world have multiplied. Thus we are now faced with a series of overlapping polygons which are split at the seams. The overlaps are international firms and foreign governments, cultures, and values.

This condition should not leave us helpless or in an overanxious state if we but recognize the normality of the unstable state, and realize how to semiclose, adjust, group, regroup, and cope. What we must cope with by anticipation, by forecasting by "prepping" (through the use of "what if" games and scenarios), are what we have loosely called externalities or environmental changes. However, many of these so-called externalities have a great deal of trouble remaining external, for example, environmentalism and women's liberation.

The bombardment of externalities hits the core of the enterprise, (that is, its strategy). Every corporation, explicitly or not, has a current reason for being, a direction or series of directions, a view of the future, a set of assumptions as to the role and directions of forces and players, a pattern to its resource allocation, a problem of fixed investments, a level of risk, a set of values firmly in hand, a culture in which it operates, and a performance level to which it reverently aspires. Every externality is either a threat to or an opportunity for the stable state and sends a cascading ripple effect through the organization.

In order to set a framework, let us return to "go" (although we do so risking illustration of the obvious and the known). What is a corporate strategy? For the purposes of this discussion, let us become somewhat global. It is the gestalt of the firm. It is its direction, velocity, style, quality, character, dimensions, and destination. It is considerably more than the classical definition of a strategy for a business of the corporation, which can be simply stated as a path down which one allocates, or chooses not to allocate, resources.

As all of us write prose, all corporations have strategies. Patterns of investments (resource allocations) exist. If the strategy, purpose, or path down which the corporation is proceeding is not explicit, it can be deduced by tracking the pattern of expenses and investments and the behavior of the principal managers, for corporations' strategies have existed in the past, are with us now, and are being shaped by the futurity of current decisions. Examples of such strategies are plans for becoming multinational; diversifying to achieve economic balance; changing the maturity of investments in businesses; concentrating on related businesses linked by technology, markets, or skills (that is, to agglomerate rather than conglomerate); changing or adopting a specific managerial system; and financing growth by internal means only.

These strategies are corporate in nature, that is, reserved to the corporation rather than to the businesses of the corporation. These strategies impact on business strategy selection and on resource allocation. Their impact sends a wave of logical consequences throughout the corporate system. The corporate strategy is, in effect, the policy that binds, directs, and redirects.

Corporate strategies are neither a matter of free choice nor set in concrete. All strategies tend to be driven more by conditions than by ambition. The game of establishing performance goals and then shaping conceivable strategies for achievement has been replaced, for the most part, by the realization that only certain strategies are reasonably achievable by any single corporation or management group. Continuous change in the conditions surrounding the corporation and within its population of employees, the competitors of its businesses, and the factors concerning sources of supplies directs and sometimes limits options and choices.

The strategies of the corporation (and they will always be multiple) are *not* the sum of the strategies of the businesses of the corporation. They cover or deal with a range of activities that are, in many instances, both different from and broader than those of the businesses. While the strategies of a business deal with products, services, competitors, markets, customers, and prices, the corporation is dealing with independence or lack thereof, sources and uses of funds, the raising of capital, and currency hedging; relating to publics, institutions, and governments; and making major managerial system adjustments to match its strategies.

This does not suggest that the corporation is not concerned with elements of the business mix or does not have impact on the businesses and their strategies for growth and renewal. However, the corporation's concern is more in the shape and balancing of growth and renewal rather than in marketplace execution. The diversified or multi-industry *corporation* has no single marketplace competitor, only competitors for resources. Therefore, when we expose clients to the range of strategies at both the corporate and business level through the device of a set or deck of strategies, only a very few of the possible choices are common between the corporation, on the one hand, and the businesses on the other.

Because of the essential variety of businesses within a multi-industry corporation—variety as to nature of industry (as to risk, for instance), maturity of industry, competitive position, strategies being executed—the likelihood is that any single corporate strategy will have a different impact on each business and/or on each "investment" in corporate functions or activity. By the same token, it can be seen that neither the sum of the available resources of a corporation nor the sum of the potential uses is to be found within the businesses of the corporation. Corporate strategies dealing with financing—and with embryonic ventures and nonoperating investments—require other sources of funds and initial allocations to other uses.

As long as resources, conditions, values, and managements grow (in size) and/or change (in composition and nature), corporate strategies and resource allocations will change—and in real time. Corporations need a series of manageable mechanisms to make these allocations. The process of coping with change, assessing and reassessing, is more critical to the organization than the exact strategy or the perfect allocation of resources at any exact moment in time. Resilience ensures the minimization of the consequences of failure—for failure to forecast all or many critical events and their ramifications is inevitable.

Perhaps the best way to describe this process of coping or creating resilience is to illustrate how one "factors in" a major external change. This should show not only the ripple effect but the strategy development process itself. Let us assume that the following developmental steps have been taken prior to the external change:

1. Economic, political, social, and technological scans have been made and a range of possible sets of future conditions or scenarios have been developed, offline.
2. Industry conditions and industry participants have been analyzed as to general attractiveness and availability.
3. The corporate management group has worked with the political, social, and economic factors to such a degree that they have designed their own best guess as to what future assumptions must be reflected or taken account of in the corporate strategy.
4. The strengths and weaknesses of the corporation have been isolated, recognized, and accepted as being valid, and are reflected or taken account of in the corporate strategy.
5. The same is true of the culture, heritage, and values of the corporation.
6. A sophisticated characterization and analysis of the array of the businesses of the corporation has been made as to both generic and specific ability to lead an industry, change competitive position, generate long-term or increased short-term earnings, generate excess cash, absorb investment, increase or decrease risk, improve managerial capabilities, and be generally congruent.

Let us now move to the spring of 1974 and factor in the oil embargo. In the best of all possible worlds, the management group that created the existing corporate strategy has been reassembled to cross-impact, discuss, and understand the implications of this event. As a result of these deliberations, the following actions are deduced. Both corporate market research and research and development are given the task to find new business and technological areas away from energy-intense businesses. Corporate planning and development is told to isolate both countercyclical industries and candidates for acquisition. The corporation undertakes to find new opportunities in solar and geothermal areas. The corporation immediately invests resources in corporate public relations functions and in the Washington office in order to influence the shape of pending federal energy legislation. The coal business receives, in the resource allocation process, double the funds of the prior 5 years. The potential shortage of oil prompts the corporation to set out policy guidelines for capital outlays of new plant construction for the businesses—install dual energy sources at a minimum, preferably gas and coal. Higher fuel costs force each business to revise operating costs and test for price sensitivity. And last, business marketeers and research and development management receive an urging from the corporation to explore products within their scope that can conserve the use of energy.

What is distinctive about this process? What is unique to this system of corporate strategy development? Certainly not the elements themselves, although the values and culture of the firm are rarely analyzed explicitly or factored consciously into the corporate strategy mix. What *is* unique, however, is the manner in which information is collected, analyzed, and used by a group of senior managers to build a corporate strategy. This core process we call a "scrum." Like the rugby faceoff, this method is rough, dirty, seemingly unorganized, but with very clear rules for the players. It is a nonlinear, iterative process that produces a result. This method of corporate strategy development is designed to facilitate an understanding of the potential cross-impacts of both externalities and internalities on both the corporation and its parts. Not only is this done to ensure the proper actions and reactions in terms of strategic response, resource allocations, and risk adjustment, but to adjust the very fabric of the organization—its culture, its managerial system, and its measurement criteria. Moreover, the purpose is to ensure as far as possible a dynamic readjustment and balancing on what we all know to be an unstable state. We are experiencing a veritable "revolution in abandoned assumptions." A method of replicating the change process is crucial whenever the corporate strategy is impacted. The corporate strategy process is the ultimate matrix game.

In conclusion, something should be said about the state of the art. Strategy systems have a great deal of currency. Providing real-time, systemic responses to external conditions is an opportunity or problem yet to be seized. The current art forms are relatively embryonic. Many corporations and their consultants are at work in the vineyard, but the list of questions remains longer than the list of answers. Depending on your attitude, this can either encourage one to proceed or depress one to inaction. We suggest that the only game in town is to engage in the task of becoming intelligently speculative and resilient, *and* that the best forum for this work is in and around the continuous development of a corporate strategy.

19 The Corporate Development Environment

S. Theodore Guild,
James W. Bradley, and
Donald H. Korn

Financing Considerations for Growth Companies
S. Theodore Guild

This chapter examines the considerations in financing emerging growth companies. These companies are not startup companies; they are established, with a record of sales and production, and a management team in place. They are profitable, but generally the personal resources of the inner circle are already at risk in the business, and the possibility of raising funds in the public marketplace is so remote as not to be meaningful. What then is the financial environment of such companies, and what options for financing their growth should be considered?

Inflation is the most significant environmental factor to a growth company. It is constantly accelerating the dollar values of their growth beyond the gains in unit sales or units produced. Inflation distorts the balance sheet and makes the necessary investments in receivables, inventory, and plant increasingly burdensome.

In other work that Arthur D. Little has done it is clear that a long-term inflation rate of 5 to 6 percent a year has serious implications for the financing requirements of the economy. The problem is particularly acute with energy growth companies. We can be sure management is working as creatively as possible with accountants to minimize taxable income and thus preserve cash flow for asset investment. Financing profit earned is the greatest single challenge entrepreneurs face. There is just no possibility that the tax collector is going to provide assistance through the extension of credit.

Given the need to provide hard dollars for growth and the tax collector, therefore, what are the possible responses? One strategic option, of course, is to accept financial limitation and adjust the growth rate to the resources available. Some slowdown in an exploding situation may not only be financially prudent, but sound in terms of management resources as well. Recognition should also be given to the fact that the management job in a company whose growth has slowed is a difficult one. Growth is an important nutrient for high morale—it restrains the young tigers who are susceptible to the lure of greener pastures. In a society where younger people are increasingly motivated by values other than salaries, growth serves to provide the challenges of problem solving, ego satisfaction, and pride in accomplishment. So before adjusting the suit to the cloth, it is important to look carefully at other possibilities.

The commercial banking relationship is vital to a growth company, and an agenda item of the highest priority is to get the right banker. Often banking relationships are established on the basis of locational convenience, prestige, or a price-cutting reputation. A growth company needs a banker with some vision, creativity, and guts, and an individual with enough stature in his organization to have his judgments respected.

It is also our belief that commercial banks are going to be experiencing a new kind of pressure—the inability to earn or find enough capital to support the loan volumes they will want to handle. Banking regulators, therefore, are going to be examining very closely loans outstanding to the very companies we are talking about—those where strong growth has impacted the debt-to-equity ratio.

This kind of scrutiny, and changing bank definitions of quality, mean that a growth company should help its chosen banker look good and protect him against the examiners. Here two important items are (1) do not immediately buy real estate, and (2) do not automatically resist giving the banker security.

There seems to be almost a nesting instinct at work in emerging growth companies which tells them to move from their original garage or low-rent building into some suburban monument. While one may sympathize with this craving for ownership, and the desire to show the world you have arrived, consider also that the offset to ownership is a large addition of debt to a balance sheet which may already be taxed by the truly working asset investment.

With respect to the issue of collateral, remember that the banker views his unsecured loan portfolio as reserved for either seasonal borrowers or companies whose loan track record of earnings he can project with comfort. A growth company does not fit. But the banker who has a pledge of the receivables, inventory, and equipment can be a different fellow. With his downside risk protected he may be quite willing to fund a significant degree of expansion—and that is the priority goal.

Another consideration that can bring a double benefit to a growth company is a restructuring of the professional support team. The lawyers, accountants, and directors who were available at the birth of the company may not be appropriate to its adolescence. A stronger professional team should not only benefit the company directly, but also serve to increase the banker's comfort level.

Trade suppliers are the next group of creditors for a growth company to consider. Frankly, the attitude of some trade suppliers is baffling—specifically those cash-rich companies that were led into cash management by the bankers and went on to make the treasurer's office a profit center—the group who are pictured in *Business Week* because they have shifted their investment portfolio from domestic Certificates of Deposit and moved overseas for another seventy-five basis points.

To this group one can say "fine, but if you're going into the banking business, why not do it in a meaningful way." Gross profit margins in banking are small, and presumably they do not compare with the margins in the company's own products. Real investment leverage might be found in strategic use of investment cash to generate more product orders.

To this group a suggestion is "If your growth customer's purchases from you are inhibited by his bank's inability to find the money for his growth, you might consider taking your offshore certificate and placing it with your customer's bank to fund his growth or helping him to get another bank."

Trade suppliers sometimes seem to feel that creative customer assistance means relaxing credit terms. A more useful definition would be the development of individualized programs for the 20 percent of the customer list where assistance will have a long-term payoff. Such actions could include inventory repurchase agreements (to give the banker comfort), leasing of new production equipment, financial counseling, introductions to money sources, and perhaps, even limited guarantees or the purchase of preferred stock.

The growth company should also explore the availability of semicquity from the public sector. There is an increasing development of financial support mechanisms for social purposes. The Small Business Administration has been around for years, but now has special programs for solar energy. Strategic location of a new plant in a farm area or a depressed labor market can turn on the faucet. This year in Massachusetts we have the new Capital Resource Company, created by the legislature to get $100 million of insurance company money loaned or invested to increase jobs. Employee stock ownership trusts can still be used to build equity with pretax dollars. And, of course, there are special incentives available for export business and tax shelters in the energy field.

Who knows, before long we may have government guarantees on certain pension fund investments or loans which are made with a socially desirable purpose. This could serve to begin the mating dance of the prudent trust officer and the risk-taking entrepreneur—a very interesting scenario.

Financing a growth company has never been easy. There are occasional cyclical windows when equity is available with risk money cheap and looking for employment. At the opposite extreme there are, unfortunately, periods when only a well-managed bankruptcy will serve to perpetuate the growth of a company. Generally, the environment will call for financial resourcefulness, ingenuity, luck, or a successful merger.

Acquisition and Merger Trends and Their
Implications for Corporate Development[a]
James W. Bradley and *Donald H. Korn*

Acquisition and merger activity in the United States has been increasing dramatically recently, with potential acquirees often sought at 50 percent or

[a]Summary of ADL Impact Services Report Published June 1978 (R780601).

higher premiums over the preannouncement market prices of their common stocks. A major force contributing to what we believe will continue to be a high level of activity is the relatively modest present level of stock prices compared to true asset values. Recent years' economic experience and the investment climate under the Employee Retirement Income Security Act (ERISA) have made investors increasingly conservative regarding equity investments. In addition, inflation factors, as revealed in replacement-cost-adjusted book values of assets, make purchases of existing companies less costly than investment in research and development and construction of new plant and equipment—even at a substantial premium over market value. At the same time, good liquidity and/or borrowing power on the part of corporate buyers allows both cash tender offers and the financing of the potentially acquired company's growth at a time when a number of growth companies lack the financial resources to capitalize on their potential and when owners prefer cash rather than stock offers.

Different valuations of future earnings potential, given the longer time horizon of corporate risk takers as opposed to individual equity market investors, often make market prices, even after a premium is added, attractive to the corporate buyer. In addition, foreign corporations, for a variety of reasons, have significantly increased their interest in acquiring operating businesses in the United States. We conclude that in this environment, the corporate development strategy of many corporations will be to grow via acquisition, and heightened acquisition activity will continue for at least the next year.

While the basic incentive for acquisition centers around the disparity between perceived risk-adjusted values and earning power compared with present stock market values, other factors have contributed to current activity. Among these are the belief that the present antitrust and regulatory environment, which has not prevented a number of acquisitions, may become more restrictive. In addition, some managements view acquisitions as a defense against takeovers, and/or regard the purchase of their company's own stock as an unsatisfactory alternative to investment in growth by acquisition. We also note the elements of a bandwagon effect and the influence of personalities and whim.

Industry sectors of special acquisition interest are those that have high sales growth and profit potentials and which to a substantial degree are benefiting from recent or emerging federal policies, although activity lately has been more widespread. We believe that, in addition to ten industries of particular interest now, acquisition activity in a number of others will become important in the future; these are shown below:

Industries of Current Interest	*Industries of Potential Future Interest*
Specialized sectors of agri- business	Dental supplies and services
Coal producers	Equipment and services related to public transport

Industries of Current Interest	*Industries of Potential Future Interest*
Energy services and energy conservation	Equipment and services for maintenance/reliability/productivity improvement
Chemical specialties, including drugs	Nonhydrocarbon energy sources and services
Communications	Precious metals, gems, and other capital preservation forms
Specialized areas of electronics	Recreation/leisure
Products and services related to the environment, fire protection, and safety	Small banks
Medical instruments	
Oil company diversification (including nonferrous mining, mining machinery, and services)	
Financial services	

Our data-base screening reveals a significant proportion of the several hundred companies in these businesses as having the financial characteristics likely to stimulate at least preliminary interest on the part of acquisition-minded firms.

Although public policy recognizes acquisitions and mergers as among the legitimate corporate growth alternatives, antitrust law frowns on those combinations that would substantially reduce competition or create a monopoly. Strength of market position—certainly a strong attraction to potential buyers—is recognized in antitrust policy as an anticompetitive weapon and thus precludes many potential mergers. At the other extreme, the "failing company doctrine" condones mergers that preserve the number of existing competitors in a field by rescuing the weak. While legal reaction to any particular merger cannot always be predicted, transactions of substantial vertical or horizontal significance are typically challenged. Often enforcement action and settlement are very long processes. The same policies that deny mergers or acquisitions to one acquirer can be sources of candidates (in the form of antitrust-forced divestitures) to other firms. The Williams Act (a recent federal statute covering cash takeovers) as well as a number of state and corporate acts may delay some transactions, but in our opinion these developments will not seriously blunt the current trend toward more mergers and acquisitions.

Today's merger activity is distinguished from that of the 1960s in several important aspects. Experience with many unsuccessful acquisitions in the late 1960s and the early 1970s has led to a more sophisticated corporate view, with far more intensive and realistic planning on the part of management. Today's merger activity is much more likely to involve more consideration by internal staff of longer-term strategic business objectives, alternate acquisition possibilities, and postmerger management issues. This deeper and longer-range consideration is leading to more soundly conceived transactions. Experience with federal antitrust policy and antitakeover laws also provides better advance guidance to corporations as to the types of acquisitions that are allowable and the tender offer and other acquisition strategies and tactics that are effective. We suggest that corporate managements intent on pursuing an acquisition strategy develop and follow a well-conceived and orderly process of protocol; one such is suggested herein.

The attractions of the acquisition route, of course, are not without pitfalls. Acquisitions and mergers are major and risky decisions. The high percentage of transactions involving divestitures indicates the extent and degree to which earlier combinations have failed. Overoptimism, lack of healthy skepticism with respect to business projections, lack of contingency planning, and the failure to see a mismatch in operations, operating styles, or management personalities are common reasons for failure. Through an understanding of the business risks involved and the management requirements of the acquired company, the hazards of failure can be minimized.

20 The Implications of New Pension Legislation

Donald H. Korn

The major recent legislation affecting pension funds includes the 1972 and 1977 amendments to the Social Security Act, and the landmark Employee Retirement Income Security Act of 1974 (ERISA). In fiscal year 1978-1979, the Carter Administration and the Congress have been considering additional actions and legislation, including a Government Pension Commission, and the Supreme Court has before it a case involving the issue of whether an employee's interest in a pension fund is a security subject to Security and Exchange Commission regulations.

In the context of pressures on funding corporate growth, the implications of the recent and prospective pension legislation are far-reaching and profound. In the related context of corporate finance, most attention has focused on the implications of and obligations under ERISA.

The indications are that industrial managers, whose traditional responsibilities are characterized in terms of operating profitability and asset management, will increasingly be concerned with the management of pension funds. At the same time, financial institutions, which have long been concerned with both investments per se and the economic strengths and weaknesses of the industries in which they invest, will increasingly become concerned with labor—with the Social Security claims on and employee retirement benefit programs of corporations whose securities they hold, and with the assumptions underlying the funding basis of those benefit programs.

Inconsistencies between actuarial, investor, accounting, internal revenue, and capital budgeting assumptions will bring pressure for additional changes in pension fund administration as well as in reporting requirements. More government control is in the offing (although the supervision and administration of pension and welfare benefit programs is being streamlined, and some agencies favor less government involvement). With increased government participation in, and regulation of, pension funds, costs to employers could increase. If high rates of inflation persist, the squeeze will likely become more severe, since politico-economic forces tend to make inflation adjustments applicable not only to personnel currently employed, but retroactively.

Moreover, at high rates of inflation, the inflation rate dominates the problem of corporate financing. It affects dramatically the magnitude of external financing requirements of capital-intensive businesses; it affects the cost of debt and equity capital; and it affects pension funding requirements. These

173

pressures are likely to cause some shift in the nature and types of pension plans offered.

ERISA established federal requirements relating to the funding, vesting, administration, reporting, and investment policy of corporate pension plans. ERISA has set a conservative tone by attempting, in effect, to legislate and control prudence and fiduciary responsibility on the part of corporate executives and pension fund managers concerned with plan assets managed under ERISA. That is, it formally establishes the liability of such people to plan beneficiaries, without precisely defining and limiting their every activity.

ERISA also established the Pension Benefit Guaranty Corporation (PBGC), which is somewhat analogous to the Federal Deposit Insurance Corporation for commercial banks (FDIC). PBGC collects premiums from plan sponsors for insurance against termination of plans having unfunded vested benefits. PBGC also has plan termination and subsequent administration authority for plans in difficulty. In assuming plan assets and liabilities, PBGC is empowered to attach up to 30 percent of a business's net worth to meet its unfunded liability. Moreover, ERISA provides the Internal Revenue Service (IRS) with taxing authority to meet funding deficiencies in plans meeting its mandatory coverage test.

The IRS has been intimately involved in the development of ERISA. This is so because corporate payments to employee retirement and pension plans may be qualified under the Internal Revenue Code as deductible business expenses. Also, pension funds accumulate capital and invest on a tax-free basis for a fund *per se*.

ERISA has caused a stepup in expense accruals and probably in actual cash outlays for funding, both to meet the required amortization of unfunded past service liability and to fund normal ongoing costs on an acceptable actuarial basis. The indications are that this increased rate of expense varies considerably from one corporation or industry to the next, and in most large publicly owned companies has not been considered onerous, especially on an after-tax basis. (This is in contrast to ERISA's annual reporting and administrative requirements, which are rather substantial and have apparently contributed to some small plan terminations.)

A larger impact on the corporation is likely to result from the employee bargaining situation in a given industry and the investment policy adopted with regard to pension plan assets. In the case of companies whose labor relations and other considerations have favored *defined benefit* plans, which are true pension funds and now account for most of the pension reserves, such plans involve the mandatory PBGC insurance coverage and the termination and assessment authority of PBGC. They also will require services of actuaries to meet mandatory funding tests. In the case of plans which are *defined contribution* plans (mainly profit-sharing retirement plans), different flexibility in investment management and different administrative costs are likely. However, both types will be affected, in terms of actual and expected funding flows from the corporate sponsor to the plan, by the investment *asset allocation* policy (for example, cash and equivalent/fixed-income/common stock holdings) and the course of inflation, interest rates, and stock prices.

There is also likely to be an important impact from the increased Social Security benefits envisaged under the new legislation and the extension of the mandatory retirement age.

Private pension funds are financially important because they comprise an enormous pool of investment capital, and one which has been growing in current dollars at roughly the same rate as GNP. Private pension funds had assets of $280 billion at the end of 1977. State and local government pension funds represent about $130 billion in assets. Both types invest primarily in corporate securities. Indeed, pension funds now constitute the single largest grouping in the market for purchases and sales of outstanding common stock, as well as for the purchase of new common stock issues.

For private pension plans, corporate contributions are now in excess of $30 billion per year, and some $15 billion per year in benefits are paid to about 7 million people. In contrast, the Social Security and Federal Retirement Trust Funds total only $91 billion and are restricted to Treasury securities. The Old Age and Survivors Insurance (OASI) payroll taxes ($45 billion per year paid by corporations) now cover most of the workforce, and benefits are currently paid to 30 million people.

The growth of private pension funds thus provides a potentially large and growing pool of capital—forced savings, as it were—to finance corporate growth. However, the notions of fiduciary responsibility and prudence articulated under existing ERISA authority, coupled with general business uncertainties in the post-ERISA period since 1975, have created perhaps the most conservative investment environment we have witnessed in many, many years. For example, corporations eschew major new capital projects with long payouts, unless there are such risk-sharing features as customer financing, long-term contracts with escalator clauses, or unsecured debt financing. As discussed in chapter 19, today they increasingly prefer the risk-return characteristics of acquiring other operating businesses. On the institutional investment side, increased public and private bond and mortgage financing has been the rule of late, with new equity issues down substantially. But pension funds have inherent long-range liability characteristics.[1] What about investments policies in the future?

In managing pension fund assets, many investment managers, consultants, and advisors have been increasingly embracing the tenets of so-called modern portfolio theory (MPT) in their operations. And many corporate pension plan sponsors and "Named Fiduciaries," as they are referred to in the jargon of ERISA, have also become interested in the application of MPT to the establishment of pension plan investment policy and objectives, including the basis for establishing guidelines to be utilized by their investment managers, as well as in evaluating investment performance. The recently proposed "prudence" rule published by the Department of Labor pursuant to ERISA appears to be perfectly compatible with the principles of MPT. Its hallmark is an informed investment program with portfolio holdings consistent with the risk/return and other policy objectives of the plan, stressing diversification to minimize risk—all in keeping with how an investment enterprise of like character and aims would be presumed to act.

We expect new forms of pension fund investment to result: more real estate-based investments, venture capital financing, and short-term corporate lending are likely.

Under ERISA, the actuaries, not the investment managers, have been given great powers. The trend set by ERISA is likely to put pressure on many corporations, their actuaries, and investment managers to justify their methodologies and assumptions. It is likely that along with the consolidation taking place in the securities industry, there will be a consolidation of investment management, actuarial, and other pension fund services firms to meet pension plan needs more effectively.

There will also be increased pressure to consider managing some funds inhouse, and to experiment with "indexing." Both concepts are presently practiced, although some controversy exists with respect to the impact on fiduciary responsibility. However, by 1990 we expect both inhouse fund management and indexing to have established a niche.

In light of the nature of pension funds, and ERISA's establishment of PBGC with a mandate to create a program of termination/liability insurance, Jack Treynor, editor of the *Financial Analysts Journal,* and others have pointed out some paradoxes in corporate pension plan investment behavior which may exist because of PBGC. The point to be made is that ERISA has apparently not alleviated the actual and potential conflicts and tensions among the corporation and its investors, creditors, and pension claimants. With PBGC interposed, Treynor, for example, believes that the result is to transfer risk from the beneficiary to PBGC.

When pension funds are invested in risky assets, this increases the value of the so-called pension "put option" and increases "true" stockholders' equity.[2] Fiduciaries and investment managers, meanwhile, feel that ERISA has transferred risk to them under the prudence doctrine. Critics argue, on the other hand, that investment managers may actually become less vulnerable. Treynor's brilliant work suggests, to this observer, that beneficiaries, the labor unions, and/or regulators might—even unwittingly—put pressure on corporate dividend payout policy, at a time when investors are favoring more generous payouts.

PBGC has been studying and reporting on these and related issues, in discharging its responsibilities under ERISA. New developments are underway in respect to determination of employer liability under pension plan terminations, as well as whether the existence of unfunded liabilities should be given creditor status, that is, treated legally and/or for financial accounting and reporting purposes as long-term debt on a corporation's balance sheet.

Management expert Peter Drucker has written provocatively about the trends in pension funds, including Social Security. He has voiced concern over their increasing ownership (and de facto control) of common stocks. Aside from their important role in the private capital markets, the role of private pension plans is perceived by others more in terms of providing supplementary retirement benefits to "high income" individuals. While the implications of ERISA unfold, the Social Security program may threaten the future of private pension funds, politically and economically.

Benefits are indexed and raised under the recent Social Security amendments; and there is an increased tax on corporations and employees. Moreover, Social Security dollars are perceived as nearly a perfect substitute for pension dollars, as has been provocatively argued in a recent study by Munnell of the Federal Reserve Bank of Boston. Since Social Security is a pay-as-you-go system now, one effect of substituting Social Security dollars is to claim capital which would otherwise flow into private pension funds and hence through the private-sector capital markets. The resultant future impacts on capital allocation in the economy, and the impact on government finance, can be profound.

Notes

1. Given their dynamics and demographic characteristics, a typical corporate pension plan would not achieve "steady-state" liabilities in an actuarial sense before 80 to 120 years.

2. See J.L. Treynor, P.J. Regan, and W.W. Priest, *The Financial Reality of Pension Funding Under ERISA* (Homewood, Illinois: Dow-Jones, Irwin, 1976).

**Part VI
The Productive Use of
Technology**

21 Overcoming Barriers to Innovation

Bruce S. Old

At the outset it should be pointed out that the process of innovation—the process by which an idea or invention is translated into the economy—is indeed a difficult one. While we all draw immense benefits from our inventors, our knowledge of the motivations and environments which lead to invention is limited. Our educational system seldom encourages students to become inventors, nor does it seem vitally interested in exploring the conditions for invention. Perhaps this is because text books deal with background information, whereas inventors seek new possibilities.

Within our economy we have grown to expect our innovations to stem largely from our investment in research and development (R&D). While economists differ on the degree to which R&D affects economic growth, all agree it is substantial. The estimates indicate that R&D accounts for between 5 and 30 percent of the factors which explain our economic growth. This chapter briefly discusses three different aspects of work at Arthur D. Little which bear upon the subject of innovation.

Measuring Investment in Present and Future Technology

We have performed studies of the administration and operation of hundreds of corporate (and government) R&D laboratories, which assignments we call "technical audits." From many of these studies of industrial laboratories we have noted that a major barrier to effective R&D is lack of top management attention and understanding. Just establishing a corporate R&D function is not enough.

We have developed a new method of measuring corporate investment in technology which is aimed at gaining better top management attention. Shortly after World War II the National Science Foundation began reporting corporate R&D expenditures as a percent of corporate net sales. This is a meaningless ratio—the average figure for all U.S. industry is 2.2 percent, which gives a completely misleading picture of the actual size and importance of the investments being made by industry.

We have proposed two major changes in measuring corporate investments in technology. These are aimed at providing new and more meaningful data to top management, and data in a form that will be more understandable to the board of directors as well as top management.

The first change is that we believe top management should consider investment in technology from two standpoints, the future and the present. Future technology is represented by current investment in R&D. Present technology is represented by current investment in new plant and equipment based on existing technology developed through past investments in R&D, wherever performed in the world, where such investments exclude mere replacement expenditures.

The second change is that these corporate investments in technology should not be related to net sales but to cash flow (income after taxes plus depreciation). Cash flow is the shareholders' money which the board of directors and top management are called upon to allocate as wisely as possible between dividends paid to stockholders, capital investment in plant and equipment, R&D, and so on.

The measure of investment in future technology must take into account that R&D is an expense before taxes, so that only one half the investment is at risk. Thus the ratio which correctly measures the extent to which top management is willing to invest in future technology is

$$\frac{\frac{1}{2} \times \text{R\&D expenditures}}{\text{Cash flow} + \frac{1}{2} \text{ R\&D expenditures}} \times 100 = \text{R\&D Investment Ratio}$$

The ratio which correctly measures the extent to which management is willing to invest in present technology is

$$\frac{\text{Capital invested (technology based)}}{\text{Cash flow}} - \text{tax credit} \times 100 = \text{capital investment ratio}$$

The combination of the two expressions is the total corporate investment in technology and can be expressed as follows:

R&D investment ratio + capital investment ratio = technology investment ratio

When this method of measuring corporate investment in technology is utilized, top management can gain a completely different understanding of the importance of technology investment. To illustrate this, Arthur D. Little obtained data from companies in three different sectors of industry in order to compare the proposed method of measuring investment in present and future technology with the older method of measuring R&D as a percent of sales. The results are presented in table 21-1. Several things should be clear from a study of table 21-1. One is that while companies in different industry sectors may invest quite differently in terms of future technology, the capital-intensive industries,

Table 21-1
Comparison of Arthur D. Little Method of Measuring Investment in
Technology with Conventional Method

Industry Sector	R&D Investment Ratio	Capital Investment Ratio	Technology Investment Ratio	R&D as Percent of Net Sales
Chemical	18	60	78	5.2
Electrical machinery	46	68	114	5.3
Iron and steel	3	63	66	0.5

such as steel, practically come out the same in terms of total technology investment because of large investments in new plant and equipment which utilize current technology. Another is that companies in all three sectors invested a majority or an excess of their cash flow in technology. Once this major investment in present and future technology in many industries is understood, no one in top management can fail to pay strict attention to all aspects of technology. Finally, the last column, relating R&D to net sales, provides no insight into the importance of technology, nor any true comparison between industry sectors. It seems clear that more attention might advantageously be paid to the newly suggested measurement techniques.

In the end, corporate top management would like to have some measure as to how much of corporate cash flow should be invested in present and future technology. This will depend on the strategies adopted by the competition as well as on those chosen by the subject corporation. To take advantage of any such investment strategy requires the attainment of adequate profitability by the corporation.

Understanding Barriers to Innovation

The second aspect of Arthur D. Little's work concerns a study we performed a few years ago for the National Science Foundation, which resulted in a report entitled "Barriers to Innovation." The study was somewhat unique in that we interviewed about 200 key people in several industry sectors, in labor unions, and in the federal government to determine what they perceived to be the important barriers to innovation. Within industry we spoke not just with R&D executives but with individuals in top and middle management—chief executive officers, sales personnel, manufacturing managers, counsel, engineers, etc.

The outstanding barrier turned out to be the vagaries of the marketplace. Lack of faith in market forecasts makes it very difficult to launch new products, since uncertainty and risk are perceived to be large. Often we were told that capital investment and manufacturing costs could be estimated rather accurately, but that total market and share of market numbers were perceived to be shaky.

How to overcome this barrier is not at all clear. More research on marketing might help. The federal government could assist in certain instances by aggregating markets in which it buys rather than fragmenting them. This is certainly a subject for further consideration since it is a real barrier in many, many companies.

The second key barrier was federal regulatory policies, which now affect many industries. One possible way to overcome such barriers is to have a continuing technical dialogue with the particular federal agency affecting your decision to proceed. We have recently had successful discussions of this type with the Environmental Protection Agency. Another suggestion has been that the executive branch establish a coordinating activity to overcome conflicting regulatory actions between federal agencies. This might be a utopian thought.

A third barrier perceived by many individuals was the effect the risk of introducing a new product or process might have on his career pattern. Would the potential rewards outweigh the risks? This immediately brings up the whole subject of short-range profit goals versus long-range corporate growth and profitability, and the corporate environment established by top management. Some of these matters will be covered by others.

Other barriers included lack of "seed capital" for individual entrepreneurs, uncertainty on payout of invested funds, concern about the Department of Justice attitude on multicorporate joint projects on capital intensive programs, etc.

Managing Inventions

The last aspect of this work concerns our invention management activity, which has operated at a profit since its inception in 1957. Its goal is commercializing proprietary inventions made by Arthur D. Little staff members and by outside individuals or companies. Often outsiders lack the skill to evaluate the technical or market aspects, or are not interested in making or using a new product or process which differs significantly from their present businesses.

Once again, it should be stressed that commercialization is not easy. Arthur D. Little Enterprises reviews on the order of 400 submissions annually. Historically we select less than 5 percent after evaluation, and somewhat more than a third of these become optioned and licensed.

Because of its success in the development and licensing of new technology, Arthur D. Little Enterprises has broadened its objectives to include: (1) exploring a totally new market segment for a product already fully commercialized in a different field, (2) providing assistance to small firms lacking the necessary managerial-technical talents or finances to capitalize on valuable technology, (3) cost sharing in the development of new technology, and (4) joint venturing arrangements. By virtue of our depth and breadth of resources, we are able to draw from a large pool of professionals and specialists in the major disciplines to perfect and commercialize new technology. We can then combine our knowledge of industry patterns and the marketplace with an ability to reach appropriate decision-making individuals to consummate optimum new product venture and licensing/marketing agreements.

22 The Interaction of Research and Development Planning and Total Corporate Planning

Derek E. Till

Three examples of planning procedures serve to illustrate the points at which interactions occur between research and development (R&D) and corporate planners. The first of these is planning from the top down (see figure 22-1). In this style, the chief executive plays a leading role. He takes into account pressure for growth from stockholders, the stimulation of the board of directors, opportunities for executive growth, and personal ambition. While the last is usually neglected in discussions of planning, it can play a dominating role if the chief executive is determined that the corporation should move into the Fortune 500 or for the company to become a billion dollar enterprise before he retires.

From these inputs emerge a sort of corporate objective, usually financial, which may then be turned into a strategic growth plan. Typically, the growth plan will have a growth segment based on existing products, a projected contribution from new businesses developed through R&D activities, and the additional factor of acquisitions.

It still happens, (although less frequently today than 10 years ago) that the R&D executive who is responsible for developing the new businesses is assured that because the corporation is financially healthy, it will be able to capitalize on any new line of endeavor. A "typical" R&D plan which responds to this challenge will envisage new products stemming from laboratory evaluations, new technical fields to exploit from monitoring research publications and contacts, and the possible acquisition of outside technical property through encouraging inventors to bring their ideas to the corporation.

From these diverse activities, the approaches which emerge are evaluated internally and the most promising submitted to corporate management for their approval to proceed further. At this stage, significant capital investment for scale-up is often required.

It is at this point that frustration often begins. In many cases, the ideas which are proffered never seem to quite fit with the corporate needs. The R&D executive looks for clues in the reasons given for rejection, then starts to refine the criteria by which he judges his output and plans his programs. The pass/fail ratio will be very unfavorable until the criteria are honed or refined.

Is it possible to develop initial criteria so comprehensive that disappoint-

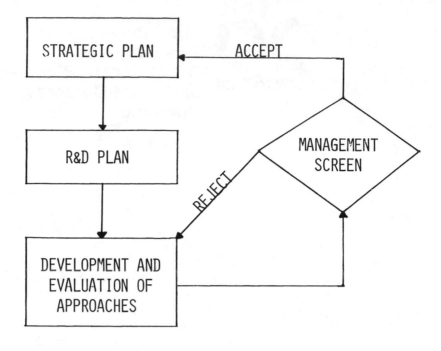

PROBLEMS: INITIAL CRITERIA FOR ACCEPTANCE OFTEN TOO BROAD

FEW PROJECTS PASS THE SCREEN

"AFTER THE FACTS" CRITERIA CAUSE DISILLUSIONMENT

Figure 22-1. Planning from the Top Down.

ments and frustrations will be few and far between? The answer to this is not an unqualified "yes"; nevertheless much can be done. Management sometimes holds off from becoming involved in developing detailed criteria because they believe that this undesirably constrains the research effort and good opportunities may be missed. Technical management, on the other hand, faced with the seductive possibility of a broad-ranging research opportunity, may unconsciously hold back from too hard a look at the long-range implications. Experience suggests that criteria will be satisfactory only after they have been tested against concrete examples—and even then they will be a moving yardstick, vulnerable to after-the-fact modification.

The second example of an approach to planning is that of the corporation in which plans are generated at the operational level and are then funneled up to a planning function, which, in conjunction with inputs from top management, produces an overall plan (see figure 22-2). Like any other organic entity, R&D organizations like to grow. Their plan is likely to include programs which they regard as offering long-term opportunities for corporate growth. These opportunities seem rational, the technology as presented seems to be "do-able," and it becomes part of the plan. As time goes on, the targets seem to recede further away, and the technological hurdles more difficult and more expensive to overcome than was anticipated.

If this process is repeated at regular intervals, one finds a disenchantment or even cynicism about the believability of R&D plans and concern about the competence of the R&D organization.

Why does this happen, even in organizations which appear to be sophisticated and in which the technical competence would be expected to be unquestioned? The answer, we believe, is in (1) the nature of the R&D process, and (2) the different styles of assessing and handling uncertainties.

In the first case, technical people always approach the R&D process as if progress will proceed smoothly toward a goal, even though experience shows that this very rarely happens. We do not use this experience, perhaps because the real (as distinct from the idealized) process sounds too much like a confession of inadequacy. Thus in planning and budgeting, estimates of time and level of effort are almost invariably low.

Second, the assessment of the probability of success of a project may be capable of a variety of interpretations and assessed by others in more optimistic terms than the estimator intends. If a technical person states that a project has a "good chance of success," he may mean that the probability is about 51 percent, because he is used to living with a world in which the average rate of success is not high, particularly for more forward-reaching, innovative projects. On the other hand, the planner or nontechnical executive may interpret a "good chance of success" as meaning 90 percent, because he is living with a more rational and quantifiable view of life.

It follows, therefore, that a really hard-nosed appraisal of long-term R&D efforts must be jointly carried out so that the real chances of success are understood by all sides and the risks are shared. When the real chances of success are low, even though the potential reward may be high, the prudent course of action may be to refrain from supporting speculative R&D unless a sufficiently large portfolio of projects can be funded.

The third example concerns the integration of technical and corporate

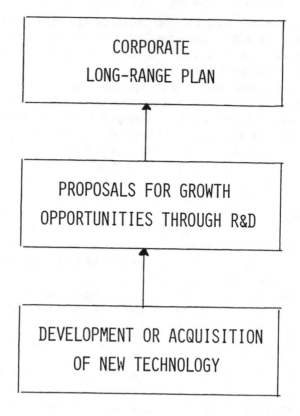

PROBLEMS: TIME AND MONEY UNDERESTIMATED
MAGNITUDE OF ADVANCE LESS THAN EXPECTED
PROBABILITY OF SUCCESS INTERPRETED IN DIF-
FERENT WAYS

Figure 22-2. Planning from the Bottom Up.

planning, using the product-maturity cycle as the basis for developing strategic plans for particular product lines (see figure 22-3).

One form of strategic profiling we successfully use divides the "rise and fall" of a product or product line into four segments: embryonic, growth, mature, and aging. Each portion of this cycle demands different techniques for

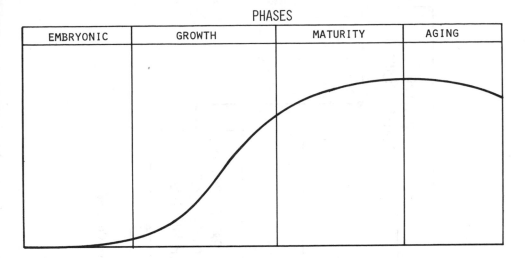

Figure 22-3. The Product Maturity Cycle.

management, marketing, financial consideration—and deployment of R&D resources.

There are two important aspects of the strategic profiling process which can affect the technical posture of the organizational unit. The first of these is the effect on R&D planning and the second (perhaps the potentially more important) is the contribution R&D can make in appraising whether or not the product maturity cycle must run its traditional course, or whether the cycle can be perturbed through R&D activity.

Let us assume that a business unit or strategy center has developed a strategic profile of the business and on this basis it develops plans for that strategy center (see figure 22-4). The important questions which R&D may be able to answer are "Can technology change the profile?" Two general considerations can be taken into account. If the strategy center is positioned as "embryonic" or "growth," are there technical developments on the horizon which, if successful, could significantly shorten the time cycle so that the product becomes mature before it reaches the anticipated peak of its growth? Second, if the center is positioned as "mature" or "aging," is it possible that a technical innovation could change the product form so drastically that the business acquires an important competitive advantage and the business center moves into a growth cycle? Or could the revolutionary (rather than evolutionary) process so change the economics that growth can be achieved at the expense of competition, or the latter stages of the maturity cycle prolonged significantly?

If the answer to any of these questions is "yes," then the strategic planning

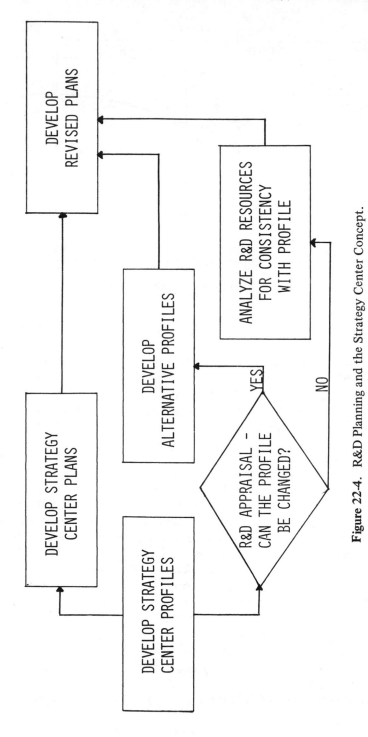

Figure 22-4. R&D Planning and the Strategy Center Concept.

process may need to develop an alternative contingency plan. Of course, the answer might be "yes," *but* the risk attendant in the R&D plan might be too great compared with the cost of the effort. Here is where the business center must deal with the problem mentioned earlier—that is, the realistic assessment of probabilities of success.

In any event, the outcome will be important from the standpoint of R&D planning. In table 22-1 is a very simplified view of the impact of the positioning of the business within the product maturity cycle on the types of R&D resources which are required. The emphasis shifts from research through shorter-range activities to the eventual focus on cost reduction, not only with respect to the product and the process but also with respect to R&D itself. What is often missed in planning the appropriate use of R&D, however, is that the shift in emphasis does not simply mean a shift in programs—it may have an important bearing on the types of people involved. For example, the creative engineer who develops a new process may well be tempermentally unsuited to efforts that are required to remove cost by painstaking evolutionary work. The chemist who demonstrates an inventive flair in the embryonic and growth phase may consider cost reduction through materials substitution and reformulation demeaning work. Thus, as the product line becomes mature, it is not simply a question of periodically reconsidering the program and the level of effort, but also serious attention must be given to whether the staff which played such a vital role in the early phases can adapt to the latter phases.

To sum up: three key aspects of the integration of strategic and R&D plans can and should be considered. The first concerns problems inherent in satisfying a vaguely expressed corporate need for diversification through new products. The second involves the better appreciation of uncertainties inherent in long-range R&D projects; and the third, the constructive role that R&D can (and should) play in strategic profiling.

Table 22-1
Impact of the Product Maturity Cycle on Research and Development

	Research	Product Development	Process Development	Cost Reduction
Embryonic:	X	X		
Growth:		X	X	
Mature:			X	X
Aging:				X

23 Organizational and Interpersonal Components of Technical Problems

William I. Rogers

Some people think that technical problems are more complex now than they were 10 or 20 years ago, and that they will be even more complex 10 years from now. This is not generally true. Realistically, however, technical problems today *seem* to be more complex than they seemed to be 10 or 20 years ago, and they will *seem* to be even more so 10 years hence. But they actually will not be more complex because scientists, technologists, and engineers are always pushing the state of their art. As analytical tools become sophisticated, so do their solutions and so do their next problems. There is an apparent contradiction, therefore, between what is and what seems to be.

What's Going on Here?

What's going on here is something that managers of technical companies are realizing more and more each day. As market, regulatory, and business opportunities, pressures, and expectations continue to appear on the horizon, more complex *organizational solutions* to technical problems will be required. The overall problems are actually becoming more complex while their technical components are not becoming more complex relative to the current state of technology. This book is replete with examples of technical problems which require both organizational *and* technical solutions. They include (1) the more productive use of technical units *by linking* technical planning with strategic business planning, and (2) a decreased risk from untimely actions of regulatory agencies or from representatives of the private sector *by linking* risk assessing and hazard managing into corporate planning, as well as into strategic business planning.

The value of interdisciplinary technical problem-solving is discovered by more companies every day. First, they are finding that there must be a more effective, operational, *translated* link between business and technical planning. And second, they are finding that there must be a more effective link between the actual work of relevant sets of organizational units, such as research and development (R&D), engineering, operations, marketing, quality assurance, finance, and top management. It is in these two areas that much progress is still required. When such progress is made by companies, it reliably correlates with more productive, effective, and timely solving of problems with technical content.

Caution: Different Cultures at Work

Unfortunately, when different organizational units with their different functional specialties and their different languages are forced by business, market, and regulatory pressures to solve technical problems together, they discover that the techniques of the social sciences are not as clearly developed as is the technology of the physical sciences.

Social science techniques are used to facilitate interunit and interpersonal functioning, thus enabling people with different cultures to be productive together. Because these techniques and their application are limited and not widely used by many organizations, the technology of the physical sciences is not now utilized cost-effectively.

What Can Be Done?

What are organizations doing about the problem? How are we helping organizations to cope with the problem? The answer seems disarmingly simple at first. However, it becomes complex as it begins to be applied in real-life situations.

The answer is that technical problems become easier to solve if they are *defined in operational terms* by first separating out their organizational and interpersonal components, leaving the purely technical problems to be solved *after* or *while* the organizational and interpersonal problems are being solved or resolved.

The key organizational and interpersonal components which require separate, concurrent work are (1) attitude and climate, (2) communicating, and (3) roles and responsibilities. The strategy is to separate the organizational problems from the technical problems. The result is that the technical problems have a clarity which enables them to be addressed effectively.

1. Attitude and Climate

The following are positive statements about some organizations:

The organization (management) is willing to try new approaches to grow and to learn.

The organization (management) gives people responsibility and regularly rewards good performance.

The structure and staffing of the organization provide an opportunity for achievement and advancement.

Conflict leads to open discussion and joint problem solving.

Responsibility is delegated to the lowest competent level of the organization.

The organization has high standards of performance and so do its employees.

There is a balance between the goal of smooth relations among employees and the goal of employees being resources to achieve organizational goals and objectives.

R&D is in productive conflict with other organizational units because R&D's first priority is to cause change while the first priority of other units is to manage the status quo.

These statements, if not positive for an organization, become potential organizational issues which represent important clues to problems in an organization's attitude and its resultant climate.

Solutions to problems of attitude must start at the top of the organization. Our premise is that people with authority can foster or block improvements in attitude. By the time organization development consultants are asked to help, there is at least a positive attitude embodied in management's decision to improve the situation. This positive attitude by management is the important first step in creating the climate for change.

What Can Be Done Specifically about Problems of Attitude and Climate? Here are two possibilities in synopsis form:

1. Conduct an *attitude survey*. Do not use a packaged survey. Create one with key people who share the problem. They know which questions they wish you would ask them so they can answer *anonymously*. Share the results with them and provide them with the power, ownership, and a potential sense of accomplishment by involving them in developing and implementing ways to improve the situation.

2. Hold a *series of interviews* with key people who share the problem, using the following model:

a. "What should be *continued*? Be positive and constructively critical.
b. "What should be *started*? Get information to build on that positive base of the things to be continued.
c. "What should be *stopped*? Learn what is in the way of effective technical problem-solving.

Follow these interviews with planning of next steps to achieve desired results. Include all parties to the problem. Be careful about how feedback is given. Feedback is frequently about the person rather than about the problem; negative feedback is frequently quite specific, whereas positive feedback is often general. Stick to the problem and provide specific positive and negative feedback.

Such interventions generally lead to the identification of problems in the organizational climate created by negative descriptions of the attitudes previously described. They also lead to problems of communicating, and problems involving roles, responsibilities, and sense of accomplishment. The results and recommended actions are generally constructive because information has been shared, dilemmas were discussed, and people know that informed decisions were made. There has been good communicating and problem solving. The organization appears to participants and its other members to be open to *learning about the way it works.*

2. Communicating

Notice that the discussion is about communicating, not about communications. Communicating ends in *ing,* and *ing* words are action words. Organizational or interpersonal components of technical problems are commonly action problems, not philosophical problems. In this chapter the emphasis is on action: what can actually be done and how it can be done.

Communicating is about collecting facts, transmitting messages, testing reception, clarifying messages, comparing perceptions, and responding. Paying attention to substance and to personal actions. Creating a climate for open communication among people and between organizational units. Communicating is critically linked to controlling and directing, planning, organizing, staffing, learning, and other managing functions.

When technical problems are complicated with organizational and interpersonal problems, there are three points for diagnosis: (1) common language, (2) translation of requests and orders, and (3) the quality of feedback.

Ask yourself first: Does my organization have a common language? Do the marketing people talk marketing to the R&D people? Do the R&D people talk in such a technical jargon that the marketing people do not understand? If so, all organizational units may not be meaningfully, relevantly, and productively engaged in work to achieve the organization's strategic business goals and objectives.

The managing function in which many communicating problems are found is the process of *delegating.* As people delegate they frequently talk with people in other parts of the organization who operate on different kinds of information than their superiors do. Improving market share, increasing margins, and diversifying are all familiar operational terms at one level of the organization, and understandable but not operational several levels below. Here, translation of objectives and directions becomes crucial to successful communication.

Crisis managers translate their requests or orders in their own minds before communicating. They communicate in language that is operational for their subordinates. This is an important technique in crisis management because it saves both time and energy, which are in short supply. However, it precludes learning. It does not support creative, interpersonal actions, and it does not foster a climate of open communicating among people and between organizational units. Participative managers, on the other hand, utilize the process of delegation for learning. The translation of requests or orders is made during the process of delegation. As both parties work together to develop statements of the problem in words that are operational for both levels of the organization, they are learning about each other and about the problem. They also are developing a contract together, which includes the things each needs from the other, so that the delegated work can be accomplished productively. It is at this stage, which requires closing the loop of communication with constructive feedback, that most delegators fail.

What Can Be Done Specifically about Problems of Communicating?

1. A diagnostic activity: hold a series of interviews with people who share the problem, as in point 2 under attitude and climate.

2. Hold a negative-challenge meeting. Many people in the organization know why the project might not succeed. However, without open communicating, people do not have a forum to present what seem to them as flaws which are not fatal. However, many projects fail because many of these "unimportant" flaws occur simultaneously to produce a vital flaw. There are critical times in projects to hold such a meeting, such as when the feasibility study has been completed and expensive development is about to start, or when the development program has been completed and the more expensive commercialization program is about to start. The steps of a negative-challenge meeting are simple, but the process must be carried out with care because potential negative feedback will be its major content. Feedback is frequently about the person rather than about the problem; negative feedback is frequently quite specific, whereas positive feedback is often general. Stick to the problem and provide specific positive and negative feedback.

The Steps of a Negative-Challenge Meeting:

1. *Attendees.* Representatives from all disciplines involved in the project should attend.

2. *Homework before the meeting.* Representatives from each discipline list any reasons they believe the project might fail. However, their reasons can only be their own or from others in their discipline, not from other disciplines. For instance, scientists can have scientific reasons, marketing people can have marketing reasons, financial people can have financial reasons, etc.

3. *Admission to the meeting.* Each representative must bring a typed list of reasons from his discipline with sufficient copies to distribute to all other

meeting attendees. It is important that no one comes as an observer and that no one participate without having shared his own views in writing.

4. *Understand all the reasons.* Each participant distributes copies of his list to each of the others so that each participant has a written list of all *reasons* why the project might fail from experts in every relevant discipline. No talking is allowed! Each person notes questions about any item which that person does not completely understand.

5. *Questions for understanding.* The moderator then allows each person to get clarification of any statement—to ask questions for understanding. It is critical that no discussion of problems or reasons occur at this time.

6. *Silent ranking.* Now that each participant understands the reasons of all others, he or she indicates a 1, 2, or 3 by each reason: 1 is an indicator of *immediate action needed;* 2 is an indicator that a *contingent plan* should be developed in case that reason occurs; 3 is a judgment to forget about that reason now and *live with the consequences.*

7. *Sharing data.* Compile a master list of each individual ranking of all possible reasons. It is useful to do this on flipcharts or a blackboard so that all participants can see and use the ranking data during the ensuing discussion.

8. *Priority-setting.* Any item ranked 1 by all participants should be indicated for action. Any item ranked 3 by all participants should be set aside. Any other item containing one or more rankings of 1 should be discussed by the whole group to ensure understanding of the problem by all participants. This is particularly true when everyone, except one person, ranks a reason as 3 and one person ranks it as 1. That individual might know something no one else knows—everyone could learn a great deal. On the other hand, the person might learn something during the discussion which would cause him to change his ranking. In neither case is valuable time lost by discussion.

9. *Taking action.* All items which require action or the development of a contingency plan should be assigned to a prime mover, a person who ensures that all tasks will be completed and reported to the leader of the negative challenge. A due date for each item should be established (it should be reasonable and under the control of the person responsible for achieving it by that date). Meetings or other means of communicating should be established so that all participants will be informed of progress on all items.

The main value of a negative-challenge meeting is to increase the probability of success of a project with little added effort. Another benefit is one of team building. People from different disciplines are forced to work together on an important project. The problems are not obvious to all participants, so a significant amount of open communicating is required. By forcing written communicating to start before the meeting, the level and activity of communicating among people is even. Therefore, people whose opinions are stated more authoritatively, eloquently, or loudly than others do not have an advantage. Discussion of important items is done in the languages of all disciplines before silent ranking, so that suspected problems in any one area are at least considered for their potential impact on other disciplines in operational terms. Generally, negative-challenge meetings take 1 or 2 days and are very powerful.

Experienced technical problem solvers know as they progress that they will encounter many problems. If these problems can be thought of and shared in advance, people from all disciplines of the organization can focus their creativity and, therefore, be more effective in problem solving. There is also a team effort at problem solving. People learn how to give and get feedback. People talk with each other about important issues and communicating is more effective.

These interventions can reveal problems in communicating which no one in the organization has consciously thought about in constructive, operational language. Our experience in conducting continue/start/stop interviews is that interviewees have never spent such a concentrated effort thinking about the quality of communicating—that crucial part of interpersonal and interorganizational functioning. In addition to minimizing problems of communicating, structured communicating, such as the negative-challenge meeting, provides information about complex technical problems which people more than one level apart in the organization never knew existed in those other levels. Other problems revealed while working on communicating include problems of people understanding their own and others' roles and responsibilities.

3. Roles and Responsibilities

We consulted with an R&D director who carried a 30-pound briefcase home every night. He worked 7 days a week. When we talked to the people who reported directly to him, we found they were bored. They said they had not done anything challenging in a year or two. They stayed with the organization because it was in their home town and because the organization otherwise was a good one to work for. After a series of continue/start/stop interviews we wanted to find out more about roles and responsibilities, so we asked: "What is your boss doing that you should be doing?" We filled many pages of notes with items which sounded reasonable to us. When we asked the boss, "What are you doing that your subordinates could be doing?" he said, "Not very much."

Many times people assume what their job is to be and do it. This is useful in embryonic organizations, but as organizations mature it causes much wasted talent and effort, as in the case of the R&D director. As he was promoted up the organization and the organization grew, he took with him all the jobs he could do well and assigned simple tasks to the growing ranks of his subordinates. He assigned the tasks as a good crisis manager would, translating first into the operational language of the taskworkers. As he climbed the managerial ladder he left behind him people without really challenging jobs and with little opportunity to learn and to grow. What he needed to do was redistribute the work in a way that was more meaningful. First, he needed to identify the work that could be done at lower, competent levels of his organization. Then he had to train his subordinates to do those jobs. Two basic techniques helped him do the training and delegating.

1. *An accomplishment log.* The purpose of an accomplishment log is to help individuals understand and identify their actual behavior at work—not what it should be, but what it actually is in action. An accomplishment log (see figure 23-1) is a format to record six pieces of information every time an event occurs at work.

By maintaining such a log for a full working week, trying not to be distracted by it and not to analyze as it develops, one will have objective data which can be the basis for more productive actions at work. Such actions include understanding the roles and responsibilities actually assumed, and deciding which of those to delegate to whom. On completing an accomplishment log, many people immediately change their relationships to their subordinates without analyzing the data beyond the intuitive level. Objective analysis can provide for deeper understanding and more subtle changes.

Before people act, they feel and they think. By briefly noting one's feelings after each event and thinking about alternate ways or alternate people who might have accomplished as much, some of one's unproductive or counter-productive behavior done by reflex can easily be modified in the future because the thoughts and feelings are now conscious. Thus the accomplishment log is an

EVENT	ACCOMPLISHED	ELAPSED TIME	WHO INITIATED	ALTERNATE WAY	I FEEL
Meeting	Information ex-changed	two hours	Boss	Have agenda & objectives	Wasted
Phone Call	Project approved	15 minutes	I Did	None	Successful

Figure 23-1. Accomplishment Log (Format with Two Examples).

objective way to compare your actions at work with the roles and responsibilities your job calls for and to be aware of opportunities for improvement. It is a personal process.

2. *Role gridding.* Negotiating and contracting for roles and responsibilities in complex, technical, problem-solving processes can be done in groups without tender feelings getting in the way by a process called role gridding. A role grid displays on one page the role (specific function and power to carry out that function) and the responsibility (part of the work that is to be accomplished) of each person who is needed to do the work. A simplified version of a role grid for new product development from the viewpoint of R&D people would look like the one in figure 23-2.

It can be seen from this simplified illustration that down the lefthand margin is the general flow of work with specific groups of tasks (which might have been abstracted from a Gantt chart or a PERT chart). In this illustration the major steps are the generation of ideas, determining their feasibility, developing them, and finally commercializing them. Across the top is a list of who should be involved. Everybody who is involved is in hierarchical order

Stage of Work	Technologist	Project Leader	R&D Director	Marketing	Manufact- uring	General Manager
Screening						
Ideas	PM/APPR	PM/APPR	PM/APPR	PM/APPR		PM/APPR
Criteria		PM	Concurs	APPR		
Business Potential			Concurs	PM		APPR
Feasibility						
Tech. Issues	Contributes	PM	Approves			
Marketing Issues		Contributes	Concurs	Approves		
Business Feasibility			Concurs	PM		Approves
Development						
Plan ←	Contributes	PM				
↓ Do	Contributes	PM/APPR		Approves		
↓ Control	Contributes	PM/APPR				
↓ Learn —	Contributes	PM/APPR				
Commercializa- tion					PM	Approves

Figure 23-2. R&D's Role Grid.

across the top. At the intersections of the people and the sets of tasks are the roles that individuals have in accomplishing those tasks. Their *function* as technologists or marketing people and their *relative power* are described by PM, which stands for *prime mover,* the one person who has been delegated authority to ensure that all tasks are done. He or she gets power and direction from the *approver* (APPR), the only individual who has veto (or final approval) power over the allocation of resources and the direction which will be taken in moving to the next step. People who can agree but cannot veto are *concurrers.* These are people whose functional expertise is respected and who generally have control over major functional parts of an organization. By allowing these people to agree, the *prime mover* can report to the *approver* on those who have agreed without having to take any of their time. However, if one or more disagrees, the *prime mover* can get the relevant *concurrers* to discuss the matter with the *approver.* Thus management by exception is carried out by delegation to the *prime mover,* not by abdication or procrastination. The fifth role is that of *contributor,* people who carry out specified tasks at the request of the *prime mover.*

The role grid is a powerful technique for agreeing on or negotiating roles and responsibilities, and the results are easily communicated because they can be seen at a glance. A completed role grid is useful for training and indoctrinating people in their jobs because it is readily apparent where they stand (their role) with respect to others and where their task is with respect to subsequent and consequent tasks. The role grid, combined with a PERT chart or other network of tasks and events which have a time sequence, provides a comprehensive communicating tool when a report on complex problems is made to policy-makers who need to know what is going on overall but do not need to know the intimate details of the process. It helps executives see what role is requested of them by subordinates and is an objective negotiating vehicle for specific contributions by busy people.

The role grid allows people to develop and communicate mutual expectations about what is going on in their organization; it provides a basis for delegating and decision making; it helps people understand their responsibility and accountability; and it allows people to know their power in performing the functions required of them by the organization.

To Summarize

Many technical problems today have organizational and interpersonal components. When these are separated out, the technical parts of the problem become more solvable, more amenable to solution by state-of-the-art technology. The growing field of organization development is training social scientists to develop principles and techniques which help organizations solve and resolve problems related to attitude and climate, to communicating, and to roles and responsibilities. Several techniques are described which have proven to be most useful during the past decade in addressing such problems. The descriptions are intended to indicate that effective techniques are available. Most important, it is hoped that this chapter stimulates people to be more sensitive to the need for organizational solutions to problems which seem on their surface to be merely "technical problems."

Note

Further information on the interview techniques and role gridding appears in "How One R&D Department Increased Productivity," by William I. Rogers, Stephen F. Neubert, and Frank T. Hulswit, *International Journal of Research and Management* 17, No. 5, pp. 17-22, September 1974.

24 Building Technical People into the Planning Process

John T. Funkhouser

The basic theme of this chapter is that planning should be done by representatives of all the activities that have operational responsibility for meeting the plan. This includes financial, marketing, production, engineering, research and development, environmental, and many others. Therefore, it is important to obtain the active participation of technical people in the planning process—it can be rewarding to both the participants and the plan.

This positive view is most likely to occur if the roles of the technical personnel in the planning process have been carefully conceived and explicitly described. Likewise, the final plan should strive to include:

Clear statements of goals and objectives

Quantitative estimates of benefits and costs

Valid measures of performance

Examples where technical input is important for planning purposes are rate of growth of markets from new products, production capacity and throughput from new processes, maintenance and reliability engineering on existing processes, strategic planning, and meeting environmental regulations and policies.

Using environmental planning as an example, we can describe how technical issues can be incorporated into the plan effectively. Environmental strategic planning requires: (1) assessing risks to the business that are associated with risks to the environment resulting from the operations of the corporation, and (2) quantification and priorization of business activities according to the magnitude of those risks.

Before being able to assess risk, it is necessary to understand the corporate policies and strategies that relate to environmental issues. This chapter discusses three possible strategies:

Strategy A: *Legalistic.* We will not knowingly do anything illegal, but as long as it is within the law, we will do it, and we will do just enough to stay within the law.

Strategy B: *Industry Average.* As long as it offers no more risk than that taken by industry generally, we will do it, and we will attempt to meet industry and societal norms in the process.

Strategy C: *Industry Leader.* Only if we can ensure a known level of safety based on scientific findings will we do it; we will work to ensure minimum controllable risk at all times, and we will make conservative assumptions where data are missing.

Each strategy has different consequences with respect to environmental planning.

Strategy A: Legalistic

The role of technology in strategy A is to provide adequate controls at the lowest cost and compliance data that are suitable for legal action. Regulations and laws provide technical and business managers with clear goals and objectives. In addition, the number of violations and dollars spent on environmental control are valid performance measures. In essence, this is a relatively easy strategy for building technical people into the planning process: it offers clear goals and quantitative measures and estimates.

Strategy B: Industry Average

More judgment is required in strategy B. How is industry average to be defined—dollars spent, state of knowledge, number of violations, number of uncontrolled hazards, risk to the environment, or risk to the corporation? None of the actors can decide by themselves because of their individual limited information and experience. Therefore, although not readily available or necessarily clear in strategy B, goals, quantitative estimates, and quantitative measures of performance *are* obtainable.

Strategy C: Industry Leader

Strategy C is even tougher than the others because of the difficult job of knowing when enough is enough. Some degree of leadership can be estimated, but how much of a leader are we and how much of a leader should we be are difficult to assess. Thus strategy C becomes more of a strategic risk management problem than a straightforward planning process. Goals, estimates of benefits and cost, and performance measures are more difficult to develop and less quantitative.

To meet the planning needs required under strategies B and C, the structure and process of planning is as important as the resultant output. The first step is to recognize and describe those portions of the strategic planning process and plan where technology related to environmental issues is legitimately important. As shown in figure 24-1, there are steps which are clearly technical, others which

DECISION MAKER

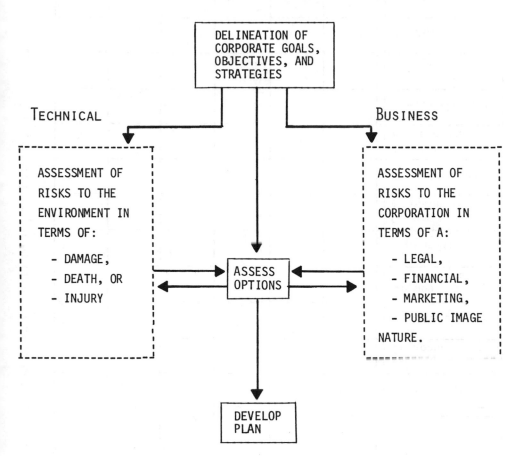

Figure 24-1. Framework for Environmental Strategic Planning Decision Process.

relate to business consequences, and still others where managers should make decisions.

The next step is to develop a clear understanding of roles and responsibilities for all participants in the process (see figure 24-2). After having developed a clear description of the decision process and an understanding of the roles and responsibilities of the participants, a soundly conceived plan can be prepared.

Roles of Participants / Steps in Decision Process	Plant Technical	Plant Environmental	Plant Manager	Division Environmental	Division Planner	Division Management	Division President	Corporate Environmental	Corporate Planners	Corporate Officers	Chairman	Board of Directors
Delineate Corporate Goals, Objectives, and Strategies												
Identification of a Hazard to the Environment												
Estimate Risk to the Environment												
Assess Impact												
Develop Alternative Approaches to Reduce Risk to the Environment												
Select Preferred Approach												

Figure 24-2. Example of Role Assignment within Process for Environmental Strategic Planning.

Part VII
Information Handling
and Communication

25 The Corporate Computer in the 1980s

Frederic G. Withington

This chapter addresses large future systems—the corporate computers. We will talk about their general character, the direction of their evolution, and then (becoming more specific) about what appears to us the likely future of the large IBM systems of the new 303X line.

We have found over 20 years of computer-industry forecasting that a good starting point is with the manufacturers' perceptions of the needs of the users. There are many things technology makes possible that are not going to be developed because the manufacturers believe they will not sell.

User needs are pretty well agreed upon these days, at least at a general level. Manufacturers believe that users want support of multiple processing environments or modes of use. They see that you want to continue using batch processing for the things it is naturally best for. At the same time, they think that you (collectively) are in the process of building and converting a substantial number of applications for the online transaction processing environment. Applications include order entry, financial systems, and manufacturing factory floor systems (one of the most interesting growth areas these days). Also, many of you want to do some kind of time sharing, for engineering design, for financial models, or for strategic planning. Very likely all three of these modes of use should work with the same corporate data base. They see that you want to employ these modes of use at your convenience, and that the system must somehow sort out the relative priorities (which vary dynamically with time), and see that everybody gets appropriate service.

At the same time you must have backward compatibility with the programming investments you have now made, because you are simply not likely to buy any new system if you have to reprogram everything for it. You also need greater usability, in the sense that the system provides the service expected, is relatively convenient, forgiving, robust, and will be available when you expect it to be. There is a new level of need for usability these days as people evolve to the transaction processing mode. If a batch processing system breaks down for an hour, typically you can run an hour late or on the weekend and make it up, but if it breaks down for an hour when the company depends on access from remote terminals, the company goes down for an hour. You need about 100 percent certainty that at least for the high-priority jobs the system will be there when wanted.

Ease of use has also become a specific market need. There are a lot of companies—maybe half a million of them—which would like to have modern multimode systems. But there are only a few thousand companies which are willing to support the staff of systems programmers necessary today to work with them. Those half million companies will not be reached until the systems have become really easy to use, meaning that they require only a handful of professional employees dedicated to the system for all purposes, with an average IQ of 105 or so. So it is a very selfish market-derived growth objective that causes computer companies to strive for ease of use.

Systems that are truly easy to use are often referred to as "virtual systems." A virtual system is easy to understand if you look at it from the point of view of the user. The lefthand side of figure 25-1 represents programmers who are preparing new programs or answering requests for new report runs that have not been done before, expressing their needs in the familiar programming languages—COBOL, Fortran, and the like—which do not seem to be changing greatly, though there is growth in APL and some of the newer languages. As they enter their requirements for compilations or tests, they encounter some software which has no generic name: we term it a "conversational scheduler and diagnoser." It says (in effect) "You didn't close this parenthesis" or "What does that asterisk mean?" or "I don't recognize that data name" or "Your credit's no good" or "Would you believe 8:00 tomorrow morning instead of 5 minutes from now?" and anything else necessary to prepare the run for execution. When the dialogue concludes, the run is performed—either instantaneously or later, as necessary.

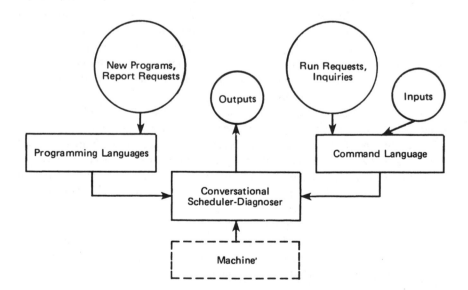

Figure 25-1. User Interaction with Virtual System.

The righthand side of figure 25-1 depicts the user, inputting data to post the files, making inquiries to the data base, asking for reports, and the like. He expresses his needs in terms of some kind of command language. The command language used to be just the job control language, but is evolving toward greater user convenience. When he pushes function buttons on a specialized terminal or points to something on a tube face, the user is employing a convenient command language. Evolution in the man/machine interfaces is occurring as these controls and languages evolve. The user's needs are expressed to the conversational scheduler and diagnoser, which then provides the data output when the need is understood and can be met.

Both kinds of conversations take place in high-level symbolic languages, and once they are concluded the user has no knowledge of what tools are used to meet the need. He is not aware of what machines are involved, or what level of what operating system is used, what the word length is, etc. He does not even know where the machine is. Maybe it is a central machine; maybe it is a distributed network. For all the user knows, the work may have been performed at a service bureau. The point is, the machine environment has become virtual; it disappears from the user's sight.

There presently exists a group of techniques in software and system architecture which, if they are all well used and meshed, make this virtual system possible in today's state of the art. Each of these techniques is in use in one or more systems; the problem is to get them together. The industry would perhaps have done a better job if it were not for one unfortunate fact about most of these techniques. They involve doing things in a standard, brute-force way which is generalized and takes care of everybody's job, but which is not optimal for anybody. They suboptimize to obtain generality, which means inefficiency and higher systems program overhead than users now experience. Fortunately there is a solution to this problem, the dropping price of semiconductor circuits.

The pace of circuit evolution today is perhaps faster than ever before. It is conservative to forecast that the cost of obtaining the present level of performance of circuitry will drop tenfold in 5 years at the component level. In other words, instead of one megabyte of memory the user can afford 10, or he can obtain something like ten times the performance for the same dollars. However, as the circuits get bigger and more complex, they become more expensive to design and prepare for manufacturing. It used to cost perhaps $10,000 to design and do the manufacturing engineering for an integrated circuit. It may now cost $100,000 for the large ones. So to obtain economy, circuits must be manufactured in large quantities and there must be a minimum number of different ones in a system. This means that microprocessors with functions determined by microcode will often be used instead of specialized circuits, and that a user getting a large machine in the future will be getting a complex of microprocessors.

Redundancy will be the route to better availability. Already Burroughs in its high-end systems offers an option of fail-soft through a continuous diagnostic procedure and multiprocessing. More likely IBM, at least, and perhaps the whole industry will eventually provide redundancy at a lower level—the level of the large-scale circuit or perhaps the board containing the circuits. For example, one approach involves designing a computer with three of every circuit and hard-wired logic for a majority vote on every function performed. If one circuit is out of step with the other two, the logic accepts the answer from the two and assumes that the third circuit failed. It is nice and neat—all hardware, very fast, with no overhead for software diagnosis. But it triples the amount of hardware required to do the job. Fortunately, circuits are getting so cheap that one can start thinking this way.

We have always known how to build associative or content-addressable memories which simplify data retrieval. One provides a compare register with every item in the file, puts the name of the item wanted in all the compare registers at the same time, and simultaneously identifies all occurrences of the item. This approach was absurdly expensive, but not any more. To add a compare register and logic circuits to a large-scale memory chip costs literally zero once the design is done; such concepts begin to become possible. Content-addressable files are a long way off because software and systems designs will be needed to go with them, but they might make quite profound changes in the way we manage files and even think of information systems.

The file storage system is critical for data-base applications. There are new technologies such as charge coupled devices, magnetic bubbles, electron beams, and holograms. The magnetic disk can improve too. It appears that the present packing density of data on the face of a disk can be increased by at least a factor of ten. A 400-megabyte spindle which is the state of the art today might contain 4 billion bytes in the future. The unit cost of disk storage will become very low, and the new technologies are not going to be able to match that cost for a decade at least. So the disk will remain the file storage medium of choice, but this means the access arms still have to be moved, which is a slow process. Fortunately the arm-movement problem can be solved by providing a large, fast buffer store and employing the same principle we are now familiar with in buffered main memory: the statistical fact that after an item is referenced there is about an 80 percent chance that the next item wanted will be within the next four or so. So if four or more records are brought into the buffer with each reference, most of the time the next one needed will be in the buffer and the disk arm need not be moved, except every third or fourth reference. So we forecast that all the manufacturers will be offering buffered disk systems, with intelligent controllers that manage the complex as if it were all a homogeneous file. The controller will probably also perform all the housekeeping functions in the file, the activities generally associated with the access method software used today. Substantial software overhead will therefore be offloaded from the main frame and put in the file controller, since its intelligence is needed anyway for managing the hierarchy.

Data-base management software usually includes a query capability so that an end user using the terms in the data dictionary can obtain data without having to work through the programmers. The user then demands capabilities to prepare reports and specify calculations and procedures. At what point is he writing programs? An interesting line of evolution. If the intelligent file system which communicates in high-level terms (the key words used in the file) also has the query language operating within it, it could be a stand-alone machine for the corporate data base—all by itself, without a big computer, serving a group of distributed minicomputer satellites where the processing is actually done.

In the input-output area, one of the more interesting developments is the incorporation of intelligence in terminals. Manufacturers have been building terminals with microprocessors for years, simply because it is the cheapest way, but this means software is in the terminal and offers the opportunity to enhance its functions. We see a proliferation of specialized terminals for more and more applications. Banking and retailing are already well along, and the latest move appears to be to the factory floor and directly to the manufacturing process itself by a microcomputer for at least monitoring and perhaps control. Manufacturing is the biggest of all data processing markets. It has grown rather slowly, but it will grow much faster in the coming years.

Nonimpact printing technologies, xerography and ink-jet in particular, have already appeared in things like the IBM 3800, the Xerox 9700, and the Honeywell Page Printer. The main virtue of these so far has been high speed. But these technologies are different, because they are not constrained to a single font as impact printers are. Any character of any size, any graphic image, any logo, in color if wanted, are all available. Over time, people will find that they can use this intrinsic graphic capability, and there will be many interesting products.

There will be greater use of the optical character recognition and computer output microfilm technologies. As electronics get cheaper, these get cheaper too. Also, paper cost and labor cost rise, so without any great conceptual breakthrough it is clear that steady growth in use of these techniques will occur.

These are some of the general trends which we forecast related to large corporate computers. Now we will apply them specifically to the IBM product line. An IBM 3033, 3032, or 3031 system today is quite conventional, containing a single processor, a memory, and a set of channels. Many observers think that the only thing new about them is their price-performance (which is indeed vastly improved). We think this is not the case—that the systems are designed to permit a great deal of evolution to take place on a modular basis in the future.

Figure 25-2 shows what we think the future 303X series system will look like. First, at the top, we show multiple processors, which IBM will get around to offering when it chooses.[1] Later, we think the present processors will be replaced by new modules which will use new electronics and will feature direct execution of high-level languages in microcode. IBM does this in some small machines (the 5100 and the 3790), and Burroughs now offers a large Fortran

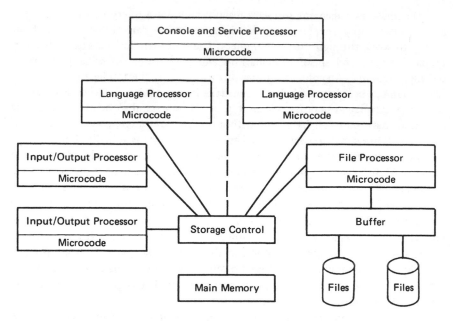

Figure 25-2. Future IBM 303X System.

processor for attachment to its big systems which runs Fortran language directly in microcode. There are some good reasons for doing this. First, it provides more speed with the same electronics: if the customer will program in the specified language, he obtains 30 to 50 percent more throughput. This induces the customer to give up assembly language and go to all high-level language programming, which IBM rightly wants them to do. Second, it enables IBM to separately price more software and to configure the products increasingly with microcode rather than with only hardware designs. This (incidentally) will make life more difficult for the plug-compatible equipment manufacturers. We think microcode control will be used in many parts of the system, not just in the language processors.

The left side of figure 25-2 shows multiple input-output processors. At present, the 303X series offers groups of six channels, each with something called a channel director. The channel director appears to be a powerful computer, not presently doing anything visible to the user. We think that at some point new microcode for the channel director will be announced and the channel group will become a stand-alone communication-switching input-output processor. The file processor described earlier appears on the right side of figure 25-2, with the hierarchy of devices—the big buffer and parallel string of disks.

We think, then, that if a user acquires a 303X system now at a single monolithic price, he will find that as time goes on IBM will make available new modules to add to it, some of which will eventually replace existing modules, and will permit the user to evolve his system into a wholly new one.

Our forecast is necessarily uncertain, but we have little doubt that the general direction of evolution which we forecast will be followed by IBM and all the other large computer vendors. Within 5 years they will all be offering something like this system; and when they are, there are certain implications to the users.

First, users will be acquiring not big monolithic mainframes in which there is a traumatic replacement of one by another, but modular, dedicated processors. The user can keep the one he has and add another or add new microcode, and mix and match pieces to meet his changing needs. This probably implies a trend toward purchase. There has been such a trend in recent years: it is temporarily stalled because of confusion over the new systems, but once this settles down it would seem that most people will buy most of their equipment or obtain it on long-term lease or some variation.

In addition, it appears that while hardware will be much cheaper per unit, this lower cost will be offset by the lower efficiency we spoke of. Now, users typically have 4 megabytes of storage for large computers. Then, they will have much more. And they will be paying separately for unbundled systems programs, mostly in microcode. Putting these two together, users will probably be paying about the same per unit of work done for the new systems as for the present ones, which is disappointing. However, what users will be getting for that money is increased ease of use, better multimode capability, availability, and usability. It does seem to us, in all fairness, that such systems will meet the user needs defined at the beginning of this chapter much better than the present ones do, and that most users will conclude they are well worth their cost.

Note

1. Since this chapter was written IBM has, indeed, announced a multiprocessing version of the 3033.

26 The Benefits of Communications Advances

Alan B. Kamman

Introduction

Let us begin this chapter by stating that communications opportunities to the 1990s lie primarily in systems and application development, not in any major technological breakthrough beyond the current state of the art. We predict for the future, a widespread application of hardware which, today, may be too expensive or perhaps be at the laboratory stage awaiting applications engineering. During the next 12 years, we see creative engineers forming usable, reasonably priced products from technically sound laboratory prototypes now in existence. We see those same engineers forming systems linking products to offer entirely new services to the public. Most important, we see highly trained, skilled marketers creating a demand for those products and services.

We do not plan to iterate a "shopping list" of items in this chapter. Rather, we prefer to use the scenario technique to deal with corporate responsibilities and opportunities to 1990, and to both confirm, but at the same time run up a gale warning flag about, the benefits of communications advances. If we were to select a subtitle for this chapter, it would be "No Place to Hide."

The Scenario

Pamela Ward, Managing Director of Electronics Therapists International's (ETI) worldwide division, sat comfortably in the Pan American SST, watching the Boeing-designed variable wings shrink from maximum to minimum surface area. The 300-passenger craft soniced into the deep blue skies above Mount Rainier, minutes after takeoff from the Seattle-Tacoma International Airport. It climbed toward 70,000 feet, where it leveled off for its hurtling flight through inner space.

Within 4 hours, Pam would face the problems of the day from ETI's international headquarters in Paris, where she was in charge of all non-U.S. activities. Her digital wrist computer registered Monday, June 6, 1990, 8:03 A.M., Pacific Daylight Time. Magnetically linked to celestial forces, that reading would automatically adjust as time zones were crossed.

Reprinted from the July 10, 1978 issue of *Telephony*, copyright 1978, Telephony Publishing Corporation.

At 8:30, a muted musical tone emitted gently from a hidden speaker within the headrest of the Boeing's contour chair. Opening the connecting arm between the two seats, Pam answered the recessed telephone. Noall Latimer, Chairman of Electronics Therapists International, sitting in corporate headquarters in Las Vegas, was calling to review the week's coming events in Europe.

Noall and Pam had worked as a team since they first met in the physical therapy department at Las Vegas' Desert Springs Hospital in 1977. Based on a deep technical knowledge of the uses of sonics and electronics to counteract muscular spasms and nerve pain, along with a physiological understanding of the human body's ligament, muscle, nerve, and bone structure, they had decided to build their own business. By the mideighties, their advanced theories widely accepted and their business position in the United States well established, they expanded to worldwide operations. Now sixty-seven ETI centers are in operation in locations ranging from Riyadh in Saudi Arabia (which by now had taken Beirut's place as capital of the Middle East) to Singapore in the Far East.

Noall's call lasted about 10 minutes, but the day's work did not cease. During the 4-hour, 9-time-zone flight, Pam handled a score of problems, originating a number of calls herself. Several were to the Paris word-processing center, where she dictated letters and memoranda.

When the office first acquired the world-processing Typeterminal equipment, Pam had recorded an 11,000 word message designed to provide an accurate "voice print" in the terminal's processor storage area. Now the processor automatically would type her memoranda directed to Paris and switch those letters or memoranda directed to other locations, where they would be typed at the receiving end. In the hyperpaced business world of the nineties, the typing and mailing of documents from the originator was minimized.

The SST roared over the fence at Aeroport Charles de Gaulle at 9:00 P.M. Paris local time and touched the runway after a completely weather-independent flight. With her "internal clock" registering noon, Pam proceeded directly to her office located in the ETI Paris center at 90 Avenue des Champs-Elysees. Her memoranda dictated while in flight were completed and in the Typeterminal outbin. She spent a half hour editing them. Pam then placed the edited copy face down onto the Typeterminal scanner and activated the device. Within minutes the copy was retyped correctly.

Placing the memoranda in her briefcase, she then taxied to Chez la Mere Madeleine to dine with colleagues. Her internal clock now registered 2 P.M. against the local time of 11:00 P.M. For this meal, her business associates were limited to fellow Americans who, like Pam, took advantage of the international 4-day work week and ultrarapid SST fleets to spend occasional weekends at home in the United States. The procedure was simple for Pam. She would work through close of business Thursday and take a 7 P.M. flight westbound from Charles de Gaulle bound for Seattle. She arrived at 3 P.M. that afternoon, taking into account the 5-hour trip against the jet stream, offset by the subtraction of 9 time zones. Invariably she could then spend 2 full days deep-sea fishing in the Pacific Ocean, her primary form of relaxation and release of tension.

Pam returned to Paris on Mondays, but considered them working days since she spent her entire flight with paper work, office routine, and telephone discussions or dictation. By keeping "American time," she also managed a working "luncheon" with her associates. She returned to the office after the meal, worked on incoming mail and routine items for another hour, and then went to her apartment at Place d'Iena. Pam's internal clock registered 5 P.M. Monday, while Paris slept at 2 A.M. on Tuesday.

Forcing herself back to the local clock, Pam arrived in the office at 9:00 A.M. The Typeterminal contained several memoranda to her, some already in answer to her transmissions from the previous evening. The machine also served as a telex, facsimile, and mailgram terminal, thus eliminating reception of messages in one central company location and subsequent delivery via interoffice mail throughout the organization. Long gone were the days of the seventies when a message was transmitted instantaneously, but then waited hours for internal delivery to the proper desk or mailstop.

As a matter of interest, Pam knew that data bits, including messages and video and digital voice transmission comprised over 80 percent of all distributed communications in Europe and North America. She had a solid working knowledge of the subject because today in 1990, voice and data communications dominated home, office, and school.

She knew that the sophisticated Eurodata networks, managed by a consortium of European telecommunications administrations, were linked with the U.S. network. Ultra-high-capacity satellites launched from the space shuttle linked the two continental networks, providing communications ranging from analog speech transmission through specialized laser-distributed data.

One message was of particular interest. A patient in Lagos had not been responding to therapy for a degenerative lower back failure. The local medical physician and the ETI therapist had asked for consultation that day at 14:00 hours Zulu. The message had been transmitted automatically to Paris and Las Vegas, so Pam and Noall could consult on the case for its therapy aspects; also, to the King Faisal Medical Hospital in Riyadh and the Massachusetts General Hospital in Boston. At Mass. General, the Head of the Orthopedic Division would consult; at King Faisal, the Head of Neurosurgery would consult.

Within communications-oriented organizations, Zulu (Greenwich mean time) is in as common use as the metric system. For Paris, 14:00 hours Zulu meant 4 P.M.; for Las Vegas, it meant 7 A.M.; for Boston, 10 A.M.; for Riyadh, 5 P.M.; and for Lagos, it meant 2 P.M., since the Nigerian community operates at Greenwich mean time.

Just prior to 4 P.M., Pam walked into the communications conference room located adjacent to the message center. Already the television screen was activated with the medical test pattern. She always marveled at this device, extending 6 feet from the ceiling and nearly 9 feet horizontally. At 4 P.M., the image appeared life size from the ETI Lagos center. With a line resolution nearly quadruple that of home television screens and a near-perfect resolution of color, there was a minimum sense of remoteness. For all practical purposes, Pam was sitting at the examination table.

The multiconference began immediately. The ETI center director called to each consultant; Las Vegas, Boston, Paris, and Riyadh answered. The transmission, direct from roof-top earth station at Lagos to roof-top earth station at each other location, gave perfect reception, and conversation was carried on as if everyone were gathered in Lagos.

During most of the conference, the life-size image was maintained. At any time, however, a consultant could ask for a close-up, and the examination room camera was moved directly to the area of the patient to be viewed in detail. The result was to fill the 54-square-foot screen with that image, hence effecting multipower magnification.

The particular examination was concluded in 30 minutes. The neurosurgeon in Riyadh diagnosed a complex disk condition pressing on certain nerves and causing the degeneration, while Noall in Las Vegas suggested electronic therapeutic treatment for a 1-week period. Should the patient fail to respond, an operation would be performed in 10 days by a surgeon in Lagos, with the neurosurgeon from Riyadh consulting via the Mediscreen.

As Pam left the conference room, she knew that her message center director already had retrieved the videocassette from the recorder and was filing the magnetic record of the conference for possible review later.

When she returned to the office, her Teleterminal chimed and she pressed the button activating the video screen. Sinking into her contour chair, she talked with Noall. He often called after these conferences to hold debriefing discussions.

Later in the day, Pam dictated briefly. Since her office had a builtin system, she merely had to press a button, and no matter where she sat or paced, the information was recorded for direct transmission to the Typeterminal. At 6 P.M. local time, deeply tired from the stress of constant decisionmaking on a global basis and from a not-yet-overcome jet lag, Pam left the office for the day.

Analysis of the Scenario

Perhaps the most important implication of the scenario is that by 1990 there will be "no place to hide." Pam and Noall conversed as one sat in an office in a western American city, while the other traveled through space above the Canadian wilderness on the Great Circle route eastward. Furthermore, the call could have taken place while Pam was on her fishing boat off the coast of Washington.

The terrestrial, marine, and aeronautical networks will link by satellite many voice and data terminals. These will be available through direct dialing no matter where the location might be. Twenty-four hours a day, seven days a week, people can be linked. If they permit it, their lives and privacy will be ruled by communications.

Communications, along with SST travel, will make somewhat of a mockery of the 4-day work week of the nineties, because as much work will be done as was accomplished in the 5-day work week of the seventies, and perhaps several months worth of the 6-day work week of the thirties.

The only piece of "hardware" that will not have been tuned to the increased workload during a decreased work period is the human body. Here is where that gale warning is hoisted. In the nineties, as in eons past, people still are the world's most important product, and they must be protected against overwhelming mental and physical tensions at work.

The second implication of the scenario is that the nineties will see a variety of hardware devices not in operation today but using principles which are known at this time. Pam made use of an air-to-ground communications link to dictate directly to a machine. Voice recognition and subsequent intelligible printout has been accomplished. Its cost is now prohibitive, and perhaps it will not be in common use until the twenty-first century. Eventually, however, profits and fame will go to the company that can get such a terminal on the market at a reasonable price.

That terminal will virtually eliminate draft typing. Many letters and almost all reports today are produced in draft form first, then edited. Even if a voice-recognition printer does a less than perfect job and, for example, translates a vocal phrase such as *therapeutical value* as *theiraputikal valu,* it can be caught in the editing and a first typing is still eliminated. Also, by making corrections with a magnetic pen in accordance with a set of correction codes, the first copy can be placed into an optical reader as Pam did after returning to her Paris office and the final copy typed—thus eliminating another manual typing operation.

Furthermore, we believe that the nineties will offer combined terminals of a size reasonable enough to be used in any office. Pam's Typeterminal combined OCR, facsimile, telex, mailgram, and typewriter, while her Teleterminal combined picturevision and digital transmission techniques for voice. As a Managing Director, her office was large, and judiciously recessed placement of several transmitters, receivers, and a video screen permitted communication without transmission loss from any part of the room.

The third implication is the overwhelming role which merged voice/data ultrabroadband networks, in conjunction with advanced communications applications, will play in the nineties. Two examples were given in the scenario. Pam received all her messages in her office. In other words, within a large company, incoming data was switched directly to the correct office. Unlike today, where the majority of messages are received at a central location, reproduced into hard copy, then carried or mailed internally to the recipient, the electronically switched digital PABX will eliminate such a time-consuming process. Just as in-dialed calls today reach the proper telephone through Centrex systems, so will messages in the nineties.

Furthermore, since the terminals will be multipurpose, the same telephone number will be used whether for voice or data. Key to success will be application programming within both the PABX switch and the end terminal itself, linked by broadband digital intrabuilding networks. These features, available on a limited basis in the seventies, will be in total common use by the nineties.

The other example of the role of networks was given in the Lagos medical examination. Today, cameras and large television-type screens have been developed in the laboratory which will give near-perfect color and picture resolution in the 1,500 to 2,500 line range. Earth station dishes of a reasonably small size can handle such messages. Microwave as well as increased capacity satellite transponders can handle the broadband transmission. For these reasons, we expect to see such a network as described in the scenario come into operation perhaps for medical applications, or for educational purposes, or for dramatic viewing of events televised as they happen, and transmitted directly to major television companies for rebroadcasting to viewers.

Summary and Conclusions

The title of the book is "Corporate Responsibilities and Opportunities to 1990." The opportunities, as depicted in the scenario, are relatively straightforward. Emphasis will be on the development of applications for current laboratory discoveries and the design of applications depending upon consolidation and integration of existing communications devices. Cost reduction, such as the ability to rent or purchase 30-second facsimile in the nineties for the same price as 6-minute fax today, is expected in the years ahead.

Applications might assume the mundane form of joint ventures (or mergers) between office furniture manufacturers and terminal equipment producers. The resulting organization will offer "one-stop" office service to the businessperson. This concept is reminiscent of the acquisition of publishing houses by computer manufacturers in the sixties, whereby the former hoped to gain textbook data to use for computer-aided instruction applications.

Emphasis will also be placed strongly on networks and network applications in 1990. Reduced cost and size of earth stations and reduced cost of satellite launches when the space shuttle replaces the giant rockets for that purpose will all contribute to network availability on a national and international basis at vastly reduced costs over the comparable 1970-1978 period.

Advances in application technology and reduction in cost will permit all reasonably sized companies to own or rent electronic, digital PABXs. Thus they will be able to switch voice and data interchangeably to a businessperson's terminal. Once again, the application, available in the late seventies, will be commonplace by the nineties.

The corporate responsibility aspect of this book raises the warning flags. The pace of business is increasing; the ability of our mental processes and bodily functions to keep pace is not. The selection within the scenario of Electronic Therapists International, and the example of the patient with lower-back failure in Lagos, was deliberate. Lower-back injuries and pain are one of the major factors in industrial lost time in America in the seventies. Nearly 80 percent are caused by muscle failure, and it is the overwhelming conclusion of therapists that poor posture primarily caused by sitting and too little exercise is the cause. There is also a school of thought which believes tension also causes lower back pain.

By 1990 it must become a corporate responsibility to enforce relaxation. This is a strange combination of words. What it means is that a person must not work on his weekends, must not postpone his vacation until the following year (or take extra salary in lieu of it), and such rules must be enforced. If a subordinate believes that his boss wants work done—weekend or not, vacation or not—that person will do the work. In the long run, the result can only be long-term illness resulting in gross lost time from the job.

Under the pressures of the nineties, seemingly made easier by instant communications, corporations must look for ingenious ways to keep their employees creative and well. The use of sabbaticals is one way; the division of vacations, perhaps two 3-week periods at approximately 6-month intervals, is another. The "annual vacation" seems a lot further off to an employee than the "periodic vacation."

It is precisely because this chapter deals with communications and because 1990 communications will provide an overpowering tool for increasing work production that it ends with the gale flag warning. The pace of work, possible because of communications advances, must be offset by a corporate responsibility to see that employees observe periods of relaxation, and that the most creative and productive employees be granted sabbatical leaves to keep them alert and healthy. Otherwise, there will be no place to hide.

27 Telecommunications: The International Issues

Martyn F. Roetter

We live in an increasingly interactive world, where no continent, let alone the average-sized or small country, is an island which can afford to ignore what is happening even in the remotest corners of the planet. The spread and improvement in telecommunications services, which still have a long way to go in most countries, are one of the factors which are rendering obsolete many, if not most, of the political and economic structures and institutions to which we are accustomed. In the fragmented continent of Europe, inevitably more people are conscious of these changes in their daily lives than in the United States, where the myth of self-sufficiency can be supported by a much broader base of natural resources. It is no accident that international direct distance dialing service is much more widespread outside North America than within it.

It was a cruel twist of fate which led the oil tanker the *Amoco Cadiz* to come to grief off the coast of Brittany in France, immediately after an election campaign in which the Left and Right had been vying with each other to see which could be more nationalist and chauvinist, each claiming to be the more vigorous defender of national sovereignty. As the oil poured out of the *Amoco Cadiz* onto the beaches of Brittany, it was only too painfully obvious that there was nothing France could do alone to prevent a repetition of this catastrophe. One of the missing elements that will be needed is a communications structure and organization on an internationally agreed basis to permit dangers of this kind to be identified and acted upon in time. Against this background of increasingly limited national power, or even national importance, we can examine a diverse group of the threats and opportunities which worldwide telecommunications technology and services do or may pose. These discussions are intended more to stimulate thought and describe areas of controversy rather than to prophesy. The areas I will touch upon include banking; data bases; mass media, especially television; regulation and protectionism; and the development of less developed countries.

Banking System

Thanks to telecommunications, we are arriving at the point where effectively a bank can stay open for 24 hours a day. No more need books be balanced at the "end" of a day, because those funds can be transferred and put to use in another town or country where the business day is in full swing. Thereby buffers have been removed which made it impossible or very difficult for similar strong changes to occur simultaneously throughout the world's financial marketplaces.

Will the new system be stable, or resistant to hysteria and panic? Will an action or a tendency in one part of the world be able to trigger a worldwide series of chain reactions leading potentially to the collapse of the banking system?

The sheeplike and substantial short-term fluctuations in currency exchange rates and stock market prices and volumes which appear to follow from ephemeral and even from false rumors or isolated pieces of evidence are not encouraging pointers. It is, of course, very easy and commercially quite profitable for authors to describe "catastrophes," but we do not wish to imply that we foresee one as being inevitable. However, it is clear that the consequences of worldwide financial telecommunications networks which permit the instantaneous transfer of funds anywhere at any time are far from being understood, and they seem to lie well beyond the competence and authority of existing banking regulatory structures.

Data Bases

The future of the economies of the developed countries is believed to be more and more dependent upon information and the knowledge to make use of that information. A fundamental question, then, becomes where shall that information be stored, and how will access to and use of the information be organized? An argument commonly heard from North Americans, and one based upon the old principle of comparative economic advantage, is that data bases should be located in the United States, because the costs of data processing and storage systems, and of data communications networks, are lowest here. Europeans, and others, often object to this line of reasoning on the grounds that it would be dangerous to depend on data bases located in a foreign country and subject to laws and regulations over which they have no, or little, influence. There is indeed a very vocal group of interests in Europe who are fiercely critical of the pricing or tariff policies of European PTTs (Postal, Telegraph, and Telephone Administrations), which can make it less expensive to use data bases in the United States rather than local European ones (just as analogously in air transport we are getting to the point where an airplane ticket from Europe to the United States can cost less than the ticket for a much shorter intra-European flight). The difficulty of establishing common, continentwide data communications networks in Europe is another reason why the simplest solution may appear to lie with a transatlantic link.

Yet fundamentally, non-Americans are quite right. The degree to which evolving legislation and regulation governing communications and data processing in the United States will take account of non-American wishes and interests is highly uncertain, and probably very small. The United States has little experience in dealing with foreign interests on the basis of equality, if only because there have been and still are no other comparable relatively coherent concentrations of economic power in the world.

The obverse, somewhat ironic side to this coin is that, in fact, in many cases the American argument may be justified; that is, a foreign organization may be able to function more effectively and at lower cost if it can exploit U.S.-based data bases and communications networks rather than be reliant upon more bureaucratic and slow-moving services in their own countries.

Mass Media

It is not entirely a result of language that one can watch more good British television programs in the United States than one can sitting just across the Channel in France. Most governments take a firm grip on television broadcasting and are not receptive to letting their citizens have a free choice as to whether to watch programs produced by foreigners.

It is intriguing to speculate what might happen were citizens of various nations able to watch the news and current affairs broadcasts of other countries. Technically there are no obstacles to this. Multilingual broadcasts (several audio channels with the same video channel) could be part and parcel of this international programming.

Of course, U.S. television programs are bought and then rebroadcast in many countries, including those ideologically hostile to the United States. These programs are for the most part of the popular, mass entertainment type ("Kojak," etc.). Conveniently, in some quarters they can also serve the purpose of illustrating the "decadence" and "cultural imperialism" of the United States. In all these instances, however, control over which programs the viewer may have access to remains firmly in national hands. Only in some of the smaller, multilingual European countries, for example, Belgium and the Netherlands, can many viewers already tune in to television programs from a number of neighboring countries, thanks to the widespread penetration of cable television networks (for whose construction the retransmission of foreign television programs was a major incentive). Canada, of course, provides large audiences for U.S. television programs, whose influence the Canadians have been trying to limit.

However, it is likely to be a long time before the television viewer in the larger countries can choose freely from among a selection of domestic and foreign programs, even in relatively open societies, let alone in Communist countries, where freedom of public expression is at best a very subordinate goal. One geographically and linguistically, although not officially favored, exception is East Germany, where West German television programs can be received directly over the air (in monochrome, since East Germany has a different color television standard from West Germany). In Eastern Europe, for example, "free" access to Western newspapers, as encouraged by the Helsinki agreements, has been interpreted to mean that in international hotels there may be a selection of the *Daily Worker, L'Humanité,* or *L'Unita* (on those days when these papers do not criticize the Soviet Union too much). At the most optimistic, one can foresee that in the major Western European nations there may be a chance by the late 1980s at least for the wider interchange of European programming. This internationalization of European television audiences would probably have to be linked to the spread of cable television networks in major population centers, if the current restrictions and even prohibition on their construction are lifted.

Regulation and Protectionism

Telecommunications in most countries is regulated by government bureaucracies. In the United States, a remarkable combination of legal and bureaucratic procedures is in force, with the legal community often having the final say. In the past 10 years, principles of competition, albeit on a controlled and limited scale, have come to be accepted in the business of providing communications services in the United States. Elsewhere, monopolistic structures continue to reign, largely unmodified. The principle of competition is also practiced for U.S. international telecommunications services, and indeed within the regulatory and governmental processes themselves. The multiplicity of levels and government within the United States may be healthy—perhaps competition between them gives the individual citizen a chance to survive—but it is bewildering to most foreigners attempting to negotiate international agreements and regulations. With whom must agreement be reached? Who has the final say? The foreigner's bewilderment can be turned to astonishment and even outrage by the growing U.S. habit of assuming that its laws and regulations, developed within and for the U.S. domestic environment, should be applied to the operations of overseas companies, whether U.S. owned or not, as soon as they come into even peripheral contact with U.S. interests (which is almost impossible to avoid).

In telecommunications, as in many other areas, the United States appears to be adopting an increasingly and uniquely litigious mode of resolving or settling conflicts, and perhaps even of creating conflicts where none should exist. Naturally enough, this mode of thinking spills over into the international arena, where, however, it comes up against cultures in which, for worse and for better, lawyers have far less influence and the adversary approach to settling conflicts is not acceptable or, more important, even workable. The degree of potential international dispute is heightened because, whereas U.S.-based telecommunications companies have not until now played a major role in world telecommunications markets (counting the European affiliates of ITT in this sense as not being U.S. based), the largest data processing company, IBM, which is the major computer supplier in all significant markets and is becoming increasingly involved in telecommunications issues, is a U.S. company. Non-American objections to U.S. telecommunications policies may, therefore, be reinforced by nationalistic determination to limit or reduce the dominance of IBM in non-American markets. The Europeans and Japanese thus have strong motivation to establish international standards in data communications interfaces which are not controlled by IBM, and to limit the international role of Satellite Business Systems (SBS) or analogous organizations outside the United States. Of course, in these efforts there are also American interests who are prepared to ally themselves to non-Americans in combating IBM's influence, to name but AT&T and American computer manufacturers as examples.

Less Developed Countries

The primary issues in telecommunications which the less developed countries face for the remainder of this century are of a different order from most of the questions discussed heretofore, primarily in the context of the major industrial nations. Telecommunications, like transport and electric power, is one of the elements of the infrastructure which countries need to build up, in line with their economic and social development. In many countries the need for substantial investment in creating a telecommunications infrastructure will exist until well into the twenty-first century. Several common questions pose themselves for these countries, albeit they will be dealt with in different ways as a function of the size and other basic characteristics of the countries involved. These are questions such as:

How much investment should be devoted to telecommunications as opposed to other basic needs?

How will telecommunications investment be financed (unless one is one of the luckier members of OPEC), that is, from international sources, from individual foreign countries, and/or from internally generated revenues?

How much of the telecommunications investment should be placed in rural as opposed to urban areas?

How does the choice of technology for telecommunications equipment (particularly where electronics is involved) affect such factors as the balance of trade, the development of local medium- and high-technology industries, and the political influence of the country or company which is the source of this technology?

These questions are perforce international in character, given that for many years to come much if not most of the telecommunications technology involved is going to be exported in one form or another from the developed to the developing countries. The advent of the electronic era in telecommunications, which is superseding a long period of relatively slow change in primarily electromechanical technologies, means that telecommunications, like computer technology, is not going to be a field where developing countries can hope to become competitive rapidly, as some of them are in more mature industries.

Concluding Comments

The unifying theme throughout this part is that telecommunications is forcing an increasing interaction between nationally based systems of law, regulation, and economic structure which are often based on fundamentally different assumptions and attitudes. The organizations which have thus far most come to grips with the clashes and compromises that are being or must be generated are the multinational or transnational corporations. Their interests and objectives cover only part of human activities, needs, and desires; and countervailing and complementary international or transnational political and economic institutions, which represent other interests of humanity, are still only in an embryonic and far from viable stage of development. During the 1980s, the gulf between economic and technical forces and the institutions trying to manage them will probably continue to grow further before the shape of an effective international framework begins painfully to emerge.

**Part VIII
Implications of Change
for the Health Care
Industries**

28 Federal Strategies and the Quality of Local Health Care

Barry Decker

Although a broader discussion is implied by the title of this chapter it will be concerned primarily with federal health programs and their effect on the quality of personal health services. These limitations impose only minor restrictions, however, since personal health services consume approximately 90 percent of all national health expenditures and federal health programs now dominate the local health scene. Medicare, Medicaid, Health Systems Agencies, and Professional Standards Review Organizations are examples of federally mandated programs that determine, regulate, and at least partially finance state and local health activities.

Since the general reader is primarily interested in public administration, annotations and technical details have been avoided. The major purpose of this chapter is to simplify seemingly complex events and to identify the trends and consequences of health legislation in recent years. The method chosen for this presentation is to select benchmark federal programs and view them from the perspective of an evolving federal health strategy. After a necessary digression into the concept of quality medical care, the chapter will evaluate the quality impacts of the following federal strategies: biomedical research, resource expansion, financing of health services, and rationalization of the health delivery system.

The quality of medical care is a complex and multidimensional concept. Perceptions of quality vary with the special concerns of different observers and specific situations. For example, patients tend to judge quality in terms of their ability to obtain care, its convenience, dignity, and personal cost. Physicians, on the other hand, usually base their quality judgments on the technical competence of the skills provided and the appropriateness of the tests or treatments to specific medical problems. Perceptions of quality also vary with the time span chosen for assessment. Traditional medical education and, consequently, most physicians emphasize the technical quality of episodic care for acute illness or injury. However, episodes are difficult or impossible to define for patients with a prolonged chronic disease or for well patients under health maintenance. In these circumstances, the continuity of care as well as episodic technical competence becomes critical to quality. Perceptions of quality will also vary with the object chosen for assessment—for example, an individual physician-patient encounter or the medical care delivered to a defined population. As these

Reprinted from the Proceedings of the Academy of Political Science, vol. 32, no. 3 (1977).

distinctions suggest, there is a difference between the quality of individual medical care and the quality of a medical care system. Although a quality medical care system requires quality individual services, it also requires an adequate volume of resources equitably distributed to the entire service population. Finally, the quality of medical care does not exist in an economic vacuum. The cost of medical services, constrained by individual and governmental budgets, must compete with other socially valued services, such as education, housing, transportation, and defense. Choices must be made between medicine and other services and among various categories or types of medical service. These choices are generally ranked as priorities in relation to economic determinants that may be random historic accidents, rational efforts to improve the system, or inadvertent side effects of well-motivated interventions. Clearly, the economic determinants actually in operation relevant to socially desired goals have a significant impact on the quality of a medical care system.

These perceptions of quality differ from one another, not because any of them lacks validity but because each observes only a limited segment of medical care. The total medical care system may be simplistically described as organized to help individuals appreciate their health needs, to express their health demands, and to have access to available resources that provide competent, appropriate, and continuing services unconstrained by costs or lack of acceptability. Clearly, patients are concerned with access, personal cost, and acceptability; physicians, with competent and appropriate individual services; health educators, with the appreciation of health needs; primary care physicians and those interested in chronic diseases, with the continuity of care; and health planners, with the availability of resources. Everyone, particularly the public administrator, is concerned with the cost of the system and its effect on taxes and Blue Cross premiums. However, quality medical care is a composite of all these concepts and can be said to be present only when criteria for each dimension of the care system and their required interrelationships are satisfied.

Criteria have been developed to describe ideal, optimal, average, or minimally acceptable medical care. Most criteria specify relationships. For example, criteria for medical services specify tests or treatments appropriate to each patient problem; criteria for resources are related to measurable service populations, their evident demand, or estimated medical need. Quality criteria may be derived from the opinion of experts (consensus criteria) or from observed measurement of existing relationships (empirical criteria). In practice, both methods of justifiction are used because the opinion of experts partly depends on prior empiric observations, and norms become criteria only with consensual acceptance.

There is an extensive and fascinating literature concerning the application of quality criteria to the assessment of medical care. Studies have been conducted to monitor or, with greater difficulty, accurately measure the technical quality of medical care, to measure the satisfied demand for medical services (utilization), to estimate unmet needs, to catalog health resources, and to measure the costs of medical services. Most of these studies are unidimensional, and none provide integrated indicators with which to assess the quality impact of federal programs.

The difficulty is that the real demand is for *health*. Medical services have value only because they are thought to protect or restore health. The rudiments of health are, of course, measurable in terms of longevity and the absence of disease. Advanced industrial nations, however, adopt more profound definitions of health, including a fulfilled life unconstrained by emotional distress. Consequently, considerable medical activity is devoted toward goals that are not readily measurable. In these circumstances, the quality of medical care is only as good as the assumptions concerning the value of specific medical services to produce health.

These observations illustrate the riddle of public health policy. National health strategies have been directed sequentially at different components of the health delivery system. These strategies have been based on the assumed value of medical services to produce health. These underlying assumptions have changed or been subject to shifting priorities. Quality medical care has therefore become a relative and time-dependent concept, and the process of national health policy formulation has reflected and partly determined modulations in the national concept of quality medical care.

Biomedical Research

During World War II it was learned that massive federal expenditures could produce rapid scientific benefits. One of the earliest federal health strategies was stimulated by this experience. In the 1950s the National Institutes of Health (NIH) were created and later expanded as a central national resource to stimulate and finance biomedical research. One of the few large hospitals in the country entirely devoted to research and the only one wholly supported by the government was built on the NIH campus to support the activities of medical scientists recruited for the intramural program. In addition, a large extramural program was developed to support scientists in various disciplines in conducting research on the campuses of the nation's medical schools.

Federal research activities were conducted in close cooperation with the academic medical establishment. Scientists of national renown were recruited for the NIH campus and others served on scientific advisory and review committees that aided and partly directed NIH activities. Extramural grants were awarded on the basis of scientific merit as judged by voluntary review committees of national experts in each field. Research associates or fellows received residency training and experience in clinical investigation in various specialties either at the Clinical Center of the National Institutes of Health or through NIH training grants awarded to various medical schools in the country. Many of these trainees are now in medical practice, but a significant number occupy positions in academic medicine.

The partnership between NIH and academic medicine provided an effective constituency that successfully lobbied for annual increases in federal allocations to biomedical research. Appropriations grew steadily while Congress, reflecting public attitudes, viewed all medical research as an unqualified public good. Recently, however, there has been a decrease in the growth of NIH funding and accounting for inflation, a decrease in total funding for some of the institutes. The granting of research awards is no longer wholly determined by scientific peer review but has become politicized. Special awards to study sickle cell anemia were used to signify interest in a minority group. War was declared on cancer more for political gain than in any expectation of a successful outcome. These new attitudes on the part of Congress and the administration again reflected public attitudes that had changed, largely because of the very success of the federal biomedical research strategy.

The success of this strategy has been witnessed by a massive increase in medical technology over the past two decades. To be sure, some of the discoveries that have expanded the scientific basis of medicine originated in other countries, and not all the research leading to successful discoveries was funded by NIH. Nevertheless, federal funding through the intramural and extramural programs of the National Institutes of Health was the largest single cause of the explosion in medical knowledge during the past generation. These advances have resulted in a clear increase in the competence of medicine to treat and diagnose various illnesses and injuries. There have been some measured, and many assumed, resultant benefits in the health status of the population. There have also been a number of unanticipated consequences that have resulted in the decreased popularity of this health strategy.

The expansion in medical technology has been accompanied by a necessary increase in specialization and subspecialization. However, changes in the organization of medical practice have not kept pace with changes in the technology of medicine. Although separate and independent physicians' offices, with their limited communication requirements, were adequate to a simpler technology, the current degree of specialization requires a greater degree of organization and communication among physicians. In the absence of such an organized system of specialists, patients experience difficulty in gaining access to the system, with referrals, and with the continuity of medical care. Furthermore, the selection and education of medical students and faculties have emphasized technology over humanism. Whether real or not, this has resulted in the perception that physicians are interested in diseased organs but not in patients. These communication difficulties and the depersonalization of medicine has resulted in the common yearning for more family physicians and the popular rebellion against more funding for biomedical research.

The size of medical schools and their faculties has increased significantly as a result of the biomedical research strategy. Clearly, the increased complexity of the required technical education demanded more resources for education. The availability of public financing, however, provided for massive growth in academic medicine during a single generation. Full-time faculty positions were once filled by the extremely dedicated or the very rich; now such positions provide a good way to make a living. The small medical faculties of the past were regarded by the rest of the medical profession as an important resource to be protected, but the large medical school faculties of today are regarded as competition. Consequently, the professional constituency in favor of biomedical research has become divided and the political lobby for biomedical research less potent.

Finally, advances in medical technology have greatly increased the cost of medical care. More patients are hospitalized because more can benefit; more tests are ordered and more drugs are prescribed because they are available and potentially beneficial. Although excessive or even inappropriate utilization may contribute to costs, they have escalated primarily because of the plethora of technological benefits made available by the explosion in medical knowledge. Despite pooled prepayment mechanisms, such as taxes and Blue Cross, medical costs have risen to the point where they compete with other desirable social goals. The average citizen and government budgetmaker feel pinched. There is a latent perception at the federal policy level that part of this cost results from the continued and uncontrolled technologic explosion in medicine. Consequently, there is a disinclination to continue funding more biomedical research.

These observations can be briefly summarized. Massive funding for biomedical research was the first of the major federal strategies to improve the quality of health care. It has been surprisingly successful in terms of technology by expanding knowledge concerning the diagnosis and treatment of disease. However, it has led to overspecialization in a largely disorganized medical care system with resultant difficulties in patient access to care and in the continuity of care. It has produced some dehumanization of medicine and a consequent lack of acceptability. It has also produced some divisions within the medical ranks, and it has contributed significantly to the threatening rise in the cost of medical care.

Resource Expansion

The second major federal health strategy also began in the 1950s and still continues. This strategy involves the use of federal funds to modernize and expand the resources of the health delivery system. The two components of the strategy were the Hill-Burton Act, which provided matching federal funds for hospital construction and modernization, and the Manpower Training acts, which provided direct federal funds to professional schools to stimulate the education of health professionals.

The availability of federal funds ensured the success of these programs. Between 1963 and 1973, short-stay, nonfederal hospital beds increased by 41 percent while the population of the country increased by approximately 16 percent. During the same interval, the number of physicians per 100,000 population increased by approximately 75 percent, and the supply of nurses increased by about 60 percent.

Several concurrent events, however, tended to modify the nature or location of these expanded resources. Increases in the number of physicians occurred while the explosion in biomedical knowledge was forcing more and more specialization on the profession. A large percentage of the additional physicians ultimately found their way into specialized practice, while the earlier supply of family practitioners aged and retired. The resultant lack of family physicians to provide entrance into the health care system, referral, and the continuity of care has only now become fully apparent to the population. Furthermore, specialized physicians depend on hospitals more and tend to settle in urban centers with better equipped hospitals. This phenomenon partly accounts for the difficulty that small towns without hospitals are now experiencing in their efforts to recruit new physicians.

The second concurrent event is the changing demography of the United States during the past 20 years. The previously established trend toward urbanization has been accelerated. A new migration from central cities to suburbia was established. More recently, there has been a migration from the Northeast and the Midwest to the sunbelt states of the South and the Southwest. Urban migrants tend to carry their concepts of social organization and demands for service with them. Consequently, small suburban hospitals have been expanded and new ones built with the aid of Hill-Burton funds, while the occupancy of older, established institutions in the central cities has fallen. Newly trained specialists followed the population to suburbia and pressed the new or expanded hospitals into providing more and more technical, specialized services. Clearly, the suburban revolution has converted sleepy country hospitals into competent minicopies of the older central-city medical centers. The expansion of resources, including both facilities and medical manpower, has therefore led to a decentralization of the health delivery system. Although at face value it seems appropriate to bring health care resources to where the people are, unanticipated consequences have made decentralization less desirable.

Decentralization has proved to be extremely expensive. The growth of hospital beds in suburbia and the movement of the population to suburbia have negated prior planning estimates for large hospitals in the central cities now only partly occupied by a new mix of patients, and this results in major budgetary dislocations. Periods of growth also tend to overshoot the mark. There are now approximately 4.5 acute short-stay beds per 1,000 population, although most experts believe that 3.0 to 3.5 beds per 1,000 would be sufficient. It is a principle of hospital administration that unoccupied beds tend to invite occupancy and increase the total cost of hospital care. Finally, many moderate-sized hospitals in suburbia, which strive to provide as full a spectrum of specialized services as possible, increase the total capital requirements for new and exotic equipment and the operating costs for necessary standby services.

Decentralization may also diminish the technical quality of medical care. Few of the expanded suburban hospitals are yet large enough to begin major medical educational programs. The absence of teaching and the associated hierarchical control, still found in older teaching hospitals in the central cities, may lead to diminished quality or at least to a reduction in the assurance of quality in suburbia. Furthermore, technical quality is often a function of repetitive performance. Fewer large medical centers could maintain standby skills or the skills required for rare treatments more effectively than could many decentralized but smaller institutions.

In summary, the federal strategy to expand hospital resources and medical manpower, fueled by federal funds, has been remarkably successful. The resources of the nation's medical system have been increased at least by half. However, the absence of firm control over the stimulated system led to a maldistribution of physicians by specialty and by geographic location, to an excess in hospital beds, and to the overduplication of expensive equipment and service. All this compounded the cost of medical care with little added benefit to health.

Financing Health Services

The third major modern federal health strategy is the financing of personal health services. Disequitable access to medical services based on financial constraints were finally addressed in the 1960s. It was assumed that the charitable services provided earlier were undignified and inadequate, and that, consequently, the medical needs of the poor were not being met. Furthermore, the elderly who were not poor lived under the constant threat of losing their life savings to pay for a major illness. Increases in the cost of health services to individuals and to the localities that funded charitable care emphasized the need for change. Medicare and Medicaid were the federal health response to this perceived popular need. Medicare provided services to the elderly through a mixture of social security payments and moderately priced supplemental insurance. Medicaid provided services to the eligible poor through a mixture of federal and state general revenues. Both programs, and in some cases a combination of the two programs, provide extensive benefits, including ambulatory care, hospitalization, and extended nursing-home care.

Medicare was implemented uniformly throughout the country by the Bureau of Health Insurance of the Social Security Administration. The program has been funded by increases in social security taxes on wage earners and employees. Since this tax is notably regressive, a disproportionately large share of the cost of Medicare has been borne by the low-income wage earner. As the cost of the program has increased, there has been a gradual increase in required deductibles and coinsurance in an effort to moderate further increases in the social security taxes that have now reached burdensome levels. It has been estimated that because of inflation, the elderly are paying more for health care now than they did prior to the implementation of Medicare.

Medicaid, which required both federal and state participation, was implemented less homogeneously. Most states quickly provided benefits to the categorical poor (those receiving cash support). Thus charitable medical costs were transferred from the localities to the state where they were offset by matching federal funds. To this date, however, Arizona has not implemented Medicaid at all. Medicaid was also designed to provide benefits to the medically indigent (those not receiving cash welfare benefits but unable to pay for medical services). There is considerable variation in the implementation of this provision from state to state; the larger, wealthier states act more quickly to provide more extensive benefits to the medically indigent. The rising costs of Medicaid have made a significant contribution to increased state taxation and to the current problems in most state budgets.

Both programs initiated specific controls at the outset because of the need to account for public funds. Standards were set to certify both individual and institutional providers who were eligible for payment. Services covered by the program were defined by regulations. Claims for payment were reviewed to ensure that unit prices were both reasonable and customary. Medicare required physicians to certify the necessity for hospitalization for each beneficiary. After an initial storm of protest, physicians soon learned that the certification was strictly pro forma. Medicare required utilization review committees within the organized hospital medical staff. Apparently, these were effective only in crowded hospitals where staff members had a personal (not a regulatory) motive to shorten hospital stays. Medicaid has instituted central studies by the state agency or intermediary to detect fraudulent claims. Current scandals reported in the media have indicated successful detective work but a notable lack of success in the prevention of fraud.

Neither program was able to institute effective controls over the utilization of services, and neither had the means to effect a more equitable distribution of medical resources in relation to the population served. In effect, uncontrolled utilization of scarce resources led to a significant medical inflation.

It is difficult to estimate the impact of Medicare and Medicaid on the quality of medical care. Certainly, there has been an increase in the utilization of all health services by the elderly and the poor. The availability of funding has expanded whole segments of the health care industry, such as skilled nursing homes and home care programs, notably by attracting proprietary resources. The poor, however, despite the availability of Medicaid, still depend on the same city and county hospitals once provided as a charitable resource. The Medicaid poor have also been the victims of "Medicaid mills," where poor-quality and high-volume practice is the rule.

There has been a suggestion of a slight downward trend in the mortality rates for the elderly since 1965. This finding is not necessarily attributable to Medicare, but it is encouraging. It is difficult to say whether Medicare and Medicaid have reduced morbidity and disability and improved the quality of life for the elderly and the poor. It is likely, however, that these groups face the possibility of medical expense with greater comfort since the passage of the legislation. These gains, however, must be offset against the price paid by the rest of the country in higher taxes, medical inflation, and the hidden but not inappreciable cost of administering these programs.

Rationalizing the Health Delivery System

The most recent federal health strategy began in the late 1960s and continues to date. The strategy is to rationalize the health delivery system—one that developed, of necessity, in response to the inadvertent and unexpected consequences of prior federal health strategies. Earlier strategies had increased biomedical knowledge, provided a greater volume of resources, and eliminated some of the financial constraints on medical care. Nevertheless, they had also produced overspecialization, a technologic orientation, disorganized decentralization, and threatening increases in cost. Despite the availability of more resources, access to care and the continuity of care were probably diminished. Clearly a strategy was necessary to address the critical elements of supply, distribution, utilization, and financing simultaneously in an integrated and rational manner.

It should not be assumed that federal efforts to rationalize the health delivery system proceeded in a smooth, logical progression. Multiple thrusts were made at different segments of the problem. These programs met with some successes and many failures. Second- or third-generation programs are now, in effect, still addressing the same issues.

The earliest programs in this strategy provided voluntary stimulants to rationalize the health delivery system. Efforts were directed at regionalization, consumer participation in planning, the development of rational micromodels, and new categories of health manpower.

Regional Medical Programs for heart disease, cancer, and stroke were created to enhance cooperative arrangements within the health delivery systems serving metropolitan areas or predominantly rural states. The program began as a legislative ambition to create fifty centers of excellence in the country, each serving a defined region. Heart disease, cancer, and stroke were selected as the original target diseases since they accounted for 70 percent of the mortality and a large proportion of hospitalizations. The proposed regional reorganization implied that other hospitals and professionals in each region would be of less stature and competence and would depend on referral to the regional center for an important segment of practice. The motives for regionalization were to improve quality and decrease total cost. Although laudable, the proposal was premature since it was presented at the end of a long period of federal effort inadvertently directed at decentralization.

Largely because of the objections of organized medicine, the Regional Medical Center proposals were modified into Regional Medical Programs. Their purpose was no longer to centralize specialty practice but to export knowledge from the centers of excellence to improve the quality of care in a decentralized system. In this form, they were accepted and rapidly implemented across the nation. Regional forums were developed, needs discussed, and a number of educational programs developed, funded, and implemented. Gradually, kidney disease, diabetes, and respiratory ailments were added to the list of concerns. Educational programs were developed more rapidly in the rural states, where the added resources were significant. Regional Medical Programs, which depended on cooperative arrangements, were much more difficult to implement in the competitive atmosphere of the major metropolitan centers.

Regional Medical Programs were implemented during the Johnson administration's War on Poverty. For this reason and because of the obvious medical needs of the poor, Regional Medical Programs began to concentrate on the issues of disequality in the medical system. Cooperative arrangements were sought, within regions, to develop programs of redistribution that would provide the poor with access to some of the medical resources available to the well-to-do. These efforts were far more politically sensitive than the earlier educational developments. The regional redistribution of medical services by Regional Medical Programs met with strong resistance and was hamstrung by their dependence on voluntarism and later by a decrease in funding. Regional Medical Programs did begin some dialogues within the medical profession and between medicine and other health care disciplines. They did institute some useful regional educational programs, conduct some research, and challenge some objectives of the health delivery system, but they never had the strength to produce any major redistribution of regional service on a voluntary basis. Recent legislation has eliminated Regional Medical Programs by combining them into new health planning units.

The Comprehensive Health Planning (CHP) legislation was the companion legislation. Voluntary participation, stimulated by matching federal funds, created local planning agencies for metropolitan areas and groupings of rural counties (CHP "b") and statewide planning agencies (CHP "a") to direct the allocation of federal monies used for health resource development in each area. The objective was to utilize planning in an effort to achieve rational regionalization. Comprehensive Health Planning incorporated two additional thrusts. One was the mandatory inclusion of health care consumers as a majority of the governing board in each CHP agency. Previously, health planning decisions governing the construction of new facilities had been made by health professionals. There was some feeling that the fox had been put in charge of the chicken coop. Consumer participation in CHP was expected to make health planning more responsive to the perceived needs of the population. The previously ignored poor and minorities were included on such planning boards in the hope that their voices would direct the planning efforts toward the medical needs of those living in poverty. The second thrust was the requirement for a long-range health plan that identified needs, set goals, and established priorities. The legislation sought to make immediate decisions governing the allocation of funds for construction and programs within the context of a rational plan to improve the health services in the region.

Because they were necessary to process and receive federal health grants, Comprehensive Health Planning agencies were rapidly implemented throughout the country. It soon became apparent, however, that they could not produce a rational, regional redistribution of medical services. A variety of factors accounted for this limitation.

First, there was an inadequate supply of trained planning staff for the number of agencies created by law. Many positions were filled by inadequately trained individuals who felt powerless when facing the local giants of medicine. Second, CHP was like an ant trying to direct an elephant. The developmental dollars that it controlled were measured in the hundreds of millions, while the government independently provided tens of billions in direct health service financing, and the private sector almost quadrupled the government contribution. CHP never had the leverage to influence significantly the delivery system. Finally, the organization of CHP became politicized, and it became relatively easy for a strong minority of health care providers to dominate the process. Providers essentially sought decentralization and individual institutional objectives and thus made any rationalization of the health delivery system by CHP impossible.

The third early leg of this federal strategy addressed the development of rational micromodels, namely Health Maintenance Organizations (HMO). HMO was a fusion of the available experience with prepaid health plans (such as Kaiser and HIP) and the Chinese custom of paying the doctor when you are well. It was assumed that services to healthy people to prevent illness were ultimately better and less expensive than treating sick people. This notion is strictly limited, however, by the scarcity of medical procedures that actually prevent disease and the fact that the few primary preventive measures, such as immunization, now available are already widely provided to the population. There are, nevertheless, opportunities for secondary prevention, where competent and continuing ambulatory care of recognized disease can prevent destructive and expensive progression or complication. In this sense, prepayment through an HMO can minimize hospitalizations by providing more and better ambulatory care, yielding better results at comparable or lower costs.

Actually, most health expenses are already prepaid through a combination of taxes, Blue Cross, and commercial insurance. The novelty, in this federal thrust, is an effort to encourage providers to accept capitation payments in exchange for the provision of all necessary health services. It is the capitation mechanism, which precisely defines the service population in relation to an organized delivery system, that provides the opportunity for micromodel rationalization. In such a setting there is an opportunity for medical management to monitor needs against limited resources and make rational priorities for the delivery of necessary services. This can be accomplished more easily in closed panel groups, such as Kaiser and a number of newer HMOs, but it has also been accomplished by the overlay of strict review programs on a decentralized, open-panel basis by Foundations for Medical Care.

The federal HMO strategy has resulted in a considerable dissemination of information about prepaid group practice and research on the required organizational modalities, but only a modest increase in the number of subscribers. Only a small fraction of the population (less than 5 percent) received their medical services through prepaid groups. Several factors account for the limited growth of prepayment. Federally funded programs have been constrained by regulations to provide a broad scope of benefits, which have diminished their ability to compete in price with the customary Blue Cross and Blue Shield programs. Perhaps more important, there is reason to believe that most people cherish their right to individual choice and are reluctant to commit all their medical funds to a single closed panel group. It is possible, however, that the prepaid mechanism prompted, publicized, and positioned by this federal strategy will become more important and attract more subscribers as medical costs rise and people experience more difficulty with medical access and in obtaining the continuity of medical care.

The final early leg of the rationalization strategy involved the development of new categories of health manpower that resulted from overspecialization, a shortage of family physicians, and the shortages in selected specialities. It was reasoned that lesser-trained assistants could be developed to augment medical manpower. Such assistants could be trained more quickly than physicians, at lower expense, and would anticipate receiving lower incomes. The potential for both economy and more available service was apparent. Accordingly, experimental programs were developed and evaluated to retrain former service corpsmen (MEDEX), to retrain nurses for this function (nurse-practitioners), and to educate personnel de novo (physician's assistants). Graduates have been placed in practice settings and have been absorbed by the health delivery system. The distribution of these new categories of personnel has not been homogeneous. Most graduates practice in rural settings, in well-baby care, and in a few organized urban programs developed to accommodate them.

Two important difficulties must be surmounted before this federal thrust can be fully utilized. The first deals with public acceptance and the residual reluctance to entrust one's health to any but the best available doctor. The second deals with the heightened needs for supervisory organization when utilizing lower levels of personnel in health care. As has been made evident already, rational organization of the health delivery system is still the most pressing need in health care. When this occurs there will be more places for lower-level personnel in properly supervised organizations and greater public acceptance of the physician's assistant.

As mentioned previously, these early federal efforts to rationalize the health delivery system were based on voluntarism stimulated by the availability of federal funds. New organizations, new categories of personnel, and the need for regional interrelationships were developed, positioned, and publicized. On the whole, however, these early programs had little immediate impact on the larger health delivery system or on the quality of health care. The second generation of programs within this strategy mandate regulatory programs to produce regional rationalization.

The first of these new steps is the current health planning legislation (PL 93-641). This legislation combines the former activities of RMP and CHP in a new network of regional Health Systems Agencies (HSAs) and State Health Planning and Development Agencies (SHPDAs). As with the prior legislation, decision making based on an overall regional plan is envisioned. However, the current act requires both a long-range Health Systems Plan (HSP) and annually updated implementation plans (AIPs), with an emphasis on continued evaluatory monitoring of the system to be used in the development of the AIP. Planning has been shifted from a reactive mode, where CHP reviewed submitted proposals, to a proactive mode, where the HSA is expected to initiate proposals for the modification of its health delivery system. The legislation requires states to implement certificate-of-need legislation giving HSAs an important role in the granting of approval for new construction and programming. HSAs have been given direct control over a local Area Health Services Development Fund and wider review and approval authority over other federal grants. There are implications of coordinated actions by the new health planning system, rate reimbursement commissions, and the agencies that make direct payment of federal funds for the provision of medical services.

A second step in the current strategy is awarding large experimental grants to state rate-setting commissions to develop and evaluate improved methods for the determination of institutional reimbursement. At the same time, the Social Security Administration has exercised its legally mandated authority to support experimental methods for reimbursement within regional systems of care designed to improve health services or reduce their cost.

The third step in the currently mandated strategy is the development of Professional Standards Review Organizations (PSROs). These are federally funded physician organizations in metropolitan areas or entire rural states charged with monitoring the necessity for, appropriateness of, and quality of the individual care delivered to beneficiaries of titles 5, 18, and 19. The initial emphasis has been on hospital care, since this is the most expensive component. However, extension of review to long-term care in nursing homes and to ambulatory care is already under way on an experimental basis.

PSROs add professional review of individual cases to planning regulation by HSAs and financial control by rate-setting commissions. Concurrent review of the necessity for hospital admission and the need for continued stay and retrospective medical care evaluations of selected topics can influence the efficiency and effectiveness of care. The required collection of data to define profiles or patterns of care will permit PSRO comparisons between regions, physicians, institutions, and selected diseases and provide data for planning and financial regulation. The development of explicit standards for quality and utilization will permit an assessment of practice and is likely to draw actual practice toward the mean.

Finally, the current strategy envisions federal intervention to limit the number of specialists trained in each field by controlling the number of residency positions, as most European countries have done. In the past, the United States has not exerted any control at all over the number of specialists and has in fact stimulated significant increases. In consequence, more surgery is done in the United States than in Great Britain, roughly in proportion to the greater number of surgeons per unit of population in this country. Nevertheless, there are no good data to indicate that the health of the American population is better than that in Great Britain as a result of more surgery. Clearly, the earlier federal strategy involving uncontrolled development of medical manpower has been modified to fine tune the number and types of specialists developed.

It is too early to project the impact of HSAs, PSROs, rate-setting commissions, and finer tuned control over the development of specialized medical manpower. It is not too early, however, to appreciate the shift in federal strategy toward integrated and mandated control over a rationalized or regionalized health delivery system.

Conclusion

National health insurance has been in the wings of Congress for a number of years. It is clear that some form of this apex of predictable federal health strategies will be enacted soon. To quote a conservative member of the House, Representative Richard Fulton of Tennessee, "The idea of national health insurance is an idea whose time has come. The question is no longer whether or not we need a national insurance plan. The question is what plan? And when can we develop one that works?"

There is clear and unequivocal evidence, summarized in this brief review, that legislation which focally addresses biomedical research, resource expansion, or the financing of health care is likely to have inadvertent consequences which will diminish some important aspects of the quality of the health delivery system. Fortunately, there is also clear evidence, again summarized in this brief presentation, that this lesson has been learned. It appears that the current federal health strategy attempts to mandate control over the diverse aspects of resource development and distribution, planning, and the appropriateness of individual care.

To preserve or improve the quality of health care will require a system that provides individual access to competent and appropriate continuing care at an acceptable cost. Each of the necessary elements of such a program has been positioned in currently existing federal programs. It is unlikely, however, that any strategy can fully anticipate all the complications that will occur. The success of national health insurance, in terms of each dimension of quality, will depend on superb broken field running and an exquisite sense of timing by those charged with its administration.

29 Management Perspectives in Health Care Developments

Richard L. Hughes

Changing Environment

Changes in the delivery of health care have had a profound impact over the past 30 years. The shift of medical care from private to public control has occurred. In chapter 28, Dr. Decker identified some of the forces supporting this shift and what resources are needed in this unsettled environment. There is not going to be universal agreement on the "rules" governing health care. There is going to be more contention and a search for a common ground in which judgments and agreements can be made. Implicit in the changes is a shifting to a more controlled environment. Corporate executives must work aggressively and diligently with the increasingly regulated environment as it evolves.

Planning for the next 5 to 10 years is most challenging because of the uncertainties. Although we believe past "relationships and rules" will not be a useful guide for the future, we do not know yet what the "rules of the road" will be. All of us are attempting to make wise decisions, recognizing that they will be based on imperfect and quite often limited information. Scientists should continue to have positive outlooks and, therefore, reasonably expect to continue to play an important role and make valuable contributions. However, what we want to do is influenced partly by what we are able to do. Thus industry decision to invest in technology is increasingly affected by social issues because the approbation and approval of society is needed to make the developments successful. The payback period is determined by the endorsement and reimbursement of various agencies. To use the investment in technology resource effectively, a good definition is needed for what society wants and is willing to accept.

This raises a fascinating challenge to management: assessing the implications of shifting basic socioeconomic patterns. Recently, Arthur D. Little, Inc. analyzed the likely environment in the year 2000. We were forced to consider the realities of scarce resources—not only identifying them but also considering whether they should or would be controlled, and if so, how. In that environment, strong social pressures shift basic demand patterns. For example, in a limited-resource setting, social pressure demands that resources be shared and managed more effectively. Thus our freedom to manage technology in health care can be dictated by social needs and our use of it curtailed if the resource is not managed effectively.

If the activities of the last 20 to 30 years are analyzed, we can track a shift toward Uncle Sam playing a stronger role in dictating what should be done. We suspect that we will see a continuation of this trend, with industry and government agencies developing a stronger cooperative working relationship.

Continuation of Change

1978 is not very different from what has been experienced in the past, or from what we began to see in the studies we reported a decade ago. In 1967 we talked about the growing importance of chronic care and treatment of long-term conditions. Dialysis, for example, has developed to such an extent now that further growth seems scarcely possible. This single disease now represents over 1 percent or $2 billion of total health care expenditures. In chapter 28 Barry Decker spoke of the last decade's increasing availability of health care to large numbers of the population and the impact of this on diagnostic testing. Past Arthur D. Little reports predicted greater government involvement in financing health care and in evaluating the quality of health care. Government's role in directing, financing and evaluating health care delivery will continue. With respect to research, of course, basic medical problems also will continue to influence future new developments.

In 1967 we observed that the Federal Drug Administration (FDA) would be reorganized and would become more active in regulating the health care industry. We also pointed out that the FDA probably would cause problems for industry which could increase operating expenses. Our assessment today reinforces the point that long-term trends indicate cost increases which will exceed sales gains, thereby resulting in profit erosion. Looking ahead, a more controlled environment emphasizes this, as does the additional challenge to price increases posed by a greater demand for identification of the elements of cost reimbursement on a formula basis. Also, there is the growing importance of standardization and third-party review. Research and development (R&D) budgets are increasing faster than sales. Success in upgrading product mix can contribute directly to profit gains, but the generation of new useful products generally requires efficient management of R&D resources. The challenge then becomes how to invest effectively in technology and also how to exploit the impact of technology. We expect the health care industry to continue being technology intensive. But the ability to leverage that skill is becoming increasingly difficult.

We also predicted, in 1967, more congressional investigation. If we examine the past few years we see that the Washington syndrome which Barry Decker spoke of has become stronger. More elected officials are becoming concerned about the availability, quality, and reimbursement of health care. In view of the health care industry's move from private to public, we expect to see even more congressional investigations and consequently greater control of industry activities, ultimately tending toward the regulation of profits.

Implications

The management implications of the unsettled conditions over the next decade are clear—substantial challenges including intervention in a broad range of activities; challenges to existing product lines, distribution, and marketing systems, as well as R&D. There have already been questions concerning DNA/RNA research, including its purpose, safety, and implications. These challenges have strong implications for industry—the ability of public concerns to influence investment decisions. Rather than spending money on what you want to do—even if you think you are doing the right thing and doing a real service to mankind—as a businessman you must acknowledge and recognize the total involvement of the population.

Difficult tradeoff decisions are required—investment in pioneering research which may not receive social approval versus maintenance and/or regulatory research in low growth margin areas—alternatives previously rejected by management are now increasingly considered as possibilities. To respond, industry must have solid data to offer for public approbation. The alternative is to become assimilated into an increasingly regulated environment.

If one examines operating costs (that is, marketing, distribution, general administration), one finds that management is being forced to control operations quite carefully in order to maintain margins. In truth, rather dramatic shifts have occurred in marketing and distribution which are not reflected in the bottom line. The size and caliber of the sales force have changed (fewer detail persons, but better trained), more direct shipments are made to key buyers, and there are fewer advertising pages and less direct mail. A key question facing management is "How far can you cut back without sacrificing your viability?" If we measure profitability before taxes in the health care industry, there has been an erosion over the past 5 years which will continue in the current environment.

Despite all these constraints and interventions, there also will be approbation for new developments, particularly those meeting medical utility and cost-efficacy guidelines. Firms able to satisfy these demanding tests will be rewarded. Thus we see selective opportunities rather than broad exploration. As a result, dramatic changes will take place in the health care industry, in part as a continuation of the consolidation trend. Firms more broadly positioned in several product arenas of health care can continue to be profitable and earn a satisfactory return on investment. The health care industry is one of the largest in the United States and has had one of the strongest growth rates. Significant opportunities remain to be discovered. The watchword is selectivity.

Part IX
The Chemical Industry
in Change

30 The Outlook for Basic Chemicals and Chemical Specialties

Donald R. Gibbons and
Samuel C. Fleming

Investment/Profitability Cycles in Basic Chemicals
Donald R. Gibbons

In recent years we have heard a lot of talk about the fact that the chemical industry is becoming a cyclic industry. We certainly know it is a maturing industry within an overall maturing economy, and its growth rate is slowing moderately. We would contend that it has always been a cyclic industry, that this is not a new factor in evaluating the future of the chemical industry but one with which we have lived and will have to continue to live into the future, and further that the chemical industry's management is better able to cope with this cyclicality than they have been in the past. We have developed some data which compare the expenditure of capital for expansion as a percentage of value added in constant dollars and compared this with net after-tax income as a percent of net worth for chemical products between 1949 and 1977. Figure 30-1 certainly shows a degree of cyclicality from the start.

Let us first talk about new capital expenditures. We made this a ratio of value added in constant dollars because the rapid increase in raw materials, particularly of energy, which is a major component in basic chemical costs, would distort the actual percentages if we used data such as shipments or industry sales. Furthermore, most of the capital invested ends up in the new production plant that creates the value added to the purchased raw materials and energy. One of the problems with any statistic is trying to get numbers which are consistent and compatible over time; this chart suffers from the constantly changing base and definitions upon which most statistics are collected, but nevertheless it is sufficiently accurate for our purpose. Taking a fairly arbitrary level of annual new capital expended as equivalent to 10 percent of value added, notice that this level was exceeded only during 10 years of the past 29 years and not at all in the last 10 years. The last rise above 10 percent was during that period of frenzied expansion in 1965, 1966, and 1967 which led to the steady erosion of prices and margins through 1972, as can be seen in the upper line which is based on the First National City Bank's estimates of returns on net assets after taxes for major chemical companies. These are the traditional basic chemical companies, although again their product line is so varied that this measure must also be looked upon as somewhat rough but indicative of trends.

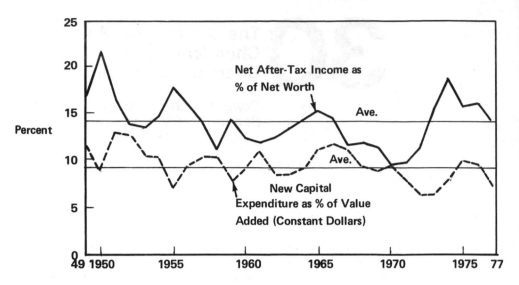

Figure 30-1. U.S. Investment/Profitability Cycles in Basic Chemicals.

While there is no clearcut data showing what triggers the capital investments, in many instances we see new capital investments rising in the year that profits start their decline. This certainly happened in 1950; it happened in 1955 and in 1959; it does not seem to apply in the early and midsixties; and it was off by one year in 1973-1974. It is interesting to note, too, that new capital investment often started its decline at the very time business picked up. The industry is not noted for very much countercyclic investing.

What has happened since the boom year of 1974 when income reached a level of nearly 19 percent of net worth, although much of it through inventory inflation, seems to show a different behavior pattern. We see a rather prudent or, perhaps we should say, conservative reinvestment policy being followed by the industry where they are investing at a rate of about 8 percent per annum of their added value. This is in constant dollars, remember, so it should reflect volume somewhat more realistically than would a current-dollar basis. When we look at the average of new capital expenditures as a percent of value added over the period 1949 to 1977, we find it about 9 percent, a level slightly above what is being accomplished currently. Similarly, we notice that a net after-tax income as a percent of net worth averaged about 14 percent over these 29 years, somewhat lower than the industry has achieved since 1973; and if we eliminate the effects that these latter years have had on the average over the entire period, we might even say average profits were significantly lower than those experienced in recent years.

You might ask: What does all this mean for the future? We do not pretend to attempt to project the cyclic aspects into the future, but it seems clear that the industry has been prudent in its new capital investment. While its pricing policy has not fully reflected the impact of inflation, its profitability has been good. We would anticipate that productive capacity in the basic chemicals (with the exception of petrochemicals) will be comfortably utilized, and in fact, in some cases more than fully utilized, in the future few years. Assuming we do not have a significant downturn in business in 1979 or 1980, a firm supply/demand balance for basic chemicals (again excluding petrochemicals) should permit the industry to maintain its profitability close to or above the average experienced during these 29 years. One should be able to expect an upturn in new capital expenditures over the next few years, although we have no reason to believe that it will reach the high levels experienced in the early fifties or mid sixties, both of which led to overcapacity and price pressure.

To conclude, the industry has been and will continue to be cyclic. Second, it is maturing and its growth rate is slowing. Third, basic chemical industry management has been prudent in its investment policy and perhaps is better able to handle cyclicality than in the past. And last, with less money plowed back into expansions and a good supply/demand balance, profits should remain attractive, providing the industry follows an inflation-oriented pricing policy.

The Outlook for Chemical Specialties
Samuel C. Fleming

Both sales and net income for chemical specialties—chemically based products sold on the basis of their function rather than their chemical specification—grew about 12 percent in 1977, as measured by our computer-based composite of public companies in the field. Sales and net income for industrial chemicals and synthetics (SIC 281) grew about 9 and 5 percent, respectively, in 1977. As noted in figures 30-2 and 30-3, we expect both sales and profit growth for specialties will continue to outstrip that for basic chemicals in 1978 and 1979. In 1980, we expect sales and profit for basic chemicals to increase at a faster rate than for specialties, as operating rates and prices firm for basic chemicals.

As noted in figure 30-4, return on equity for specialties increased to 17.2 percent in 1977 and is expected to remain in the 17 percent range through 1980. The return on equity for basic chemicals fell to 13.4 percent in 1977, which was below the average for all manufacturing firms. Profitability for basic chemicals is expected to increase to the 14 percent level in 1979 and to the 15 percent level in 1980.

Figure 30-5 illustrates that the profitability for specialties companies declines and becomes more volatile with decreasing company size. For companies over $1 billion in sales, return on equity has not varied significantly from the 18 percent level even during recessions. In contrast, for companies with less

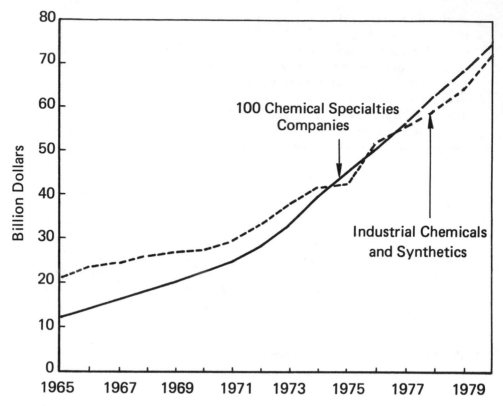

Sources: Federal Trade Commission for 1965-1977 data on Industrial Chemicals and Synthetics; company reports for 1965-1977 data on 100 Chemical Specialties Companies; Arthur D. Little, Inc., estimates for 1978-1980.

Figure 30-2. Chemical Sales by Product Type, 1965-1980.

than $100 million in sales, return on equity has varied from a low of 12 percent during the 1974-1975 recession to a high of 18 percent in 1966. Profitability for even the smallest specialties companies has exceeded that for basic chemicals in every year except 1974 and 1975.

Figure 30-6 illustrates that consumer-oriented chemical specialties companies experience a generally higher profit level and less cyclical results than do industrial-oriented companies. However, for 1977 the gap between the profitability of the two types of firms has narrowed considerably.

The high level of acquisition activity continues in chemical specialties. From early 1977 through March 1978, fourteen leading chemical specialties firms were acquired or were in the process of changing their ownership. In mid-1978, Diversey and STP reached agreements to merge with Molson and Esmark, respectively. As a result of this high level of acquisition interest, the remaining attractive independent companies in chemical specialties are being besieged with

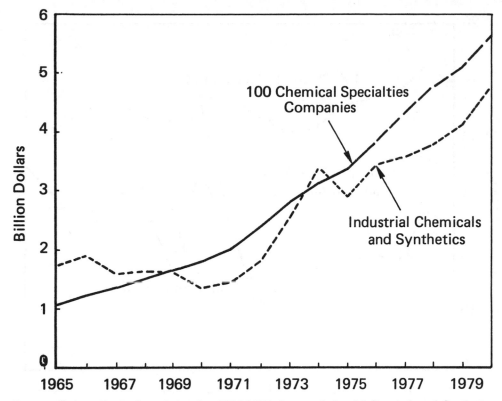

Sources: Federal Trade Commission for 1965-1977 data on Industrial Chemicals and Synthetics; company reports for 1965-1977 data on 100 Chemical Specialties Companies; Arthur D. Little, Inc., estimates for 1978-1980.

Figure 30-3. Chemical Net Income by Product Type, 1965-1980.

acquisition approaches, and premiums paid to acquire companies in the field have escalated sharply. Perhaps a more interesting consequence is the likelihood that recent acquirers will selectively divest chemical specialty operations of the acquired companies that do not fit well with the objectives and resources of the parent.

As has been the case in the past, the most attractive future opportunities in chemical specialties will be those which derive from either or both of the following forces:

1. Long-term trends that upgrade our standard of living.
2. Situations where chemicals contribute economic benefit disporportionate to their cost.

Examples of emerging opportunities include the following. The long-term trend to microminiaturization of electronics is creating a myriad of new

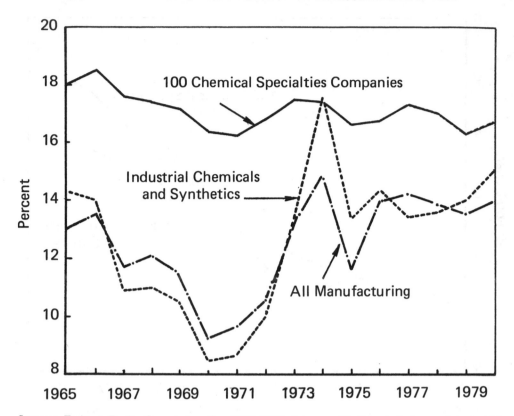

Sources: Federal Trade Commission for 1965-1977 data on All Manufacturing and Industrial Chemicals and Synthetics; company reports for 1965-1977 data on 100 Chemical Specialties Companies; Arthur D. Little, Inc., estimates for 1978-1980.

Figure 30-4. Chemical and All Manufacturing Return on Equity, 1965-1980.

high-value-in-use applications for chemical specialties in the electronics industry. Similarly, the high costs of new capital projects and energy have stimulated greater interest in high-performance chemical specialties to extend the useful life of buildings and equipment and to conserve energy via friction reduction.

In summary, we believe that the market opportunities for chemical specialties are sufficiently great that this industry will continue to enjoy superior sales and profit growth for at least the next 5 years. However, it is becoming increasingly difficult to enter this field because the high level of recent acquisition activity has substantially reduced the number of successful independent companies of significant size.

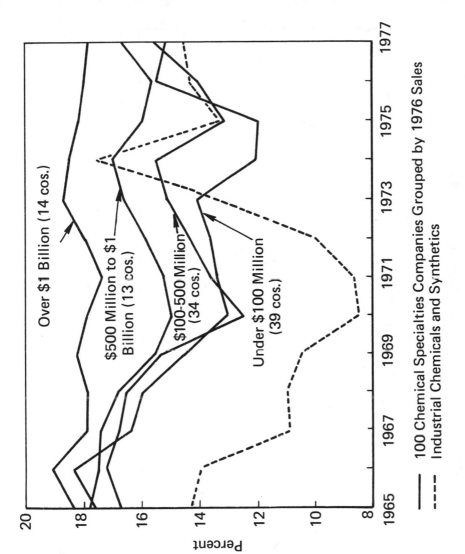

Sources: Federal Trade Commission for Industrial Chemicals and Synthetics; company reports for 100 Chemical Specialties Companies.

Figure 30-5. Chemical Return on Equity by Company Size, 1965-1977.

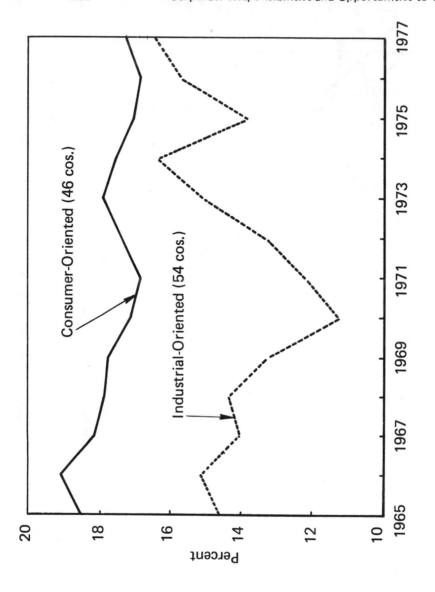

Source: Company reports.

Figure 30-6.   Return on Equity for Chemical Specialty Companies by Market Orientation, 1965-1977.

31 Petrochemicals, Plastics, and Synthetic Fibers

George B. Hegeman,
Charles H. Jenest, and
Richard F. Heitmiller

World Outlook for Petrochemicals[a]
George B. Hegeman

The worldwide petrochemical business remains a growth industry, though one faced with increasing risk. The outlook over the next decade is for an expansion at roughly twice the worldwide real economic growth rate. Worldwide consumption of petrochemicals was $145 billion in 1977. We expect consumption to grow about 9 percent per year—7 to 8 percent per year in physical volume plus 1 to 2 percent per year in real price increases—over the next decade.

The plastics business remains the key to future petrochemical growth, as synthetic fibers and synthetic rubber give signs of increasing maturity. The overall outlook remains positive because of the wide variety of products which the industry supplies that are vital to providing food, clothing, shelter, transportation, and health care to the consumer. Substitution of natural products by synthetics will continue as the prices of natural products increase and the demand for petrochemical products expands.

Despite the petrochemical industry's strong growth outlook, there is increasing risk associated with the underlying cyclicality in demand derived from serving major consumer markets such as automobiles, home construction, and clothing. Compounding this risk is the uncertainty involved in establishing secure feedstock supplies. Increasing seasonality in the cost and availability of heavy-liquid feedstocks will force primary petrochemical producers to maintain maximum flexibility in their feedstock supplies and production operations. Although government regulation of feedstock supplies will continue to create confusion, we expect the supply of oil and gas hydrocarbons will be adequate to satisfy the expected growth in petrochemical production at least through the mid-1980s.

New petrochemical investment in the United States has been relatively stable in constant dollars over the past 3 to 4 years, indicating that future

---

[a]Summary of the Arthur D. Little Impact Services report, published August 1978, R780802.

overcapacity fears may be exaggerated given continued economic growth. Worldwide the industry will need to invest about $13 billion per year (1978 dollars) in the early ?980s to meet expected demand.

The petrochemical business is truly international; eight of the top dozen largest participants are headquartered outside the United States. These twelve companies accounted for nearly $60 billion of petrochemical sales in 1977, or about 40 percent of the world total. Multinational firms will be the prime beneficiaries of the growth in petrochemicals.

The oil companies, which now account for 18 to 20 percent of petrochemical sales, face a difficult test, since independent chemical companies successfully weathered the 1974 feedstock supply crisis and are in a strong position to compete effectively until the next energy crisis emerges. Even assuming a major crude oil supply/price realignment in the mid to late 1980s, we believe the outlook would be for improved petrochemical profits for both chemical and oil companies in a repeat of the price increase that occurred in 1974 following the Arab oil embargo and the release of U.S. price controls.

Increased government intervention in the petrochemical business is inevitable. However, we do not expect a regulatory environment that will create either upset conditions or structural change over the next decade.

The Outlook for the Plastics Industry through 1981 [b]
Charles H. Jenest

Over the 5-year period 1976-1981, we expect the resin industry to grow in constant-dollar terms at about 12 percent per year, or roughly three times as fast as projected real GNP growth. This rate compares with about 14 percent per year, or five times real GNP growth, over the 1971-1976 period. The resin business, valued at approximately $11 billion in 1976 and nearly $13 billion in 1977, is the fastest growing major segment of the chemical industry. Growth in physical units—estimated at nearly 31 billion pounds in 1976 and 34 billion pounds in 1977—will continue at the 9 percent per year rate experienced since 1971, but down from about 12 percent per year between 1956 and 1971. However, resin prices are expected to increase about 1.5 to 2 percent per year faster than general inflation over the next 5 years. Resin sales (in constant dollars) will therefore grow at over twice the 5 percent per year rate experienced between 1956 and 1971, when average resin prices declined about 6 percent per year in constant dollars (including inflation, which reduced the purchasing value of the dollar 3 percent per year during that period).

Building and construction products and packaging materials are by far the largest end-use markets for plastic materials—together they account for over half

[b]Summary of the Arthur D. Little Impact Services report, published February 1978, R780201.

the total. Motor vehicle manufacture is the third largest market. Substantial market-penetration opportunities continue for plastics in the construction and automotive markets and to a lesser extent in packaging. Fabricated plastic products (for example, pipe, panels, bags, bottles) will continue to exhibit favorable inplace cost/performance in comparison with competing products based on metals, wood, paper, and glass.

Meeting existing and future government regulations—for example, in the areas of environmental protection, occupational safety and health, and consumer safety—will continue to add cost and constrain the growth of the resin business somewhat. However, we do not expect regulatory pressures to limit the market potential for plastics seriously at least through 1981.

The availability of raw materials for resin manufacture (primarily oil- and gas-derived feedstocks and primary and intermediate petrochemicals) will be more than adequate to support the projected resin tonnage growth of 9 percent per year. Resin production now uses only about 2 percent of the total oil and gas consumed in the United States, and resin has a much higher value-added component than do energy products. U.S. resin production costs, which are now the lowest in the world, will increase somewhat in real terms (faster than inflation), assuming the domestic price of petroleum and of oil- and gas-derived feedstocks increases to more nearly approximate world market prices over the next 5 years. Since resin prices will also increase in real terms (although at a slower rate than real costs), the profitability of resin manufacture will remain at acceptable levels to attract the necessary new capital investment, even though the returns may be reduced somewhat from current levels. Returns on resin investment (for example, on total assets) are now higher than the average of all chemical manufacture, and a positive differential is likely to continue through 1981. Projected levels of return will result in somewhat higher relative research and development spending (including process development) than has been the case in the past several years. In general, supply and demand will be in reasonable balance for most resins through 1981, with low-density polyethylene in the tightest supply and polystyrene in the most ample supply among the large-volume commodity resins.

The oil and gas companies, which now account for about 30 percent of commodity thermoplastic resin production, will increase their market share somewhat over the next 5 years. Raw material integration to basic hydrocarbons is necessary to be fully competitive in the commodity resins over the longer term (beyond 1981).

The trend to greater inhouse fabrication of plastic parts by the automotive and other OEM companies (which now account for about 30 to 35 percent of total resin processed into plastic products) will continue. Conversely, the captive use of resin for fabricated products by resin producers (now about 15 to 20 percent of all resin processed) will continue its slow decline.

The fabrication of plastic products for merchant sale from purchased raw materials is still largely a small-business industry dominated by private owner-ship. This situation will not change appreciably by 1981; approximately 4,000 independent fabricators process about half of all resin and will continue to process about 45 percent in 1981. Proprietary products (for example, the Glad line of Union Carbide) that command a premium price are required for a large company to be a financially successful fabricator of plastic products.

Non-U.S. demand for resins in regions other than Western Europe and Japan will grow faster than domestic use. U.S. exports of resin, now about 8 percent by value of total U.S. resin sales (about $900 million), will increase less rapidly than domestic sales as U.S. resin production costs approach world levels. Excess capacity for resin will exist in Western Europe through 1981, and resin plant construction is proceeding at an accelerated pace in Canada and the developing countries (such as Brazil and Mexico), which are important export markets for U.S.-produced resin. The construction of resin plants in Eastern Europe is also proceeding at a relatively fast pace. Plastic materials and fabricated products, which produced a positive trade balance of about $1.7 billion in 1976, will continue to exhibit a substantial positive trade balance, however, through 1981. Production of resins in the Middle East and other OPEC countries (for example, Algeria and Venezuela) will still be relatively minor through 1981 and will not adversely affect the U.S. resin business or the non-U.S. sales of resin by U.S. companies.

Those producers which should realize the highest return levels from their U.S. plastics operations over the next few years include Dow Chemical, DuPont, Eastman Kodak, General Electric, Mobay (owned by Bayer), Shell Oil (con-trolled by Royal Dutch/Shell), Union Carbide, and Upjohn. DuPont and General Electric will benefit primarily from their strong positions in specialty resins (and in polyethylene in the case of DuPont); Union Carbide and Dow Chemical, particularly from their polyethylene sales; Shell and Eastman, from their dominant positions in epoxies and cellulosics, respectively, and relatively favorable positions in polyolefins; and Upjohn and Mobay, from their strong overall positions in urethanes.

World Outlook for Synthetic Fibers
Richard F. Heitmiller

In 1969, just 30 years after nylon was first introduced, nylon, polyester, and acrylic fibers had captured 20 percent of the world's fiber market with 4,270,000 metric tons of production. By 1976, just 7 years later, synthetic fiber production had risen to 8,695,000 metric tons and world market share increased to 33 percent.

The rapid penetration of synthetics into the world fiber market can be attributed to a number of factors. They were exciting—new, and in many cases, functionally superior—a merchandiser's dream. The raw materials for their production were cheap and readily available from a young, robust, and growing petrochemical industry. They fitted well with the existing business in the chemical industry and required relatively low investment cost for production facilities; and last, but not least, they were fantastically profitable.

While synthetic fiber production was initially confined to a few companies in the United States and Western Europe, expiring patents and the lure of the glamour and profit of the new synthetics opened the field to a host of new producers all over the world. In 1967, synthetic fiber producers experienced their first "minirecession." Worldwide production capacity utilization fell to 78 percent. This caused the first major break in synthetic prices, and in spite of a resumption of demand growth, prices continued to fall through 1972. Because of the reduction in potential profits caused by lower selling prices, the rate of new investment in synthetic fiber production facilities slowed. During the period 1967 to 1973, production of synthetics increased at a rate of 19 percent per year, but new capacity increased at a rate of only 15 percent per year. By 1973, world synthetic fiber production facilities were straining at a 95 percent operating rate and prices were increasing.

Encouraged by strengthening prices and surging world demand, substantial new capacity expansions were committed all over the world. These capacity expansions, for the most part, came on stream in 1974 and 1975 when synthetic fiber demand declined for the first time. In a very short period of time the tight supply situation of the early seventies turned into a nightmare of overcapacity.

It is instructive to note, however, that this overcapacity problem was not felt with the same severity in all parts of the world. Capacity utilization rates in 1976 compared with 1973 fell 7 percent in East Europe, 11 percent in Japan, 17 percent in the United States, and in Western Europe capacity utilization for synthetics fell 23 percent. Worldwide capacity utilization rates for synthetics in 1976 were 80 percent compared with 78 percent in 1967. Despite the slightly higher operating rate, however, profitability for fiber producers in 1976, and in 1975, was disastrously low or nonexistent because of the inability of fiber producers to raise selling prices fast enough to offset rising manufacturing costs. Low selling prices and low capacity utilization are the twin reasons for the current depressed state of the synthetic fiber industry worldwide.

Current world capacity for natural and synthetic fibers is about 31 million metric tons, broken down in thousands of metric tons as follows: wool, 1.5; cotton, 14.7; synthetic fibers, 10.7; cellulosic fibers, 4.2; and a total of 31.1. The world fiber recession that occurred in 1975 was unprecedented in severity. In that year production fell 3 million metric tons from the previous year. In 1976, however, production recovered sharply, a full 2.2 million metric tons, and world growth of synthetic fibers continued reaching new highs.

Between now and 1986, world requirements for fibers of all types are projected to reach 37.3 million metric tons, an increase of 11.8 million tons over

1976. This increment is approximately equal to the total world's fiber consumption in 1952. While there is ample fiber capacity now to meet world needs by 1986, an additional 6.2 million metric tons of new capacity will be needed. Where will this capacity come from?

As noted, in 1976 there was approximately 10.7 million metric tons of synthetic fiber capacity in the world. This year, world synthetic fiber capacities are around 12.8 million metric tons. Synthetic fiber production capacity is approaching 50 percent of the world's total fiber demand. There is still a large surplus of world capacity for synthetic fibers over world demand, and yet capacity additions are still increasing at a faster rate than demand. This fact is significant in the outlook for future world fiber demand. Continued overcapacity in the world for synthetic fibers will virtually ensure that current low synthetic prices will continue for the foreseeable future. With current prices at or near cost, continued penetration of world fiber markets by synthetics seems virtually assured.

In view of the world overcapacity for synthetic fibers and their low profitability, why are new plants being constructed? There are a number of reasons, some of which are rooted in national policy considerations. The construction of synthetic fiber plants in countries like Iran or China tends to make these areas more self-sufficient in their domestic fiber supply. Countries like Egypt and Turkey are constructing synthetic fiber plants, not only to supply domestic demand, but also for eventual export as yarn, fabric, or apparel to developed countries whose current markets are dominated by synthetics or blends. Italy is increasing synthetic fiber production as a means of generating employment and hopefully a greater degree of prosperity in their southern provinces.

The specific rationales vary, but the underlying reasons are simple. Synthetic fiber production technology is readily available all over the world. Synthetic fiber plants are relatively cheap to build; and last but not least, the informed consensus of textile people all over the world is that synthetic fiber production will be needed to meet rising consumer demand. This latter point becomes a self-fulfilling prophecy. The more synthetic fiber plants that are built, the more synthetic fiber will be produced and consumed. As world fiber demand increases, synthetics will be consumed because they are available.

While all classes of fibers will grow over the next 10 years, slower growth rates for wool, cotton, and cellulosics will cause them to continue to lose market share to the synthetics.

By 1981, the world supply and demand of fibers should be about in balance. Geographically, this could occur sooner in Western Europe and Japan if further planned cutbacks in these areas are executed. A firming of the world supply/demand balance for all fibers including synthetics should allow an opportunity for a significant price improvement, particularly if the prices of synthetics remain as they are today, below the prices of either cotton or wool.

The combination of increased prices and increased capacity utilization should lead to substantially improved levels of profitability which will be welcomed by producers and investors alike.

32

Strategic Implications of Environmental Regulations

Richard Williams

Faced with a lengthening list of environmental abatement regulations, corporate managers have typically been concerned with the requirements for compliance, the cost of compliance, and in some cases, potential new market opportunities. For many companies, environmental regulations have, and will have, far more profound implications. These regulations can alter the relative competitive position of firms within an industry and between competing products.

Environmental regulations are here to stay, and the outlook is for increased capital expenditures over the next 10 years and for a continuing, and perhaps increased, level of uncertainty about future requirements. This is particularly true for the chemical industry with the implementation of the Toxic Substances Control Act.

Environmental regulations do not have uniform cost impact on plants or firms. The regulations do not uniformly affect the ability of firms to build new plants and introduce new products. These two factors mean that the relative competitive position of companies can be changed as a result of environmental regulations.

Any one company or plant can have its position improved or deteriorated in a relative sense. The relative costs of production can be changed, there can be different capital requirements for coming into compliance, the relative profitability of the business can be altered, and the potential for growth can be differentially impacted.

The conditions which cause industries as a whole, and firms within industries, to be differentially impacted by regulations are shown in tables 32-1 through 32-10. While it is true that smaller companies in mature industries with unequal control costs will be highly impacted, the strategic implications for a business will be very specific to that company and its products.

Our recommendations for managers in industries for whom environmental control regulations are important cost factors are the following:

Recognize that the regulations can have important strategic implications for the business which can be both positive and negative.

Consider, as part of the business planning process, the influence of these regulations on the current and future business environment for the company.

Understand the implications of the regulations both for your company and for your competitors.

Identify, as part of your analysis, particular opportunities or difficulties resulting from the differential impacts of the regulations.

Table 32-1
Responses to Environmental Regulations

What are the requirements for compliance?
How much will it cost?
Are there any new or expanded market opportunities?

Table 32-2
Strategic Implications of Environmental Regulations

Alter Short-Term Competitive Relationships
  Differential change in production costs
    Plants producing the same product
    Plants producing competing products

Increase Capital Demands of the Business
  Differential capital demands among competitors
  Different timing of capital demands
  Higher required capital for participation in the business

Alter Mid- and Longer-Term Relative Profitability of the Business
  Change relative return on investment of business as a whole
  Change ability to attract capital

Change Relative Growth Potential of Business and Firms
  Capital shortages
  Geographical restrictions on growth
  Restrictions on new product introductions
  Restrictions on new plant locations

Table 32-3
Major Environmental Regulations

Clean Air Act

Federal Water Pollution Control Act
  Amendment (FWPCA)

Toxic Substances Control Act (TSCA)

Resource Conservation and Recovery Act (RCRA)

Table 32-4
Pollution Control Expenditures, 1976
(Millions of Dollars)

Industry	Air	Water	Solid Waste	Total	Percent of Total Plant and Equipment Investment
Durable					
Primary metals	661	250	12	923	15.7
Electrical machinery	44	86	19	148	5.6
Machinery, except					
electrical	40	30	10	80	1.6
Transportation equipment	53	51	21	125	3.4
Stone, clay, and glass	74	25	5	103	3.9
Nondurable					
Food	90	75	10	175	4.5
Textiles	11	24	2	37	4.4
Paper	182	304	25	511	14.7
Chemicals	287	433	45	765	11.4
Petroleum	554	594	126	1,275	10.9
Rubber	20	14	3	37	3.4

Table 32-5
Incremental Hazardous Waste Management Costs

	Estimated 1977 Production Value ($MM)	Total Incremental Waste Management Cost ($MM)	Incremental Waste Management Cost as Percent of Production Value
Inorganic Chemicals			
Chlorine (Mercury Cell Process)	225	11.87	5.3
Chlorine (Downs and Diaphragm)	800	2.61	0.3
Chrome Pigments	110	1.41	1.3
Hydrofluoric Acid	200	48.57	24.3
Titanium Dioxide	625	19.43	3.1
Phosphorus Pentasulfide	45	0.02	0.04
Sodium Chromates	85	3.91	4.6
Boric Acid	25	0.31	1.2
Nickel Sulfate	10	0.16	1.6
Phosphorus	420	48.59	11.6
Aluminum Fluoride	55	3.14	5.7
Sodium Silicofluoride	10	1.43	14.3
Organic Chemicals			
Nitrobenzene	100	0.06	0.06
Toluene Diisocyanate	335	2.03	0.6
Chlorobenzene	65	1.19	1.8
Furfural	85	3.78	4.4
Benzylchloride	30	0.007	0.02
Perchlorethylene	125	13.51	10.8
Chloromethane	330	4.17	1.3
Epichlorohydrin	110	2.64	2.4
Vinyl Chloride Monomer	720	6.82	0.9
Methyl Methacrylate Monomer	290	1.09	0.4
Acrylonitrile	410	1.05	0.3
Maleic Anhydride	95	0.41	0.4
Lead Alkyls	425	0.12	0.03
Ethanolamines	120	0.72	0.6
Pesticides	3,000	22.8	0.8
Explosives	650	98.3	15.1

Table 32-6

Estimated Industrial Pollution Abatement Expenditures, 1976-1985
(Billions of 1976 Dollars)

	1976			1985			Cumulative 1976-1985		
	O&M	Capital	Total	O&M	Capital	Total	O&M	Capital	Total[a]
Air pollution	1.9	2.2	4.1	4.3	5.1	9.4	31	22	67
Water pollution	1.9	1.6	3.5	7.5	6.9	13.4	45	41	82
Solid waste	3.8	0.9	4.7	5.0	1.3	6.3	47	6.3	57
Toxic substances	n.a.	n.a.	n.a.	0.2	n.a.	0.2	1.1	n.a.	1.1

[a]Includes interest charges.

Table 32-7

Industry Characteristics Differentiating Pollution Abatement Impacts

Macroeconomic Parameter	Conditions for High Negative Impact	Example of High-Impact Industry
State of growth	Mature	Steel
Magnitude of abatement costs	High	Chemicals
Capital intensity	High[a]	Utilities
Competition from substitute products	High	Packaging
Market concentration	Low	Paper products
Distribution of abatement investment	Unequal	Textiles
Competition from imports	High	Copper smelting

[a]Pollution abatement can have a heavy impact on a highly depreciated industry that requires large, new control equipment.

Table 32-8
Company and Plant Characteristics Differentiating Pollution Abatement Impacts

Microeconomic Parameter	Condition for High Impact	Nature of Impact
Size of plant	Small	Higher relative costs of compliance
Size of firm	Small	Capital availability limitation
Age of plant and equipment	Old	High retrofit cost for installation of control equipment
Geographic location	Dense urban or rural	Constraints on ability to expand or lack available municipal treatment facilities
Present level of pollution control	Low	Higher relative costs of compliance
U.S. and foreign plant site	U.S.	Higher relative costs of, compliance
Energy intensity	High	High costs of compliance

Table 32-9
Impact of Environmental Regulations on Growth

Restrictions on new and expanded production in urban and rural areas

Higher capital demand per unit of capacity

Higher costs of new product introduction

Uncertainty about environmental acceptability of new and existing products

Table 32-10
Required Response of Corporate Management

Awareness that environmental regulations can have important strategic implications for their firms
   Both positive and negative

Need to understand the implications for their firms and their competitors

Identify particular opportunities or problems resulting from the differential impacts of the regulations

About the Contributors

Kirkor Bozdogan is a senior economist in the Managerial Economics section at Arthur D. Little, Inc. He has worked as the chief economist for studies undertaken by the White House Energy Task Force and the Department of Energy. Dr. Bozdogan received the B.S. from the University of Wisconsin, the M.A. from Harvard University, and the Ph.D. from the Massachusetts Institute of Technology.

James W. Bradley is a senior consultant in the Financial Industries section at Arthur D. Little, Inc. He concentrates on acquisition, corporate development, and planning issues in a wide variety of industries. Mr. Bradley has worked both directly for corporate clients and in conjunction with work by investment banking firms. He holds the M.B.A. from Cornell University.

Linsay R. Clark is a member of the Managerial Economics section group of Arthur D. Little, Inc. and specializes in forecasting U.S. consumer expenditure patterns. Ms. Clark received the B.A. in economics from Boston University and is currently enrolled in the M.B.A. program.

Barry Decker is a senior staff member of the Health and Manpower section of Arthur D. Little, Inc. He has managed programs in health services research and evaluation research as well as providing planning and management consultation to hospitals and communities. Dr. Decker received the A.B. from Columbia College, the M.D. from the New York University School of Medicine, and the M.S. from the University of Minnesota. He is a Fellow of the American College of Physicians.

Oscar A. Echevarria is president of Economia Ingenieria y Sistemas, C.A., a consulting firm in Caracas, Venezuela. He was formerly the economic advisor to the planning office of the presidency in Venezuela. Dr. Echevarria received the M.A. in economics from Georgetown University.

Vince P. Ficcaglia is a member of Arthur D. Little's Managerial Economics section, responsible for the coordination and preparation of short- and long-term economic and industry forecasts. He is also professor of economics in Arthur D. Little's Industrial Development Management Education Program, an accredited program leading to an M.S. in management. He received the B.A. in economics from Brandeis University and is a candidate for the Ph.D. from Boston College.

James F. Fleming is a member of the Food and Agribusiness section of Arthur D. Little, Inc. He was formerly a vice president of the Chiquita Brands Division of United Brands. Mr. Fleming has nineteen years of experience in the food industry and holds the B.S. in food technology from the Massachusetts Institute of Technology, and the M.B.A. from Harvard.

Samuel C. Fleming is a vice president of Arthur D. Little, Inc., and president of ADL Impact Services Company. He is active in acquisition and strategic planning consulting for clients interested in businesses with superior growth and profit potential. Mr. Fleming received the M.B.A. from Harvard Business School and a B.Ch.E. from Cornell University.

John T. Funkhouser is a senior staff member in the Organization Development section of Arthur D. Little, Inc. His major activities include management consulting for technically-based companies, environmental management, and management of technical risk. Dr. Funkhouser is a graduate of Princeton University and received the Ph.D. from the Massachusetts Institute of Technology.

James M. Gavin is a director of and consultant to Arthur D. Little, Inc. He joined the company in 1958 following his retirement as Lieutenant General, United States Army, after thirty-three years of service. He served as U.S. Ambassador to France from early 1961 to the fall of 1962. General Gavin received the B.S. degree from the United States Military Academy at West Point in 1929. He holds honorary degrees from the Polytechnic Institute of Brooklyn, Dartmouth College, New York University, and Babson Institute.

Donald R. Gibbons is a senior staff member of the Chemical Management Consulting section. He is a member of the American Chemical Society, the Society of Chemical Industry, the American Institute of Mining, Metallurgical and Petroleum Engineers, and Phi Beta Kappa.

Peter E. Glaser is a vice president of Arthur D. Little, Inc., and manager of the Engineering Sciences section. He heads activities in the field of solar energy and is a past president of the International Solar Energy Society. Dr. Glaser received the M.S. and Ph.D. degrees in mechanical engineering from Columbia University.

A. George Gols is a vice president of Arthur D. Little, Inc., and head of the Management Economics section and Input/Output Forecasting Center. He is involved with the analysis of long- and short-range growth prospects of U.S. industry and the economic impact of public policy programs. Dr. Gols holds the M.A. in political economy from Johns Hopkins University and the Ph.D. in economics and statistics from the University of Oregon.

S. Theodore Guild, Jr., is a member of the Financial Industries section of Arthur D. Little, Inc. His specialty is the creation of innovative financing packages for high-growth/high-technology companies. Mr. Guild has served as vice president of the National Shawmut Bank of Boston. He received the A.B. degree from Harvard College and the M.B.A. from the Harvard Business School.

Howard E. Harris works in the Energy Economics section of Arthur D. Little, Inc. and concentrates on problems of strategic planning and organization in the energy industries. Mr. Harris received the B.A. in international relations from Stanford University. He received the M.P.A. from the Woodrow Wilson School of Public and International Affairs at Princeton University.

George B. Hegeman has been responsible for a wide variety of corporate planning, acquisition, diversification, marketing research, and economic studies at Arthur D. Little, Inc. He has worked with many companies in the chemical industry on problems of strategic planning and corporate policy formulation. He is a graduate of the School of Industrial Management at the Massachusetts Institute of Technology and the Advanced Management Program at the Harvard Graduate School of Business.

Richard F. Heitmiller, a senior staff member of the Chemical Management Consulting section, has led numerous fiber-related projects. Prior to joining Arthur D. Little, Dr. Heitmiller was director of research for J.P. Stevens & Company, Inc. He received the A.B. and M.S. degrees in chemistry from the University of Delaware and the Ph.D. from the University of Illinois.

Richard L. Hughes is a vice president of Arthur D. Little Impact Services Company and director of its Health Care Industry Service Program. Mr. Hughes directs casework assessing the implications for management of technological, economic, and regulatory trends in health care, in the United States and abroad. He holds the B.S. and the M.S. from the Massachusetts College of Pharmacy and the M.B.A. from Northeastern University.

Donald A. Hurter is manager of Arthur D. Little's Automotive Technology unit and has directed numerous projects for corporate and government clients. He received the B.S. in mechanical engineering from the Massachusetts Institute of Technology and the master of engineering degree in thermodynamics and internal combustion engines from Yale University.

Michael C. Huston is a senior economist and management consultant at Arthur D. Little, Inc. He has directed or participated in a number of studies dealing with economics, investment, and industrial development. Mr. Huston received the B.S. degree in marketing economics from Arizona State University and a master's degree from the Graduate School of International Management in Phoenix.

Charles H. Jenest, a senior staff member of the Chemical Management Consulting section, has worked on a wide variety of business problems in the chemical and related process industries. Mr. Jenest received the B.S. in chemistry from Boston College and has taken advanced courses in organic chemistry and polymers at the University of Pittsburgh.

Alan B. Kamman is a vice president of Arthur D. Little, Inc., and manager of the Telecommunications Sciences section. He has carried out marketing and hardware evaluations for international clients in telecommunications. Mr. Kamman holds the B.S. in engineering from Swarthmore College and has done graduate work at the University of Pittsburgh and Drexel Institute of Technology.

Donald H. Korn is a senior consultant in the Financial Industries section. He has conducted a wide variety of company valuation and investment analysis assignments in connection with major corporate acquisitions and divestitures. Mr. Korn holds advanced degrees in engineering from Tulane University and the Massachusetts Institute of Technology.

Charles R. LaMantia is a vice president of Arthur D. Little, Inc., and head of the Chemical and Metallurgical section. Much of his work involves chemical process development, design and analysis, environmental control, and coal utilization. Dr. LaMantia received the B.A., B.S., M.S., and D.Sc. in chemical engineering from Columbia University.

Gary A. Marple, a member of Arthur D. Little's Management Counseling section, has concentrated on strategic planning and futures research problems that require observing, measuring, understanding, or changing human behavior as part of their solution. Dr. Marple holds the B.S. from Drake University, and the M.B.A. and D.B.A. from Michigan State University. He was also a post-doctoral fellow at the Massachusetts Institute of Technology's Sloan School of Management.

Richard F. Messing, a vice president of Arthur D. Little, Inc., has overall responsibility for the company's economic and business counseling in the energy, chemical process, and resource industries. Mr. Messing is a chemical engineering graduate from the University of Minnesota, and did graduate work at the Illinois Institute of Technology.

Ellen I. Metcalf is a member of the Consumer Goods and Services unit of Arthur D. Little's Management Counseling section. Her major involvement has been in the development and application of information-gathering techniques for strategic market planning studies in a wide range of industries. Ms. Metcalf received the B.A. from Jackson College, Tufts University.

Robert K. Mueller is chairman of the board of Arthur D. Little, Inc., and Arthur D. Little International, and director of Arthur D. Little, Limited (London). He has had multinational management responsibility for business development, new ventures, acquisition, corporate planning, venture capital, and diversification activities in various industries and financial organizations. He received the B.S. in chemical engineering from Washington University and the M.S. in chemistry from the University of Michigan.

Bruce S. Old, a senior vice president of Arthur D. Little, Inc., has directed studies in a variety of fields, including the nuclear power supply industry and the government's uranium enrichment facilities. Dr. Old is a former member of the President's Science Advisory Committee.

Gerard Piel, publisher of *Scientific American,* received the A.B. at Harvard College and holds a full assortment of honorary degrees as well—Sc.D., Litt.D., L.H.D., LL.D. He worked as a science editor of *Life Magazine* from 1939 until 1945 and then served as assistant to the president of Henry Kaiser Company in 1945 and 1946. In association with two colleagues, he began publishing *Scientific American* in 1948.

Martyn F. Roetter, a member of Arthur D. Little's Paris office, has been involved in several major projects concerned with the broad fields of telecommunications and new applications of computer capabilities. Dr. Roetter obtained a bachelor's degree from the University of Oxford and the Ph.D. from the Department of Theoretical Physics at Oxford.

William I. Rogers is a senior member of the Organization Development section of Arthur D. Little, Inc. He has participated in and been responsible for more than seventy organizational effectiveness, feasibility, project planning and implementation studies for companies, universities, medical centers, and governmental agencies. Dr. Rogers obtained the B.A. from Adelphi University, the M.S. from the University of Vermont, and completed his doctoral work at the University of Iowa.

Kenneth Schwartz is vice president of Opinion Research Corporation (ORC), an Arthur D. Little subsidiary, and managing director of the ORC Public Opinion Index, a continuing study of basic opinion trends affecting business now and in the future. Mr. Schwartz advises corporate clients on ways of meeting the challenges posed by social problems. Mr. Schwartz received the A.B. degree from Grinnell College and attended graduate school at Columbia University.

Derek E. Till, a vice president of Arthur D. Little, Inc., is in charge of the Product Technology Laboratories. In addition to his supervision of and participation in laboratory-based problem-solving activities, Mr. Till has been involved in casework assignments to establish technological needs and the means to supply these needs. Mr. Till studied at the University of London where he was awarded the B.Sc. in chemistry.

Polyvios C. Vintiadis, vice president of Arthur D. Little, Inc., and vice president-Middle East, Arthur D. Little International, Inc., has conducted many economic feasibility studies and evaluations of industrial development opportunities and investments. Mr. Vintiadis holds the B.E. in engineering from the American University of Beirut and the S.M. degree from the Massachusetts Institute of Technology.

John R. White is a vice president of Arthur D. Little, Inc., with professional responsibility for its domestic management consulting activities. Mr. White came to Arthur D. Little after twenty years of marketing and general management responsibilities in the industrial equipment and instrumentation fields. He holds the B.S. and M.S. degrees from the California Institute of Technology.

Richard Williams is a senior staff member in the Chemical Management Consulting section. He has the client management responsibility for several large government and private clients and has led assignments concerning the economics of the process industries, the interface of government and industry, and business strategy and planning. Mr. Williams has a degree in physics from the University of Pennsylvania. He is a graduate of the Harvard Business School Program for Management Development and the Executive Education Program in Corporate Finance.

Frederic G. Withington, a senior staff member of Arthur D. Little's Information Systems section, provides a series of studies discussing the computer industry for Impact Services clients. His work involves the study of data processing systems: their design, applications, markets, and effects on the organizations using them. Mr. Withington is a graduate of Williams College with a B.A. in physics.

Robert V.L. Wright is a senior staff consultant within the Management Counseling section at Arthur D. Little, Inc. He has developed a unique set of concepts and techniques for the development of corporate and business unit strategies. Mr. Wright has degrees in economics and history and has worked for the federal government as an economist in the Marshall Plan in Paris.

Yoshimichi Yamashita, president of Arthur D. Little (Japan), is an international management consultant for leading Japanese, U.S., and European organizations. His areas of professional competence include corporate strategic planning, long-range planning, marketing, and systems analysis. Mr. Yamashita holds the B.S. in mechanical engineering from Tokyo University and has done graduate work in systems engineering.